Participatory Livestock Research: A Guide

Participatory Livestock Research: A Guide

Czech Conroy

ITDG
PUBLISHING

Natural
Resources
Institute

DFID
Department for
International
Development

CTA

LPP

Published by ITDG Publishing
Schumacher Centre for Technology and Development
Bourton Hall, Bourton-on-Dunsmore, Warwickshire CV23 9QZ, UK
www.itdgpublishing.org.uk

First published in 2005

ISBN 1 85339 577 3

The Technical Centre for Agricultural and Rural Cooperation (ACP-EU)

The Technical Centre for Agricultural and Rural Cooperation (CTA)
was established in 1983 under the Lomé Convention between the ACP
(African, Caribbean and Pacific) Group of States and the European Union
Member States. Since 2000, it has operated within the framework of the
ACP-EC Cotonou Agreement.

CTA's tasks are to develop and provide services that improve access to
information for agricultural and rural development, and to strengthen the
capacity of ACP countries to produce, acquire, exchange and utilise information
in this area. CTA's programmes are designed to: provide a wide range of
information products and services and enhance awareness of relevant information
sources; promote the integrated use of appropriate communication channels and
intensify contacts and information exchange (particularly intra-ACP); and
develop ACP capacity to generate and manage agricultural information and to
formulate ICM strategies, including those relevant to science and technology.
CTA's work incorporates new developments in methodologies and cross-cutting
issues such as gender and social capital.

CTA, Postbus 380, 6700 AJ Wageningen, The Netherlands
www.cta.int

ITDG Publishing is the publishing arm of the Intermediate
Technology Development Group.
Our mission is to build the skills and capacity of people in developing
countries through the dissemination of information in all forms,
enabling them to improve the quality of their lives and
that of future generations.

Typeset by J&L Composition, Filey, North Yorkshire
Printed in Great Britain

Contents

Figures

Tables

Boxes

Acknowledgements

This book has evolved partly out of participatory livestock research on goats and scavenging poultry with which I was involved. I would like to thank all of the Indian and British colleagues with whom I collaborated on that research for the learnings that I gained from it, in particular: Dr A.L. Joshi, Dr D.V. Rangnekar, Dr D.N. Shindey, Mr L.R. Singh, Mr Y.A. Thakur, Mr M.H. Vadher, Dr R. Matthewman, Dr D. Romney and Dr N. Sparks. Equally, I am grateful to the several hundred livestock-keepers without whose co-operation and collaboration the research would not have been possible. The book has also drawn on the rich experience of numerous other projects and livestock specialists, particularly those represented in the case studies. I would like to thank the case study authors for their contributions and for answering my many queries. Dr Andy Catley wrote Chapter 5 on Animal Health, which draws on the pioneering work that he and his colleagues have been doing. My colleague Dr John Morton provided valuable feedback on drafts of the manuscript and selection of case study projects, and Dr Ann Waters-Bayer did likewise on earlier material that was subsequently incorporated into the book. Flavia Jolliffe gave some advice on matters relating to the use of statistics. Two independent reviewers read the draft manuscript, or parts of it, at different stages in its evolution, and made valuable comments that have enabled improvements to be made. Helen Marsden of ITDG Publishing has supported the development of the book in various ways, almost since it was first conceived in 2001. Last but not least, I would like to thank Dr Wyn Richards and the UK Department for International Development's Livestock Production Programme, and Dr Ruben Puentes and Professor Gordon Conway at the Rockefeller Foundation, for their financial support, without which the book would not have been possible. Any errors in the book are my responsibility.

Acronyms

ACIAR	Australian Centre for International Agricultural Research
ASAL	arid and semi-arid lands
ATIRI	Agricultural Technology and Information Response Initiative
BAIF	Bharatiya Agro-Industries Foundation, generally known as BAIF Development Research Foundation
BNF	biological nitrogen fixation
CAHW	community animal health worker
CBO	community-based organization
CCPP	contagious caprine pleuropneumonia
CE	campesino experimentation
CIAT	International Centre for Tropical Agriculture
DAREP	Dryland Applied Research and Extension Project
DFID	Department for International Development
DM	dry matter
EMI	Embu-Meru-Isiolo
EVK	ethnoveterinary knowledge
FPR	farmer participatory research
FRG	farmer research group
FSP	Forages for Smallholders Project
GIS	geographical information system
HI	haemagglutination inhibition
ICRAF	International Centre for Research on Agro-forestry
ILRI	International Livestock Research Institute
IIRR	International Institute for Rural Reconstruction
IPR	intellectual property rights
ISPA	Indo-Swiss Project Andhra Pradesh
ITDG	Intermediate Technology Development Group
ITK	indigenous technical knowledge
KARI	Kenya Agricultural Research Institute
KARI-NVRC	Kenya Agricultural Research Institute-National Veterinary Research Centre
KETRI	Kenya Trypanosomiasis Research Institute
KVA	Kenya Veterinary Association
LDCs	less developed countries
NARS	National Agricultural Research System
ND	Newcastle disease
NEV	non-experimental variable
NGO	non-governmental organization

NRF	nitrogen-rich fodder
NRI	Natural Resources Institute
ODA	Overseas Development Administration
PA	participatory approach **or** participatory appraisal
PJ	*Prosopis juliflora*
PM&E	participatory monitoring and evaluation
PRA	participatory rural appraisal
PSA	participatory situation analysis
PTD	participatory technology development
R&D	research and development
RD	recommendation domain
RRA	rapid rural appraisal
RRC	Regional Research Centre
RPF	resource-poor farmer
SC	scheduled caste
SDP	Smallholder dairy project
SSA	sub-Saharan Africa
ST	scheduled tribe

1 Introduction

This book is about participatory research, which covers two broad areas. The first is participatory situation analysis (PSA), in which researchers and local people collaborate in developing a sound understanding of the local situation, usually with reference to a particular topic, such as animal husbandry. This kind of research may then be followed either by participatory technology development (PTD), which is the second type of research covered in this book, or it may be used as the basis for planning some form of livestock development programme, which itself could (and hopefully would) be participatory in nature.[1] PSA could also be followed by a *combination* of PTD and broader livestock development.

PTD is a process in which local people and outside facilitators work together purposefully and creatively to identify, experiment with, and validate technologies that effectively address important problems or opportunities, while simultaneously strengthening the capacity of local communities to address other related problems and opportunities in the future.[2] Another term with a similar meaning to PTD is farmer participatory research (FPR). The term PTD is preferred here because (a) not all livestock-keepers are farmers; and (b) FPR is a broader term that does not distinguish between situation analysis and technology development.

Whether or not research and technology development are conducted in a participatory way depends primarily on the attitudes of development workers and researchers. The specific tools and techniques for situation analysis that are described in this book are those that are conducive to a participatory mode, but they are by no means inherently participatory. The inquiry or research process will only be participatory if researchers:

- respect the knowledge and skills of the farmers
- recognize that the farmers or livestock-keepers are the most important stakeholders, and that their own role is to support them.

In a participatory process farmers and outsiders discuss what, if anything, they want to research; and only if both parties agree on the desirability of

---

[1] Participatory development (PD) is a programme of development interventions in which local people are actively involved in the management and implementation, rather than passive recipients or beneficiaries – for example, a community animal healthcare programme or a dairy development programme. The main difference is that PD does not necessarily include technology development.

[2] This definition is similar to, but not the same as, that given by Veldhuizen et al., 1997.

investigating particular topics, or achieving particular objectives, is a joint process of inquiry initiated. Where a participatory process is sustained for some time it is likely to contribute to general community development on a self-reliant basis; and to foster the awareness, self-respect and self-confidence of the local people involved.

The use of PTD came into vogue during the 1980s and 1990s as an alternative to conventional forms of agricultural technology development, which were seen by many as having an unsatisfactory, if not poor, track record when it came to developing technologies that were useful to resource-poor farmers. Conventional approaches had the following characteristics:

- researchers played an active role in the technology development process, whereas farmers' contribution was, at best, largely limited to describing their circumstances and their constraints;
- researchers defined the problem to be addressed, sometimes after discussions with farmers and sometimes not;
- researchers developed the solutions to the problems, and these were then passed on to the farmers via extensionists.

The application of PTD is still relatively unusual in livestock research and development projects and programmes, as compared with crop-related research. Yet the case for PTD is just as strong in relation to livestock as it is in relation to crops; and there has been increasing recognition that livestock-related research needs to give greater emphasis to farmer participation (Sidahmed, 1995; Conway, 1999). Indeed, for the development of forage options, some researchers now believe that 'participatory approaches are mandatory' (Peters et al., 2001).

PSA is similar to what is commonly known as participatory rural appraisal (PRA). The term PSA is used here in preference to PRA, for two reasons: first, it is equally applicable in urban areas; and second, the emphasis is on analysing *a situation* as a prerequisite to further action, either in the form of PTD or PD. The very process of PSA tends to raise the expectations of local people that the outsiders will be able to help them address problems or opportunities that are identified. Ideally, therefore, PSA should not be undertaken unless the outside facilitators are confident that they will be able to follow it up with an ongoing collaboration with the local people concerned that responds to one or more of their priority needs.

Participatory technology development with livestock-keepers has the potential to increase dramatically the efficacy of livestock research for resource-poor people, and greatly to enhance the contribution of livestock to their livelihoods. However, this will only be true if it is undertaken in the appropriate circumstances, and with careful consideration of the methodology to be followed. I have written this book, therefore, with a view to encouraging the more widespread use of PTD and to assist researchers and development practitioners in determining when to adopt PTD with livestock-keepers; avoiding potential problems; and maximizing the benefits generated by it.

The book is aimed at two main audiences: government researchers who have only limited experience of participatory research in villages, and NGO staff working in the field who have little, if any, experience of participatory technology development. It does not pay much attention therefore to theoretical issues, and only covers the use of statistics in a very general way.

The book has three main parts. Part I describes the general philosophy and approach of PSA, and a wide range of tools, with examples of their application to animal production and health. Part II describes when and how to conduct PTD. Part III contains ten case studies of PTD with livestock-keepers that describe how this approach has been used to address a wide range of issues with different types of livestock in several less developed countries (LDCs).

Parts I and II of the book draw on three major experiential sources of information. One is my experiences with a collaborative goat research project in India, which was jointly co-ordinated by BAIF Development Research Foundation and the Natural Resources Institute. Another is my involvement with a scavenging poultry project in India, co-ordinated by the Scottish Agricultural College and also involving BAIF and the Tamil Nadu University of Veterinary and Animal Sciences. The third is the experiences of the case study projects in Part III.

1.1   Why livestock are important to resource-poor people

Livestock ownership
In many LDCs the majority of the resource-poor households in rural areas own livestock of one type or another, and in urban and peri-urban areas livestock-keeping can also be important for a significant minority of the poor. For example, in India more than 70 per cent of rural households own some kind of livestock, and the global figure for LDCs is similar to this. Even landless families often own a few goats or chickens – and sometimes one or more large ruminants (e.g. in Bangladesh and Kenya).

There are three broad categories of poor livestock-keepers:

- sedentary landless people, who may live in rural or urban areas;
- mixed farmers with small farms that are usually rainfed, and often located in dryland regions; and
- extensive graziers, whose main livelihood activity is livestock-keeping.

Contributions of livestock to livelihoods
Livestock contribute to people's livelihoods in a variety of ways, and their contributions tend to be particularly important (at least in relative terms,

such as percentage of income) for poorer people. These include the following.[3]

Source of cash income Sale of livestock and their products, notably milk, can be a valuable source of income, as can be seen from the example in Box 1.1.

Liquid asset Sale of animals, particularly smallstock, is an important way of generating income to deal with contingencies, such as unexpected medical needs or coping with failed crop production in a drought year.

Inputs to crop production In many countries draught power and manure are both very important inputs to crop production.

Utilization by poor of land owned by others Livestock ownership can be a means through which the poor capture private benefits, in the form of forage, from: village commons, state-owned land (e.g. forests), and other people's private farmland (in exchange for deposition of manure).

Diversification of risk/buffer to crop yields In dryland areas, crop yields are highly variable from year to year for a given locality.[4] Livestock-based enterprises are often more robust in drought years than crop-based ones, so income from animal husbandry (e.g. through the sale of milk or manure) can provide a valuable buffer against poor crop yields.

Source of food This is often a minor use of livestock for poor people, and some livestock-keepers (particularly in India) are vegetarian. Nevertheless, livestock products (notably meat, milk and eggs) can sometimes be important sources of protein.

BOX 1.1   The importance of income from livestock in Kenya

Livestock are an important source of income for households in every district of Kenya and, in 40% of Kenya's districts, income from livestock contributes more than 25% of the total income. In 78% of the districts the contribution livestock make to total household income is as important, or more important, to households falling below the poverty line as it is to those above it. In general, in the arid pastoral districts, livestock contribute significantly more to total household income for poorer households than for those with household income levels that place them above the poverty line.

Source: Thornton et al., 2002

---

[3]   The typology of contributions used here is adapted from Livestock in Development, 1999.
[4]   This reflects the variability of the rainfall, both in terms of the annual total and its distribution over the year (i.e. late rains or heavy rainfall at the wrong time often result in poor yields).

Cultural value A livestock species may have cultural or religious values in particular societies, such as the cow in India, and may be traditionally sacrificed at the time of a certain festival.

Trends and prospects in the livestock sector

The prospects for livestock-keeping are generally very good. Demand for, and production of, livestock and livestock products in LDCs is expected to double over the next 20 years (Delgado et al., 1999). Livestock production has been growing faster than any other agricultural sub-sector, and it is predicted that by 2020 livestock will account for more than half of total global agricultural output in financial terms. This process has been termed the 'livestock revolution' (Delgado et al., 1999).

The livestock revolution presents both opportunities and threats to resource-poor livestock-keepers in LDCs. The increased demand for livestock products could represent sustained, and perhaps increased, revenues for them. On the other hand, they could face increased competition from larger, more commercially oriented livestock production units. One dimension of the livestock revolution has been the industrialization of livestock production, with production changing from being the traditional local multi-purpose activity to an increasingly market-oriented and vertically integrated business (Delgado et al., 1999; Steinfeld, 2002).

There is a real danger that large-scale intensive producers could undermine the viability of small-scale livestock production, thereby exacerbating rural poverty (Steinfeld, 2002). Whether or not this happens will depend on two factors. One is government policies, and how supportive they are of small-scale production. The other is the extent to which small-scale producers are able to increase the efficiency of their operations and the productivity of their animals. Whether livestock-keepers are able to increase livestock productivity significantly will depend partly on whether researchers can work with them effectively to develop technologies and systems for easing or removing productivity constraints. It is intended that this book will make a positive contribution to that process.

1.2 Livestock constraints and failure of conventional research

Despite the important contribution commonly made by livestock to poor people's livelihoods in LDCs, the productivity of these animals tends to be well below what is possible due to a variety of problems that livestock-keepers and their animals face. If these constraints could be overcome the benefits to huge numbers of resource-poor people would increase significantly. Unfortunately, the contribution of animal science research to developing effective ways of addressing these constraints has been disappointing (Waters-Bayer and Bayer, 2002).

Constraints

Some of the most important and widespread constraints to livestock production and productivity are listed in Table 1.1. It can be useful to make a distinction between constraints that limit the numbers of livestock that a family is able to keep, and constraints that limit the productivity of the animals kept, although many constraints may affect both. Some constraints (e.g. theft, labour availability) primarily affect the numbers of livestock that a household is able to keep; while others (e.g. gastro-intestinal parasites) limit productivity, but not necessarily numbers.

Most of these constraints are 'researchable': that is, it is feasible that research could identify ways of easing or overcoming them. Large sums of money have been spent on research to address many constraints, particularly those relating to feed and nutrition and to animal health, but the results have been disappointing as far as the impact on resource-poor livestock-keepers is concerned. The reasons for this will now be discussed. The next section describes the general weaknesses of livestock research in relation to resource-poor livestock-keepers, and then two more sections look at more specific weaknesses associated with research on forages and feeds, and animal health, respectively.

General problems with traditional livestock research

Animal science research in the South has been strongly influenced by that in the North. The latter has a history of being orientated towards meeting the needs of estates, and more recently 'factory farms', and being geared to increasing the production of livestock and their products (Waters-Bayer and Bayer, 2002). Specialization and commercialization have been common

Table 1.1 Types of constraints affecting livestock production and productivity

Constraint	Affecting	
	Numbers (production)	Productivity
Insufficient feed year-round	✔	
Insufficient feed during particular seasons		✔
Inefficient utilization of feed	✔	✔
Water scarcity, particularly in dryland regions	✔	✔
Life-threatening diseases	✔	
Productivity-reducing diseases		✔
Labour requirements, particularly for herding	✔	
Poor access to markets	✔	✔
Predation (especially of smallstock)	✔	
Theft	✔	
Poor management	✔	✔

themes. Another feature of this research has been manipulating the environment so that it contributes to maximum production or productivity: for example, feeding systems are based on the nutritional 'demand' of the animals, rather than on the availability of various feed resources at different times of the year (Bayer and Waters-Bayer, 1998).

The traditional 'northern' or 'western' paradigm of animal science research for developed countries has been dominant and pervasive. It was transferred *directly* to LDCs by researchers from the North who turned their attention to these countries; and *indirectly* by its influence on the education of animal scientists from LDCs. If scientists had been more sensitive to the needs and priorities of livestock-keepers in the LDCs, they might have re-oriented their research so that it was more appropriate and relevant to them. However, they were not particularly sensitive or responsive, they often failed to understand the circumstances of small farmers (Roeleveld and van den Broek, 1996), and the old paradigm persisted. They were aware that traditional systems in LDCs were often substantially different from those in the textbooks, but they saw these traditional systems as backward and in need of change. Hence they did not make much effort to understand why these systems were different, and it did not occur to them that resource-poor livestock-keepers might have different objectives to resource-rich, commercially oriented ones. They failed to take proper account of the fact that most livestock in LDCs belong to farmers, and are an integral part of a mixed farming, crop–livestock system, providing inputs into crop production (in the form of draught power and manure) and receiving inputs (e.g. crop residues) from crop production.

Another reason why old attitudes, methods and beliefs persisted was that researchers' contact with resource-poor livestock-keepers was quite limited. (For an example of attitudinal barriers, see Box 1.2.) They did most of their research on the research station, because that was more convenient and also because it enabled them to exert more control over treatments and non-experimental variables. This in turn meant that they could produce sound scientifically valid results that were publishable in journals, which has been more important for scientists' promotion than has the usefulness of the results for farmers (Bayer and Waters-Bayer, 1998).[5] It is hardly surprising, therefore, that there has been a 'lack of participation and interest among animal scientists' in on-farm animal research (Amir and Knipscheer, 1989).

Furthermore, scientists' accountability to resource-poor livestock-keepers has been almost non-existent, and there has been little pressure on them

---

[5] Reward systems in research organizations tend to be strongly dependent on the extent to which staff are able to publish articles in respected scientific journals. Such journals tend to be prejudiced against material based on on-farm trials, particularly participatory ones, because it may not satisfy conventional criteria for experimental design and statistical rigour (Chambers, 1997; Morton, 2001).

BOX 1.2 Barriers to participatory approaches to animal health research: the example of Kenya

Participatory approaches (PAs) were introduced in the early 1990s. These PAs were institutionalized in the Kenya Trypanosomiasis Research Institute (KETRI), the Kenya Agricultural Research Institute's National Veterinary Research Centre (KARI-NVRC) and other parts of the national agricultural research system (NARS) during this period, shifting the emphasis of their work from being primarily laboratory-based to primarily field-based. This change was partly due to shifts in policies of some development partners, who gave priority to research that was demand-led by farmers. Donor support (e.g. from DFID) for some projects was dependent on the incorporation and use of PAs in research activities.

Attitudinal barriers

Biophysical scientists tended to have negative attitudes towards these approaches: they were initially apprehensive and reluctant to adopt PAs, for three reasons. First, they considered them to be overburdening (due to their lack of skills to conduct studies using the PA methods). Second, they saw them as an interference with scientific etiquette. Third, they were also concerned that the results of qualitative studies carried out using PAs would not be accepted for publication in scientific journals.

They also feared losing control of the research projects to other collaborators with a comparative advantage in the use of PAs. The initial negative attitude to PAs by the biophysical scientists was a major constraint to their institutionalization in the NARS.

Organizational barriers

The organizational mandates were narrow, and did not facilitate research by a single institution on all aspects demanded by client farmers. The mandate of KETRI limits it only to tsetse and trypanosomiasis research and control, while the NVRC mandate limits it to specialization in selected animal health constraints.

The negative attitudes of biophysical scientists, coupled with lack of appropriate personnel to undertake the bulk of participatory assignments, presented obstacles to the incorporation of PAs in existing research projects. Both KARI-NVRC and KETRI, as government research institutions, found it difficult to retain highly trained and experienced scientists, especially those trained in PAs: a significant number of staff moved to the private sector and international organizations. This made it difficult to implement effective follow-up of planned activities, as some of the projects were linked to individual scientists with whom the respective communities identified.

Participatory approaches were also complicated by lack of appropriate quality control standards (standard operating procedures) to guide the conduct of participatory studies and thus allow for comparison of data across study sites by different institutions. Initially, the linkages between and within the institutions to enhance the learning process in the use of PAs were not well established.

Source: Okuthe et al., 2002

to work with these groups. Where research has been geared to livestock-keepers' needs it has been primarily addressing the needs of relatively resource-rich, commercially oriented groups, because they have more influence, and also because traditional research is more likely to be relevant to their needs anyway, as their production systems tend to be more similar to those in the North.

An additional factor that has inhibited a shift to research that is more relevant to the needs of the resource-poor is the fact that most research, until quite recently, has been discipline-based, rather than system-based. It has been reductionist, with researchers focusing on components rather than on systems, and hence failing to understand what the system was and how the component fitted into it. For example, researchers focused on increasing milk production in cattle breeding programmes, and paid little attention to the ability of bullocks to plough effectively. As a result, when high-yielding breeds of dairy cattle became available to resource-poor farmers in India they were often not interested because these breeds were ill-equipped to meet what to them was a more important need, namely draught power (for ploughing, etc.).

Finally, there has also been a perception that on-farm experimentation with animals can pose serious challenges. For example, it has been observed that animal scientists have been slow to adopt on-farm research due to the following complexities:

'[b]ecause of the small number of animals on farms, high cost, and close personal ties between the farm family and its animals, on-farm experimentation with animals becomes more difficult than with crops. Failure of a treatment, or even animals' adjustment to new feed sources, may lead to a drop in milk production, loss in weight, or listlessness. Disease effects can have more serious repercussions for livestock researchers than will reduced grain yield in a farm field ...' (Hawtin and Havener in Amir and Knipscheer, 1989).

Livestock forage and feed research

Scientists have acquired a tremendous amount of knowledge about the feed resources and nutrition of ruminants, both large and small (Acharya and Bhattacharyya, 1992). Despite this, the adoption of feed-related technologies developed by researchers (e.g. for enhancing forage production or improving grazing management systems) has been disappointing, particularly among resource-poor livestock-keepers (Acharya and Bhattacharyya, 1992; Sidahmed, 1995; Peters et al., 2001).

This is partly because feed technologies have often been developed without the involvement of the intended users, and without an adequate understanding of their farming systems, needs and constraints. Forage research and development has usually been undertaken 'with no involvement of farmers, except as labourers for experiments and contributors to questionnaires and surveys' (Horne and Ibrahim, 1996). Consequently, researchers have failed to take account of farmers' criteria for assessing forage species, which are often different from those of researchers (Horne and Ibrahim, 1996).

Inappropriate feed technologies include: (a) forage crops, which the farmer cannot grow because (s)he does not have enough arable land and they compete with food or cash crops; (b) urea treatment of straw, which is only appropriate under a limited set of conditions;[6] and (c) inputs that have to be purchased, such as compound feeds or concentrates, and are too expensive and may not be available locally. Some of the common weaknesses found in forage research and development are listed in Box 1.3. Two of the case studies (G and H) describe initiatives that have avoided these problems.

Animal health research

Veterinary researchers have made tremendous progress in understanding diseases and their causes, and in developing drugs and vaccines to combat them. A whole raft of commercial products is on the market, even in LDCs. Unfortunately, as few as 15–20 per cent of the livestock populations in LDCs have enjoyed regular and affordable access to modern veterinary medicine and 'there is little prospect that these percentages will change much in the foreseeable future' (McCorkle et al., 1999). Some livestock-keepers do not have easy physical access to modern veterinary medicines, but for most of them it is the cost of the products that is the principal problem.

In some LDCs government veterinary services have, in principle, been free of cost; but in practice they have not been available to resource-poor farmers. One general trend has been that, as the cost of providing veterinary services increases, the level of government services decreases (Heffernan and Sidahmed, 1998). There have not been enough drugs for everyone, with

---

[6]   The required conditions are: (a) fine straws are in good supply; (b) green fodder is relatively scarce; (c) a plentiful supply of water is readily available; (d) plastic covering and urea can be obtained cheaply and reliably; and (e) high market prices for animal products allow the purchase of inputs (Bayer and Waters-Bayer, 1998).

BOX 1.3 Common mistakes in forage research and development

Some of the common weaknesses experienced in forage research and development are listed below.

■ Taking insufficient account of the effects of rainfall variability on plant growth and forage yields, especially in arid and semi-arid areas.

■ Expecting livestock-keepers to pursue government objectives, such as growing forage for higher milk or meat production, instead of their own objectives, such as feeding for traction or manure production.

■ Failing to understand the existing forage husbandry system, especially the role of crop residues and other multi-purpose plants, and therefore promoting special forage crops only.

■ Introducing forage species that grow well in one area into another without considering limitations to the plant's adaptability.

■ Assessing the 'advantages' of a new forage species by comparing it with natural pasture or another cultivated forage rather than with the performance of the existing forage–husbandry system.

■ Overestimating potential yields and underestimating risks, such as crop failure on account of disease.

■ Making incomplete assessment of the economics of forage improvement, by not taking alternative uses of land or labour into account.

■ Allowing insufficient time for the process of improving forage husbandry.

Source: Bayer and Waters-Bayer, 1998

salary costs often accounting for most of the budget; and corruption may lead to officers selling the products. For example, in India extension services are characterized by biases that result in them tending to neglect poor rural livestock-keepers (Matthewman et al., 1998). Most extension organizations there focus primarily on large ruminants and on intensive systems, and tend to be concentrated in higher potential areas. In other words, livestock-keepers in relatively remote areas, particularly those with smallstock, are unlikely to be reached by state veterinary services.

There is a need, therefore, to develop health-related technologies based on locally available materials or expertise. Where these technologies are based on indigenous technical knowledge they are generally categorized as ethnoveterinary medicine. Two of the case studies (B and C) describe the validation and development of indigenous technologies for controlling mange and gastro-intestinal parasites respectively.

Genetic improvement

Research on genetic improvement has been primarily concerned with cross-breeding, and with ruminants there has been a particular focus on increasing milk production. The characterization of indigenous breeds has often been neglected, as has their improvement. Case study J describes one of the small number of cases of research into improving an indigenous breed, namely the Chiapas sheep of southern Mexico, which is kept primarily for wool production.

1.3 The advantages of participatory research

The advantages of participatory situation analysis

PSA is an essential prerequisite to a sound understanding of farmers' and livestock-keepers' situations and priority needs. While more formal and structured types of surveys and needs assessment exercises can yield useful information, relatively unstructured discussions have a greater probability of revealing people's perceptions and of generating a holistic picture. Information from PSA should ideally be influencing the agendas of research organizations and the nature of specific research projects, and also the priorities of livestock development programmes.

The advantages of participatory technology development

A participatory approach to technology development can help to ensure that new technologies are appropriate to farmers' and livestock-keepers' needs and circumstances, and hence increase the likelihood of adoption (Reijntjes et al., 1992; Conroy et al., 1999). Numerous examples of such technologies are given in the case studies in this book (see Part III). A list and short description of the case studies can be found in Table 1.2.

Greater participation of the intended users can mean that:

- applied and adaptive research will be better oriented to farmers' problems;
- farmers' knowledge and experience can be incorporated into the search for solutions, and highly inappropriate technologies can be 'weeded out' at an early stage;
- the performance of promising technologies developed on-station can be tested under 'real-life' agro-ecological and management conditions;

Table 1.2 List of case studies

Project	Country	Type of livestock	Research subject
Animal health			
(A) Control of Newcastle disease	Mozambique	Poultry	Assessing the suitability of different ways of administering vaccines for the control of Newcastle disease
(B) Dryland Applied Research and Extension Project	Kenya	Small ruminants	Indigenous mange control methods screened and validated
(C) Ethnoveterinary Knowledge Research and Development Project	Kenya	Sheep	Three ethnoveterinary remedies for internal parasites in sheep validated
Feed/nutrition research			
(D) Re-allocation of concentrates during lactation	Kenya	Dairy cattle	Effect of temporal re-allocation of concentrates during lactation on milk yield
(E) Easing seasonal feed scarcity for goats	India	Goats	Supplementation of tree pods during critical periods to improve productivity of female goats
(F) Enhancing the integration of livestock into LEI crop systems	Mexico	Pigs and poultry	Amount, quality and complementarity of feed sources; possible livestock/crop interactions
Forage research			
(G) Forages for Smallholders Project	Indonesia, Laos, Vietnam, Thailand, etc.	Not applicable	The evaluation of forage crops and development by farmers of forage systems
(H) Legume supply and cultivation adapted to facilitate adoption	Kenya	Dairy goats and cows	Improving the availability and adoption of forage crops (*Desmodium*)
Tools research			
(I) Development of a donkey traction technology	Sudan	Donkeys	Development of donkey traction technology
Genetic improvement			
(J) Participatory breed improvement of the Chiapas sheep	Chiapas, Mexico	Sheep	Improving wool production of Chiapas sheep

- researchers will be provided with rapid feedback on the technologies tested, and promising technologies can be identified, modified and disseminated more quickly, reducing the length of research cycles and saving time and money;[7]
- farmers' capacity and expertise for conducting collaborative research is built up and becomes a valuable resource both for them and for future research programmes (Conroy et al., 1999).

---

[7] More conventional procedures have involved 'pre-screening' by researchers, followed by a minimum period for running trials to generate statistically valid results before making 'recommendations'. These might then have to pass through a committee structure before being 'released'. When farmers participate more actively in the technology screening process, they also formulate their own recommendations while doing so (Sutherland and Kang'ara, 2000).

PART I Participatory situation analysis

2 General aspects of participatory situation analysis

2.1 Introduction

This part of the book describes most of the participatory situation analysis (PSA) methods that are relevant to livestock, and gives examples of their use with reference to particular topics. It also describes some potential pitfalls associated with their use in livestock research that need to be avoided, and various ways of enhancing the application of these methods.

Several general guides to PRA have been published, but most of the material in them relates to crop production, and the application of PRA in livestock development has been relatively neglected.[8] Nevertheless, most of the tools of PRA are common to various development sectors, so these general guides can also be useful to the livestock professional.

The information collected using the participatory methods described below should provide a sound basis for planning development interventions, or for planning research to develop new technologies to address the priority constraints identified. It will ensure that interventions address priority needs and that the benefits to livestock-keepers are maximized.

Further information may need to be collected using more formal methods (e.g. regarding the nature of diseases, or the nutritional value of certain feeds), but often more detailed information can be collected in parallel with development interventions. In other words, it may not be necessary to collect all of the information during a planning phase. It is important to keep this phase as short as possible so that the interest of livestock-keepers is sustained and they do not become disillusioned by what they may perceive as unnecessary delay and inaction.

It is assumed that the reader is already familiar with the basics of PRA/PSA through training and/or practical application in the field.

---

[8] General guides include: Pretty et al., 1995 and Reitbergen-McCracken and Narayan, 1998. Livestock-related PRA has been covered by three specific publications, but these may not be easy to obtain. They are: RRA Notes 20 (IIED, 1994); Waters-Bayer and Bayer, 1994; and Catley, 1999.

Nevertheless, this introductory section briefly re-states certain key points that are sometimes forgotten or overlooked.

Participatory methods for analysing situations

PRA/PSA is more than a collection of techniques. No data collection method is inherently participatory. PSA is a general approach, whose effectiveness depends heavily on the attitude of its practitioners: it will only work well if they listen to and respect the views of the local people with whom they are working. Whether or not the data collection process has been participatory depends on the way in which the method is applied and the data are used.

Nevertheless, some methods are particularly associated with PRA and participatory research. Visualization techniques, such as mapping and diagramming, are well suited to a participatory mode: they can be intelligible to all, including the illiterate, and provide a tangible focus for discussions. The general approach used in PSA is semi-structured interviews, combined with various visual techniques. These include:

- Timelines/historical profiles
- Mapping and modelling
- Ranking and scoring (showing proportions)
- Matrices
- Diagrams (such as seasonal calendars and transects).

Group discussions are usually used, particularly in the initial stages, because they are an efficient way of obtaining a general picture. Where appropriate, individual interviews and other methods, some formal and quantitative, can subsequently be used to collect more detailed information (see Chapter 6).

Visual techniques are used because they encourage people to get involved in the process, to express the information in a way that is easily intelligible to them, to discuss issues among themselves, and to add to, refine and correct this information. When people have made the diagram or map it provides a useful basis for questions and discussion. There may be high levels of illiteracy among disadvantaged groups, especially women. Where this is the case, by utilizing symbols, rather than words and numbers, mapping and diagramming make it possible for these people to be involved in the process as much as literate people.

PRA/PSA has a few basic principles or characteristics. One is that it should be conducted in a *relaxed* way, not a hurried way. For example, a transect walk should be done in a leisurely fashion, stopping along the route to ask questions about things that are observed, and to ask questions of people encountered. Driving along the route in a jeep is not a transect walk and is not PRA/PSA.

A second principle of PRA/PSA is *triangulation* – which basically means cross-checking information from different sources and using different approaches. The reason for doing this is that without cross-checking there is a danger of producing findings that are not entirely correct. This can be due to: misunderstandings between the survey team and the participants; or only getting part of the picture; or participants deliberately giving false information; or unrepresentative individuals dominating the discussions. An example of triangulation is the collection of information on forage resources in three different ways: through mapping, a transect walk and production of a seasonal feed diagram. The use of triangulation does not guarantee that the information generated will be accurate, but it certainly increases the likelihood it will be.

A third principle of PRA/PSA is *optimal ignorance.* This means that we only seek information about things that are relevant to our aims, and to the level of detail that we require: we do not collect information that is not relevant, even if we find it interesting personally. Some livestock professionals have difficulty acting on this principle. One important reason for adopting this principle is that the time of the people we are surveying is precious, and we do not want to waste it. Another important reason is that experience has shown that the collection of large amounts of detailed, quantitative information during the diagnostic or needs assessment phase tends to create problems. Analysis of the data is a lengthy and complicated process that creates a long delay before any technology development work or intervention is implemented, and as a result local people rapidly lose interest and their participation is undermined (Roeleveld, 1996a).

Direct observation

Another important way of learning about various aspects of livestock production is by direct observation. Apart from general casual observation there are a number of specific types of observation that can be adopted. Ones that are specifically related to livestock production include:

- village walks that take in the major sources of forage, such as common grazing areas, crop fields and private wasteland or fallow land;
- accompanying the herder(s) for a day; and
- types of learning by doing, such as milking animals and feeding them.

Getting organized for PRA

It is important to be clear about the **purpose** of any survey work before it is undertaken, so that neither livestock owners' time nor development workers' time is wasted. Being clear about the purpose will help to focus the topics to be covered, and may also influence the selection of villages to be covered. One should also be aware that undertaking participatory situation analysis is likely to raise people's expectations of the development agency bringing material benefits to the community, as some of the case studies note. The purpose of the work should be clearly explained to the community at the outset, so that they do not have false expectations, and so that they have a basis for deciding whether or not they want to become involved.

Data collection requires resources – time, money and skilled staff – some of which may be in short supply, so the **resources available** should also be taken into account before any work is undertaken. Before starting participatory studies full use should be made of any existing sources of information, such as previous surveys of villages in the locality, reports on livestock production that rely more on formal data, and livestock census data.

The responsibilities of team members should be identified in advance: at least one member should keep a detailed record of the discussions and should copy maps/diagrams that are produced, while another asks most of the questions and facilitates the discussion. This will enable the information collected to be used to maximum effect, and will avoid duplication in the future.

Topics and sequencing

This will depend on the purpose of the PRA/PSA, and on what is known already. As the term implies, *semi-structured* discussions should be flexible as to: (a) what they cover, and (b) the sequence in which topics are covered; and they should allow the villagers to influence the topics through some open-ended discussions. Particularly in exploratory PRAs, the survey team should not dominate the discussions and limit the topics covered. The structured aspect concerns the prior identification by the survey team of certain key topics that it would like to cover during the discussions: these are normally noted in a checklist that is made available to all team members. One general guideline that follows from the need for flexibility is that the discussions should start off at a fairly general level, and only gradually focus more narrowly on specific topics that the survey team may have identified in advance. For example, one possible sequence would be to:

- start with general matters – **livelihood systems;**
- move on to **livestock production in general for each of the main livestock types found in the village** (production objectives, benefits, marketing, constraints); then
- gradually focus more on important issues that have emerged.

A more detailed illustrative (and optimistic) schedule is given in Box 2.1. This process needs to be repeated for each major sub-group (e.g. landless, farmers).

Timing of PSA

PSA needs to be conducted at a time of day, and of the year, that is convenient for the livestock-keepers; for example, a group of agro-pastoral livestock-keepers once said to me, 'we're busy right now – come back in six weeks' time please, after we have harvested our crops'. In addition, once a time and date are agreed with them the researchers should honour it. Discussions and

BOX 2.1 An illustrative survey schedule with a focus on forage and goats

Day 1 Livelihood systems

- Introduction

- Identify and rank activities making up the livelihood systems (matrix ranking)

- Seasonality of activities, labour and cash flow (seasonal diagram)

- Identify and analyse long-term trends affecting people's livelihoods (time-line)

- Daily schedule of activities for men and women, including livestock-keeping (activity schedule)

Day 2 Livestock production system, benefits and constraints

- Historical trends in livestock ownership (timeline)

- Benefits/reasons for keeping small and large ruminants (SRs and LRs) (matrix ranking)

- Production constraints for SRs and LRs (ranking)

- Goat production system over a year – showing feed resources, breeding and kidding seasons, disease and marketing times (seasonal calendar)

Day 3 Forage resource mapping and transect

- Forage resource map (participatory mapping)

- Two dry season forage maps – for an average year and a drought year – showing: (a) tree tenure – owners' trees, communal, and purchased lopping rights; (b) typical daily herding route

- Village walk, visiting key forage resource points, possibly accompanying herders

Day 4 Feeding systems and seasonality

- Seasonal feed calendar – showing feed types by month and/or by source

- Discussion about whether or not there is a goat feed problem – and its precise nature.

- Discussion about what happens to goats in the dry season (average and severe) – liveweight gain, milk production, herding time, etc.

- Coping strategy in average and severe years (e.g. distress sales, longer dis-tance migration)

- Preliminary discussion of possible interventions/solutions (if there is a scarcity problem).

interviews may need to be spread over a few weeks in order to avoid placing excessive demands on livestock-keepers at any one time.

Women tend to be particularly busy, and may be available for relatively limited periods only at certain times of the day. Similarly, landless labourers may only be available in the evening. If researchers choose a time that is not particularly convenient for livestock-keepers this could have a negative effect on the quality of the PSA. It may:

- hinder the development of mutual trust and respect;
- result in less people being available for discussions;
- result in an unrepresentative sample taking part; or
- make the livestock-keepers less focused on the discussions, because they are thinking about the tasks that they need to do.

2.2   The use of statistics in PSA[9]

The use of statistics in PSA and PTD could be the subject of a book in itself, and it is not possible to cover it comprehensively in this book. A few key issues are discussed here, but it is strongly recommended that livestock professionals consult a statistician when any studies are being planned, and at later stages in the process. Contrary to what many people think, statistics can be just as relevant in PSA as in studies using more structured and quantitative methods. The main roles of statistical ideas and techniques are to assist in the interpretation of data, and to help design studies in such a way that it will be possible to produce the type of data that researchers want and to interpret those data in a useful fashion.

Statisticians are experienced in design and measurement issues in surveys, and should be able to ask pertinent questions and offer valuable advice, provided that they recognize the practical constraints under which participatory researchers are operating. For example, to maximize the value of the information collected through PSA, careful consideration needs to be given to what the information is being collected for and how it will be used. Statisticians often help researchers to sharpen their thinking on such issues.

Survey objectives
One of the first steps in survey design is to define which group of people or units is of interest. The full group of interest is called the 'target population'. This will depend on what the survey objectives are. Objectives vary, but common ones include:

1. providing an overall picture of a population (e.g. livestock, ploughs, farms, landless households) in a given area

---

[9]   Some of the issues covered in this section are also discussed in section 8.3, with particular reference to participatory technology development.

2. making a comparison of the existing situations in areas that are clearly different
3. categorizing households, communities or other units into groups that may be studied, sampled or reported separately or which become 'recommendation domains'.[10]

An example of a type 1 objective might be identification of the main constraints facing camel-keepers, and their frequency, in a particular region. An example of the kind of results arising from a survey with a type 2 objective is given in Table 2.1. The two districts in this comparison are different in terms of their human populations' wealth status and ethnicity. People in the Udaipur sample are tribals, who are generally poorer than the Hindus in Trichy. Scavenging poultry-keeping is also far more commercialized in Trichy.

Table 2.1 A comparison of egg spoilage and chicken mortality in villages in two semi-arid districts of India

	Trichy District, Tamil Nadu	Udaipur District, Rajasthan
Spoiled eggs (%)	18.2	27.3
Mortality during first 6 months (%), of which	23.1	41.9
■ Disease	7.0	16.6
■ Predation	14.7	21.9
Total losses[a]	41.3	69.2

[a] i.e. spoiled eggs plus mortality. The spoilage and mortality data are not strictly summable – they are not a percentage of 100. They have been aggregated here simply to give an overall picture of the losses, to facilitate comparisons between each district.

Source: Adapted from Conroy et al., 2003.

Comparative studies may reveal both differences and similarities. Table 2.1 shows that total losses in Udaipur are much higher than those in Trichy, which is perhaps not surprising given the socio-economic differences between these districts. It also shows a few patterns that are common to both districts, such as the finding that predation causes more deaths than disease. The fact that the situations in the two districts are very different suggests (but does not demonstrate) that the common findings may not be peculiar to the survey districts. Whereas, if the survey had only been done in similar villages in one district, unexpected findings (such as the predation versus disease finding) might provisionally have been interpreted as a peculiarity of the geographical area or sub-set of villages that was studied.

Regarding the type 3 objective, an example of categorization of livestock-keepers is given in Box 2.3 (see page 32). A survey might aim to place goat-keeping households in a particular area into one of these three categories.

---

[10] See Chapter 11 for a discussion of recommendation domains.

Researcher bias

The flexible and less structured nature of participatory methods makes it easier for researcher bias to creep into the way that topics are investigated (e.g. by asking leading questions) and reported. For example, when recording what farmers have said in group interviews some researchers also intersperse their own interpretations of what farmers have said, without distinguishing between the two. This can be either deliberate or unintentional – sometimes they see their interpretation as fact, not recognizing that there may be other interpretations. Members of the survey team should monitor each other to check that none of them is introducing bias in these ways. Researchers' interpretations or observations can be recorded separately.

Choosing the sample[11]

There is usually no need to cover the whole of the target population in a survey, and constraints on the time and money available often make it impossible to do so. It is necessary, therefore, to select a sample of the target population. If there is to be any claim to representativeness of the sample, or generalizability of the findings, careful consideration needs to be given to the selection of units. This should be done in an objective way that is not influenced by the personal preferences of the survey team – except where practical issues (e.g. accessibility) are so important that they become explicitly recognized as part of the selection criteria. Consulting a statistician about this is likely to improve the efficiency and effectiveness of the design.

Where generalizability is sought, the PSA exercise will need to be repeated in several units. Where group exercises are the research tools, the unit required could be groups of villagers or groups of people from a particular village sub-group (e.g. buffalo-keepers or landless livestock-keepers). Where

Table 2.2 A hypothetical example of multi-stage sampling in a poultry survey

	Stages			
	1 *State*	2 *District*	3 *Village*	4 *Household*
Possible selection criteria	Two states: (a) with semi-arid regions; (b) with markedly differing degrees of commercialization; and (c) in which survey agencies have operational presence	One district in each state: (a) that is semi-arid; and (b) in which poultry-keeping is widespread	Three villages in each district: (a) in which poultry-keeping is widespread; and (b) particular ethnic groups predominate	Random selection of 10 households in each village that: (a) keep poultry; and (b) belong to particular ethnic groups

[11] This section draws on Statistical Services Centre, 2000.

household-level data are required the data will need to be collected from a number of households, and it may be necessary to standardize which type of household member is interviewed (e.g. husband, wife or household head). For example, the Udaipur data in Table 2.1 are based on data collected from ten individual women belonging to different households in each of three villages.

Formal, structured data collection exercises have developed the use of various sampling methods to minimize bias in the selection of the people who form the sample. Users of participatory methods have generally been less systematic in their approach to selecting a sample of individuals for interview or participation in research. This can be a major weakness of survey findings, because it means that they could be biased.

Sampling is often multi-stage, involving different units at different stages or levels – for example, state, district, village, household, individual. Table 2.2 gives an example of multi-stage sampling that is quite similar to what was used in the study whose findings are shown in Table 2.1. This is sometimes called stratified random sampling. Stratification refers to situations in which the population divides naturally into segments that differ from one another, but are internally relatively homogeneous. Internal homogeneity, if it can be achieved, means that a relatively small sample will serve to typify a stratum reasonably clearly, so this can lead to efficient sampling.

The survey team (which may include representatives of the livestock-keepers) has to use its knowledge and judgement to assess how homogeneous the population is. For example, in the poultry survey mentioned above the survey team determined in advance of the survey that there were three slightly different scavenging chicken production systems in Trichy district (see Table 8.2); and they decided to make the production system an additional level of stratification. They selected survey villages in which all three types of production system co-existed. This was done because if they had studied each production system in a different village this could have introduced other differences – for example, in distance from markets.[12] They then selected ten poultry-keeping households from each of these production systems.

The survey findings showed that there were marked differences in mortality, hatchability, etc. between the three production systems, so if this additional level had not been added, and the data had not been disaggregated accordingly, there would have been far more heterogeneity or variability within the households. (The data in Table 2.1 are the aggregated data for the three groups: the disaggregated data are presented in Table 3.7.)

---

[12] Then it could have been difficult to determine whether differences in survey findings were due to differences between production systems or differences between villages – two variables would have been compounded. Where the sample size is large statistical techniques might be able to separate the influence of different variables, but in this case the sample size was very small due to resource constraints.

Selection of villages The selection criteria will depend on the purpose of the work to be undertaken. Where the objective is type 1, there are two common scenarios. First, a development agency may want to analyse the situation in *all* villages in a particular area, because it plans to implement a programme of work in that area. Another common scenario, particularly in research-oriented work, is that the agency wants to cover a representative sample of villages in a district or region, to get a reliable overview of certain conditions or practices. Another criterion that may be important in some situations is the need to have a good rapport already with the community where the situation analysis is to be undertaken.

Trade-offs may be necessary between the extent to which the villages included are representative and other criteria (need for good rapport, resource costs involved, accessibility, etc.). **A guiding principle is that well-informed choices, based on clear criteria, are always preferable to the selection, by default, of non-representative situations** (e.g. adjacent to research stations, major roads, previous projects, or a researcher's home village).

Selection of groups Where the survey methods involve group discussions and exercises there is a risk that those present may not be representative of the village or sub-group concerned, and that certain individuals may dominate the discussions, which could result in the findings being biased. It is important to be aware of this possibility, and either to do whatever is feasible to prevent it, or to take account of it (for example, by noting who was present, and to which sub-group they belong).

It is sometimes the case that the survey team is aware of particular sub-groups (see section 2.3) within a village (e.g. landless versus farmers, men versus women) and is clear that it wants to have separate discussions with each, or only wants to talk to particular ones (e.g. only poultry-keepers). In such situations it may be possible (as well as desirable) to ensure that only people from a particular sub-group are present, particularly if the survey is planned with village representatives who recognize the importance of stratification.

Selection of individuals or households Where PSA is being done with individuals careful consideration should be given to how they are selected, particularly where the research team intends to make generalizations from the survey findings. Random selection of individuals is possible in principle if the survey team has a list of all households in a village or sub-group, and such lists can be obtained from census data or through social mapping (see section 2.3). Each household can be given a number. Each number can then be written on a separate piece of paper and pieces of paper can be drawn from a hat or other container, preferably by villagers themselves. Making the selection process transparent in this way increases the likelihood that villagers will understand the process and recognize that it is fair and unbiased. An example of random allocation of villagers to different experimental groups is given in Box 7.5. However, sometimes villagers might have difficulty understanding the rationale for it, in which case insisting on random sampling would be non-participatory and likely to have a negative effect on the relationship with the villagers.

If villagers are not selected in a systematic, objective fashion then it may still be useful to classify them on the basis of characteristics that are thought to be relevant and important. For example, they could be classified by wealth category (see section 2.3), by livestock production system used (see Box 2.3), or by whether or not they are landless.

Sample size What the sample size should be is a complicated, yet very important, issue in field-based studies, and this is a good reason for consulting a statistician (see also section 9.2). The following quotation sums up the factors that need to be considered (Statistical Services Centre, 2000):

> 'There is no clear-cut sensible method of producing an answer to the question, "How big a sample do I need?" You have to think it through in the light of the objectives, the field data collection conditions, the planned analysis and its use, and the likely behaviour of the results. There are several situation-specific aspects to this; there is no universal answer.'

When undertaking comparative studies, such as the poultry study described earlier, the survey team will probably want to know whether any differences they identify between different groups of livestock-keepers and their livestock are 'genuine' or due to chance. Tests designed to address this issue are commonly referred to as 'significance tests'. This has implications for sample size, because when samples are very small it may be impossible to answer this question. Conversely, if the samples are very large it may be possible to show that even small differences between groups are not due to chance. What is needed is a sample size that is large enough to enable meaningful statistical analysis to be carried out, but not so large that it makes the survey burdensome or too costly.

Statistical analysis of data collected using participatory methods

In the analysis of data the discipline of statistics has two major functions. First, it can assess whether apparent effects demonstrated by the data are 'genuine' or whether they could be due to chance. This prevents over-interpretation of the data. Second, statistical analysis may be able to separate the effects of different factors that may be partially confounded.

PRA/PSA methods have sometimes been distinguished from more traditional survey methods on the basis that the former generate *qualitative* data and the latter *quantitative* data. Qualitative data from different groups or villages are inherently difficult to summarize and aggregate, which can be a weakness if one wants to present a summary of PSA findings. However, the qualitative/quantitative distinction is not entirely correct: some PRA/PSA tools **do** generate quantitative data, and these data can be aggregated provided that they are collected using a common format.

Standardizing formats, however, involves a loss of flexibility, so there may be a trade-off to be made. Some of the benefits of participatory inquiry can be lost if researchers concentrate on collecting numbers from livestock-keepers, rather than facilitating discussion and exploring their knowledge and ideas. In veterinary epidemiology, Mariner (2000) has warned about the dangers of quantification and advises that:

> 'Flexibility and much of the potential to discover new ideas, perspectives and insights would be lost in the interests of statistical significance. The process would be longer and less comprehensive than true PRA as the same key questions and exercises would have to be repeated'.

It was also suggested by Mariner that repetition of methods would lead to expert teams (as used in participatory appraisal (PA)) taking on the role of enumerators and their attention would be directed towards ensuring methodological consistency.

A general guideline here is that it is advisable to test and modify a format in a pilot survey, and only to use it in a large-scale survey if it has been developed to the point where it appears to be suitable for a wide range of situations and respondents. In addition, it may be possible to build in a certain degree of flexibility. This can be done by having an 'other' category – for example, where causes of mortality are being recorded; and by complementing the standardized components of the methods with open-ended discussion of results each time they are used.

The participatory clutch history method (see section 3.3), which was used to generate the data in Table 2.1, and some of the methods presented in section 5.3 are examples of participatory methods that can be standardized and repeated to produce numerical data. Each of the methods described in section 5.3 comprises a quantitative and qualitative component. They allow numerical data to be recorded in a systematic way and enable agreement between informants to be assessed. Informant agreement indicates reliability that in turn indicates (but does not prove) validity.

2.3 Social groups, livelihood systems and livestock

Identifying different sub-groups and production systems
Different socio-economic groups may have different livelihood systems, and hence different livestock systems; and different livestock systems may have differing constraints and may require different interventions to remove those constraints. Thus, the identification of different sub-groups should be one of the first activities of any situation analysis, and the analysis of various aspects of livestock production will need to be undertaken separately with each sub-group.

Even within one village there may be several sub-groups with quite distinctive livelihood systems. Important influences on livelihood systems include ethnic group, wealth and size and quality of landholding. For example, one sub-group may be landless and may depend primarily on wage labour for their survival; while another may be farmers who do little, if any, wage labour. The principal criteria for determining sub-groups will vary from village to village, and region to region.

Wealth-ranking Wealth ranking is a tool by which sub-groups within a community can be differentiated in economic terms. Only a brief description is given here, and other references should be consulted for detailed guidance on how to do it (e.g. Grandin, 1988). The first stage of wealth-ranking involves members of the community identifying those criteria that they consider to be most important and relevant for this purpose, and identifying a number of wealth categories on the basis of them. (One way of doing this is described in Box 2.2.) The second stage involves getting two or three members to place all households in the community into the appropriate category. An example of wealth categories and criteria identified in one wealth-ranking exercise is given in Table 2.3. Wealth can be a sensitive subject, and this kind of exercise needs to be handled tactfully, particularly the second stage.

It is not always necessary to do the second stage of wealth-ranking. It may be sufficient to identify the categories and then to say that you want to have separate meetings with a few people belonging to each category. When you have the meetings you can ask the individuals present for the relevant information, to check that they do belong to that group.

BOX 2.2 Eliciting information about wealth categories

This box describes one way of getting a general overview of the proportions of households in different wealth categories, and the characteristics of these households in the views of local people, that is both easy and fun. Sit with a group of villagers and make a big pile of beans, each of which should represent a household in the village. Then divide the pile into, say, three smaller piles, calling them 'rich', 'medium' and 'poor' households, and putting most of the beans in the 'rich' pile.

The people in the group will soon correct you and start moving the beans around to make the piles closer in size to 'reality' (at least the reality they want to convey to you). This process will generate discussions about what makes the households in one pile different from those in another – for example, the participants might tell you that the people in the 'poor' pile have few or no livestock. In one case in Sudan, the villagers decided to divide the poor pile into two piles, one of which was the 'very poor'. This group had no livestock whatsoever, whereas the 'poor' had some goats.

Source: Ann Waters-Bayer, personal communication

Table 2.3 Wealth categories among tribals in Naganwat Chotti, Jhabua District, Madhya Pradesh

Category	No. of households	Characteristics
Very poor	3	They have 2 acres of land, no bullocks and food grains last up to 2 months. Families are dependent on migration, and have to abandon property, leading to degradation of private land.
Poor	22	They have up to 3 acres of land, food grains for up to 4 months, and they have insufficient bullocks for ploughing. Most members of the household migrate for up to 6–8 months. They have no silver ornaments, and it is difficult for them to buy a wife.
Medium	30	They have up to 6 acres of land, and food grains for up to 10 months. They have 2 bullocks and men migrate for 2–3 months/year.
Better-off	9	They have food grains for the whole year and sufficient bullocks. They can easily get money from moneylenders and save the money that they earn when they migrate.

Source: Turton et al. (1996)

Social mapping Social mapping is widely used for identifying all of the households belonging to a particular hamlet or village. The livestock owned by each household can also be shown on the map: this will enable the survey team to get an overview of the pattern of livestock ownership in the village, and to see whether there is a relationship between this and particular sub-groups found in the village (e.g. castes in India).

If the relationship between the survey team and the community is not conducive to wealth-ranking (e.g. if community members are suspicious about your intentions), social mapping can be a less sensitive alternative approach to identifying sub-groups. Information about livestock and land ownership (if the latter is not too sensitive) may provide a reasonable basis for this.

Working with women

Women often play a lead role in livestock-keeping, particularly in the case of smallstock, such as goats and scavenging poultry. Where this is the case, it clearly makes sense to do the PRA work with them, as they will be more knowledgeable than men. At other times it may be desirable to work with both women and men (although preferably in separate groups), so that any differences in views and priorities can be identified. When working with women, the survey team should include a female member if possible. The importance of having a woman in the team will, of course, depend on the culture and religion of the people with whom the team want to work.

Gender division of labour A daily activity schedule (see Table 2.6 for an example) will provide some insight into this, and so will direct observation. Group discussions specifically on this subject are also useful, as some activities, like marketing and disease control, may only happen at certain times of the year. It is important to discuss this with men and women separately – to avoid men dominating the discussion, and because men's and women's views on how tasks are divided between them sometimes differ a little. The gender division of labour should be discussed at an early stage, as this may have implications for whether further discussions on particular topics should be with men or women.

Gender differences in the ranking of constraints The different responsibilities of men and women in livestock production are liable to affect their perceptions of what are the main production constraints or problems. This is illustrated by Table 2.4. In this village, the men were responsible for disease management, while the women were responsible for collecting drinking-water from the village well and carrying it back to the home for the goats.

Describing and analysing livelihood systems

A livelihood comprises the capabilities, assets (including both material and social resources) and activities required for a means of living. People's livelihood systems can determine whether they get involved in keeping animals, the types of animals they keep, the ways in which they look after them, and the constraints on livestock production that they face. This is why it is important to obtain a good understanding of what their livelihood systems are. These linkages are illustrated by the examples given in Box 2.3.

Assets People may have, or have access to, various kinds of assets. Five general types of capital assets have been identified (Carney, 1998), namely: natural, social, human, physical and financial. These are briefly described in Box 2.4. Natural capital includes forage and water resources, so there tends to be a relationship between the natural capital assets to which people have access and their ownership of livestock.

Livestock themselves are assets: they could be natural, physical or financial capital. For example, a cow is a form of natural capital, from which milk is derived; a bullock is part of the equipment (physical capital) used for land preparation and transporting goods; and a goat that is kept as a 'savings bank' is a form of financial capital.

Table 2.4 Gender differences in the ranking of constraints on goat production in Kumbhan village, Bhavnagar District, Gujarat – scheduled castes

Rank	Men	Women
1	Disease	Water scarcity
2		Forage scarcity

BOX 2.3 Livelihoods and goat-keeping systems in India

Smallholder agro-pastoral systems These systems can be subdivided into those of small ruminant specialists and non-specialists. In South Rajasthan, there are many tribal people, who are non-specialists, who sometimes live in the same village as specialist castes. What they have in common is that the feed resources include: crop residues from their own land, forage from their private wasteland and forage from common lands. Specialists have larger herds, comprising mainly sheep, with flocks of 50–150, which are kept for their meat and wool, but also some goats. They tend to be more self-sufficient in feed resources; and the animals are herded by adult males. Non-specialists keep goats rather than sheep: they have smaller landholdings and hence depend more on common grazing lands around the village, where the goats are herded by children or women. Adult non-specialists are often involved in seasonal migration for wage labour, which may be a constraint on the numbers and types of animals that can be kept.

Landless wage-labourer system In Bhavnagar District, Gujarat, some of the scheduled caste goat-keepers are landless and their livelihoods depend primarily on wage labour, usually by both adult males and females. Most wage labour is agricultural labour, and there are about 4 months in the year when there is little, if any, available. These households keep 1–4 breeding does. The feeding system is a combination of stall-feeding, with forage collected in the fields where they work or on their way home, and some herding by elderly family members or children. Families who do not have any members available for herding tend to pay the livestock specialists, Rabaris, to do the herding for them. Milk for subsistence use is the main product, and people of higher castes would not want to purchase milk from them anyway (social stigma).

Marginal/landless livestock specialist In Bhavnagar, the Rabaris are the specialist livestock caste. They tend to be landless, or only own a small amount of land, which may be of poor quality; at certain times of the year some of them do wage labour. Their livestock include goats and large ruminants. Some of them spend most of their time herding their animals. Being landless, they graze them primarily on common lands and on other people's agricultural fields after harvesting. Nearly all of their income comes from livestock production: milk production is the major source of revenue, with some income also from the sale of manure and the occasional animal sale.

Enterprises/activities To understand fully the contribution that livestock make to people's livelihoods we need to know what people's livelihood systems are. Livelihood systems include a number of activities or enterprises, each of which may produce benefits in terms of cash and/or subsistence products. We need to know what these activities are, and to get an idea

> **BOX 2.4** Types of capital
>
> **Natural capital** The natural resource stocks from which resource flows useful for livelihoods are derived (e.g. land, water, wildlife, biodiversity, environmental resources).
>
> **Social capital** The social resources (networks, membership of groups, relationships of trust, access to wider institutions of society) upon which people draw in pursuit of livelihoods.
>
> **Human capital** The skills, knowledge, ability to labour and good health important to the ability to pursue different livelihood strategies.
>
> **Physical capital** The basic infrastructure (transport, shelter, water, energy and communications) and the production equipment and means which enable people to pursue their livelihoods.
>
> **Financial capital** The financial resources which are available to people (whether savings, supplies of credit or regular remittances or pensions) and which provide them with different livelihood options.

of their relative importance. Common types of activities in rural areas are crop production, animal husbandry, wage labour, collection and marketing of forest products, and various non-farm activities (e.g. barber, locksmith). It may be useful to disaggregate wage labour into agricultural and non-agricultural (such as house construction, or working in a mine or quarry). It is also important to know whether there is seasonal migration for work, as this may have significant implications for livestock-keeping.

Matrix scoring and ranking is a useful tool for assessing the relative importance of different activities in people's livelihoods, and for obtaining an indication of the importance of livestock. Once the main activities have been identified, participants should be asked what criteria (the column headings in Table 2.5 are examples of criteria[13]) they think are important when making comparisons between them. When these have been agreed, the activities can be compared and scored, and then ranked in importance through matrix scoring and ranking.

A hypothetical example of this is given in Table 2.5; scoring is on a scale of 0 to 5 (maximum). It should be noted that the total scores for each enterprise will not necessarily correspond with the rankings. This is because different criteria may have different weights (importance) in the minds of the participants. In this example, wage labour is ranked more highly than forest

---

[13] Other criteria that people sometimes use include: enterprise available most of the year, and flexibility (work can easily be fitted in around other activities).

Table 2.5 Scoring and ranking of livelihood activities

Enterprise	Income	Food	Other subsistence products	Total score	Overall rank
Crop production	3	5	1	9	1
Animal husbandry	1	2	1	4	4
Wage labour (non-agriculture)	5	0	0	5	2
Forest products	2	1	3	6	3

products, despite having a slightly lower total score, because *income* is considered more important than *other subsistence products*.

Seasonality of activities, labour and cash (income and expenditure) This can best be explored through the construction of a seasonal calendar, showing: when the various activities are undertaken during the year; peaks and troughs in labour demand; and peaks and troughs in income and expenditure. (See Table 3.5 for a calendar that looks at income.) When discussing labour try to clarify who does what, so that a general idea is obtained of the gender and age division of labour. Construction of a seasonal calendar can be time-consuming, but is worthwhile. The information about labour and cash should help to identify when the use of these factors of production is most constrained, and will thus give an indication of when different types of intervention (capital-intensive or labour-intensive ones) are likely to be most and least feasible.

Daily activity schedule/profile Livelihood systems can also be usefully looked at in relation to people's **daily cycle of activities.** This can be done by asking men and women (separately) to construct a daily activity schedule, showing what they do during the course of a normal day, from the time they get up to the time they go to bed. Daily activity schedules are another way of obtaining information about the gender division of labour. It is advisable to construct at least one schedule for each season, since the daily pattern of activity may vary substantially over the course of a year. Livestock-related activities should be included, so that we can see how they fit in with other activities. An example, relating to small ruminants, is given in Table 2.6.

Long-term trends affecting people's livelihoods

Information about long-term trends in natural resources and other variables is important, as it can improve understanding of some of the main factors shaping the pattern of livestock ownership and the direction in which this is changing. This can be explored through a general discussion about changes that have taken place during people's lifetimes. Discussions with older people will obviously give a longer-term perspective. Construction of a **timeline**, showing key events in the community's history, can provide a useful time-frame and reference points within which the changes can be located.

Table 2.6 Daily routine of rural women – village: Patiyo Ka Kheda

Monsoon season (June–September)	Winter season (October–January)	Summer season (February–May)
1. 04.00–06.00h Women wake up and do household work	1. 05.00–07.00h Women wake up and do household work	1. 04.00h Women wake up
2. 06.00–06.30h Clean house and animals	2. 07.00–07.30h House cleaning and cleaning of animal sheds, collecting of cow dung	2. 04.00–06.00h Household work
3. 06.30–07.0h Feeding of goats, sheep, cattle and buffaloes and feeding of concentrates	3. 07.30–08.30h Feeding of goats, sheep, cattle and buffaloes, and feeding of concentrates	3. 06.00–07.00h House cleaning and cleaning of animal sheds, feeding concentrates to dairy animals and then milking
4. 07.00–07.30h Women milk their animals	4. 08.30–09.00 Women milk their animals	4. 07.00–09.00h Boil milk and prepare tea; prepare chapati and feed family members; dairy animals go outside village for grazing
5. 07.30–08.00h Boil milk and prepare tea	5. 09.00–09.30h Boil milk and prepare tea	5. 09.00–12.00h Women go to fields for hoeing, weeding and collection of grasses from the fields for dairy animals
6. 08.00–08.30h Prepare chapati for family	6. 9.30–10.0h Prepare chapati, feed family members and send dairy animals to graze in pastureland out of village	6. 12.00–14.00h Women have complete rest due to heat
7. 8.30–9.0h Kids and lambs separated from adults and adults taken to graze in common or government grazing areas	7. 10.0–16.00h Women go to fields to do hoeing, weeding, cutting and collecting of grasses for their dairy animals	7. 14.00–17.00h Again women work in fields for spreading manure and breaking clods
8. 09.00–13.00h Work in their own or other peoples' fields if they do not have their own land. During this period women cut and collect grass from the fields for dairy animals	8. 16.00–17.30h Women return to their home, children bring dairy animals back home, animals tied and water provided and then milking is done	8. 17.00–19.00h Women provide water to dairy animals as they come back from pasture lands, feed concentrates and milk animals
9. 13.00–14.00h Women rest	9. 17.30–18.00h Bring water from the well	
10. 14.00–19.00h Women work in fields	10. 18.00–20.00h Women prepare chapati	
11. 19.00 All dairy animals come back to the home from pasture lands and some are milked	11. 21.0h They all sleep	

Typical key events are: severe drought, and completion of various types of community infrastructure, such as a temple, school, village pond or road. People generally find it easier to relate information about trends to key events than they do to calendar years, so use of key events can improve the reliability of the information they recall. Key informants may be able to say in which years the key events took place.

The timeline can be used to help answer the following questions:

- How has asset status (including natural capital and livestock) been changing over time?
- Are people on an upwards or downwards trajectory with their different assets?
- What are the root causes of changes and how do they vary between different wealth and social groups?

Having traced important historical trends, people can then be asked what changes they expect to take place over the next 10–15 years or so.

Information about long-term trends in **livestock ownership** can either be collected along with information about changes in natural resources, or as a separate exercise. It can be difficult, however, to collect this kind of information in such a way that its meaning is unambiguous and that we find out everything we want to know. One potential problem is distinguishing between trends in livestock numbers per household and numbers for the whole village. This distinction may be complicated by the fact that the number and proportion of households keeping a particular type of livestock has increased or decreased markedly over time.

Table 2.7 summarizes one attempt to obtain data on long-term trends in livestock ownership and two other types of natural capital, farms and trees. Its strengths are that it gives data that are unambiguously on a per household

Table 2.7 Long-term livestock and natural resource trends in Patiyo Ka Kheda, Bhilwara District, Rajasthan

| Caste/tribe | 1976 | | | 1986 | | | 1996 | | |
	Gujar	Balai (SC)	Bhil (ST)	Gujar	Balai (SC)	Bhil (ST)	Gujar	Balai (SC)	Bhil (ST)
Number of households	25	6	2	30	10	5	40	18	8
Large[a] ruminants	75%	75%	25%	40%	50%	Nil	25%	25%	Nil
Small[a] ruminants	25%	25%	75%	60%	50%	Nil	75%	75%	100%
Trees	++++			+++[b]			+[c]		
Farm size (ha)	7	1	1	3.5	0.5	0.5	1	1[d]	1[d]

[a] The livestock figures refer to the percentages of large and small ruminants per household.
[b] One reason given for this decline was increased demand for timber for building.
[c] Further decline was because of the use of trees for fuel wood.
[d] Balai and Bhil farm sizes increased because government land was redistributed to them.

basis, and it distinguishes between different socio-economic groups. Its weakness is that all the data are percentages, so we do not know how *total numbers* of livestock have changed, nor whether the changes in percentages are due to small ruminant ownership increasing or large ruminant ownership decreasing. To get a more precise and accurate picture of livestock population trends it may be necessary to conduct individual interviews with one or more members of each household.

3 Getting an overview of livestock-keeping

3.1 Reasons and benefits

We saw in Chapter 1 that the keeping of livestock can contribute to people's livelihoods in several ways. Matrix scoring is a very useful tool for exploring the advantages of keeping different types of livestock and the benefits they provide.

Tangible benefits

Matrix scoring generates quantitative information and is a technique that people enjoy using. Livestock-keepers are asked to construct a matrix or table on the ground, with one column for each type of livestock that is widely owned by their group, and one row for each of the kinds of benefits that livestock may provide. It is important to have a good discussion about these things before the matrix is made, so that no benefits are overlooked. Each benefit is illustrated by a symbol (e.g. a jug or drink container for milk, or a piece of dung for manure), as is each type of livestock. The animals can be depicted through drawings: for example, drawing an outline in the soil with a stick, and covering it with ash or coloured powders; or using chalk on stone.

Scoring involves indicating the relative importance of each benefit for each type of livestock. For example, people might show that 50 per cent of the benefits provided by goats takes the form of sales, 30 per cent milk and 20 per cent manure; whereas for bullocks 80 per cent of the benefits might be from animal traction (ploughing, etc.) and 20 per cent from manure. An example of matrix scoring of benefits is given in Table 3.1.

Advantages of different types of livestock

Matrix scoring of material benefits, as illustrated in Table 3.1, does not give a complete perspective on why people are keeping different types of livestock. It is also useful to ask people about the **advantages** of different types of livestock. This line of questioning reveals other important factors, such as: ease of milking, ease of sale and ability to survive a severe dry season. For two examples, see Tables 3.2 and 3.3.

Table 3.1 Matrix scoring of livestock product benefits by tribals in Khakad, Udaipur (%)

Benefits	Buffalo	Cow	Bullock	Goat	Poultry
Manure	15	20	15	5	
Milk	25	12.5		12.5	
Ghee	30	12.5		5	
Income	25	50		50	50
Meat[a] (home consumption)				5	50
Draught power			80	5	
Leather	5	5	5	5	
Liquid asset[b]				12.5	

[a] In some areas/societies, there is a custom that goat-keepers do not consume their own goats; thus, the score given to meat may need to be interpreted carefully.

[b] As this is not a tangible product, goat-keepers may not identify it without prompting. In this example, they were deliberately prompted by the survey team, who wanted to know the relative importance of sales to meet contingencies versus sales to maximize net income.

Table 3.2 Livestock species ranking, sheep and goats

Farmers' criteria	Score	
	Goat	Sheep
Require less grazing land	*********	**
Diseases are less	********	*****
Ability to produce young	******	*****
Market demand	******	******
Total	29	18

Source: ISPA Bulletin

Table 3.3 Livestock species ranking, cows and buffalos

Farmers' criteria	Buffalo	Cross-bred cow	Local cow
Utilization of straws	7	4	6
Milk price	8	5	5
Disease problems	7	3	6
Milk production	4	6	1
Produces bullocks	1	3	9
Total	27	21	27

Source: ISPA Bulletin

This scoring/ranking exercise was done in Anmaspally in Andhra Pradesh, India. The reason shepherds ranked goats more favourably than sheep in grazing land requirement is that Anmaspally is a forest area with plenty of browse trees, and is therefore more suitable for goats. The availability of browse in good quantity made goats healthier and more disease-resistant than sheep in this situation.

When comparing different types of large ruminants (see Table 3.3), people gave higher scores to buffaloes and local cows than to cross-bred cows. Although cross-bred cows scored highest on milk production, they were considered to be more susceptible to disease, and produced bullocks that were inferior to those of local cows.

3.2 Describing the livestock production system

Seasonal dimensions of the production system

A general **livestock production calendar** can give a very useful overview of some key aspects of a livestock production system. It can be used to show breeding and kidding/calving/lambing seasons, the temporal distribution of disease, marketing times and the utilization of feed resources (in general terms). Different calendars can be produced for each major type of livestock.

It is best to show the information on a monthly basis, not just by season, as this gives a more detailed and informative picture. The seasons should be illustrated through the use of symbols, so that illiterate people can easily contribute to the preparation of the calendar. If the people identify three seasons, then columns can be made under each season to indicate months.

It is also advisable to show festivals on the calendar, so that everyone is clear when a season starts or ends. Different sub-groups may have different ideas about this (for example, one group may regard a particular festival as coming towards the end of the winter season, while another thinks it comes at the start of the summer season). Clearly, if this is not done it may appear that there are major differences between the calendars of different groups, even though there are not.

The use of a seasonal calendar like this can reveal patterns and possible inter-relationships. For example, it may show that most disease occurs at the start of the rainy season, and this may suggest that there could be a link between weakness due to feed scarcity in the dry season and susceptibility to disease. Table 3.4 is an example of a goat production calendar. The data in this table have been converted from Anas (the old Indian currency) to percentages. The numbers in each row add up to 100 per cent. (Villagers think of 16 Anas as 100 per cent, 8 Anas as 50 per cent, etc.)

Table 3.4 Seasonal calendar of goat production for Gujars in Indrapura, Asind Block, Bhilwara, Rajasthan (%)

Topic	Rainy			Winter			Summer		
Breeding			25					37.5[a]	37.5[a]
Kidding		37.5	37.5			25			
Sales	25					37.5[b]	37.5[b]		
Disease[c] –kids			12.5		25		9.375		
Disease[c] –adults			25		25		3.125		

[a]They select these months for breeding because of the availability of nutritious *Acacia nilotica* pods.

[b]They sell at this time, when the kids are 5–6 months old, because of problems with male kids mounting and fighting. If they had a castration facility they would like to keep the kids for 12 months before selling them.

[c]Sixteen Anas (100 per cent) were allocated to disease as a whole i.e. both kids and adults.

The seasonal production calendar provides a basis for questions and discussion. Any apparent contradictions should be clarified. For example, 'you have shown goat kidding as occurring 4 months after breeding, but the gestation period is 5 months – can you clarify this, please?'. Issues like **breeding** and **marketing** of livestock or their products can be explored. Why does breeding take place at this time? Is breeding time controlled, or does the availability of a particular feed trigger oestrus?

Sale of livestock products, marketing and income

The production calendar can provide a basis for discussing questions like:

- Why does marketing take place at these times?
- Are these preferred times because of prices being higher, or are some of the sales 'distress sales'?
- To whom do you sell your animals, and for what sort of price?

Seasonal calendars can be used to describe how prices of livestock and their products vary during the year. If small ruminant keepers are selling their animals to traders they may not know much about the ultimate destination of their animals, which could be in a major city a few hundred kilometres away. Therefore to gain an understanding of the marketing system, it may be necessary to talk to traders, butchers and other key informants.

Where livestock are producing multiple marketed products that vary seasonally, it may also be useful to produce a **seasonal product calendar**. Table 3.5 is one example, which was prepared by Rabari women in India, and which was used to analyse seasonality of income for Rabaris. Milk production was shown per animal, in percentage terms, since different households represented in the group had different numbers of animals. The vast majority of the milk is sold, so the quantity produced is synonymous with income. The women said that cash was scarcest in late summer, when milk production has fallen to a low level. During the rainy season they earn money from agricultural labour, which helps them cope with the fact that income from sale of animal products is lowest at that time.

Exploring relationships between livestock production and the farming system

Given the importance of crop residues as a feed for livestock, it is important to obtain a good understanding of what crops are grown and when. This can be done through preparation of a **crop production calendar**, which can depict the relative quantities of each crop as well as the growing season. Such a calendar can give a preliminary indication of the quantities of forage available to the owner's animals from the farm, provided that certain points are clarified. If any fodder crops are grown these should be distinguished from food crops, and clarification should be sought as to whether any of the fodder crop is sold. Also clarify whether it is only the owner's animals that graze on crop residues in his/her fields, or whether other people's animals also

Table 3.5 Rabari women seasonal livestock product and income calendar

Percentage milk production	Winter		Summer		Rainy season	
10	8 ✳	8 ✳	8 ✳	8 ✳	8	✳
20	8 ✳	8 ✳	8 ✳	✳		✳
30	8 ✳	8 ✳	8 ✳			✳
40	8 ✳	8 ✳	8			✳
50	8 ✳	8				✳
60	8 ✳	8				✳
70	8 ✳	8				✳
80	8 ✳	8				✳
90	8 ✳					✳
100	8 ✳					✳
Sale of LR manure					2.5 cartloads	
Sale of animals	*********				*********	

8 = goat milk, 100 per cent = about 2 litres.

✳ = cow milk, 100 per cent = about 4 litres.

********** = sale of one lactating goat each year @ 1000 Rs.

********** = sale of large ruminant (LR) for 4000 Rs once every 4 years = 1000 Rs per year.

enter his/her fields. Information about the contribution of crop residues can also be obtained through a general forage calendar (see Table 4.4).

3.3 Collecting more detailed information about animal productivity

The majority of PRA/PSA methods described in this book are based on exercises involving *groups* of livestock-keepers. They have the advantage of providing a general picture relatively quickly, as compared with discussions with many *individuals*. Once the general picture has been obtained, and one or more critical issues identified, it may be desirable to obtain more detailed information about livestock productivity: for example, regarding mortality rates, or calving/kidding rates or intervals. In principle, this can be done either by:

- *monitoring* animals over a period of time; or
- interviewing individual livestock-keepers and asking them to *recall* the relevant information.

Many field-based livestock projects have incorporated detailed, but unfocused, long-term herd monitoring (of productivity parameters) studies in their early stages, usually lasting for at least 2–3 years (Roeleveld, 1996a). Herd monitoring has the advantage of generating reliable information, but there have been a number of disadvantages to this approach, namely:

- there is a significant time lag between the initiation of the project and the commencement of on-farm trials;

- substantial resources are required to implement such studies, making them costly;
- the livestock-keepers being monitored are liable to lose interest in the research early on, as they tend to see little benefit in it;
- such studies are largely quantitative and descriptive, and do not necessarily shed much light on the reasons why livestock productivity is good or poor, or contribute to the identification of research topics or the development of interventions.

Single-visit surveys, based on recall of herd history by the owner or another knowledgeable person, have been used as an alternative in some projects; two particular methods have been termed 'Herder recall' and 'Progeny history' (Iles, 1994; Waters-Bayer and Bayer, 1994). These can provide satisfactory results under certain circumstances (Roeleveld, 1996b). However, there are disadvantages (potential or inherent) with this approach too, notably:

- the reliability of the method depends heavily on the skill of the researcher/enumerator;
- the accuracy of recall may be less for lower value animals, such as small ruminants;
- as numbers of animals increase recall tends to become more difficult and hence less reliable; and
- such methods have generally been used in an extractive, non-participatory fashion.

The ideal method would combine speed with reliability. As with villages (see section 2.2) careful consideration should be given to the basis on which people or herds will be selected, particularly where it is desirable to have a representative sample.

Participatory herd histories

To address the issue of recall errors, the author and counterparts in BAIF Development Research Foundation have developed a way of collecting detailed livestock production information that we call the 'participatory herd history' method. It involves making an inventory of the current herd, and working backwards over 1–2 years to document what changes to the herd have taken place and when, either in terms of acquisitions or removals. (In the case of small herds of goats, the owner's recall appears to become increasingly unreliable after 1–2 years.) Thus, it provides information about births, deaths, slaughter, sales, purchases, abortions and still-births. It can be used to investigate various issues, some of which are described in Box 3.1.

A key difference between the latter method and conventional recall methods is that the herd history method uses symbols, and is a form of diagramming; whereas with the other methods the enumerator records the data in written form. This gives it two advantages. First, it makes it more 'participatory', in that the livestock owner is recording the information and can see it her/himself – goat-keepers with whom we have used the method have said that they found it useful.

Second, it improves the reliability of the data because: it makes it easier for the livestock owner to recall the information; it encourages her/him to think carefully before recording any information; and it makes it easier for the development agency staff to understand, or to spot any gaps or apparent anomalies, thereby reducing the likelihood of any omissions or misunderstandings between them and the livestock-owner. In fact, for goat herds with numerous animals, the extractive methods tend to be unreliable, making the herd history method essential.

The survey team (or livestock-keepers themselves) prepares a set of cards for the species being studied, each of which represents one animal. It helps if large cards are used for adults, and small cards for young animals; sometimes an intermediate size might also be appropriate. Each card has a picture of the animal drawn on it, and the pictures of adults indicate their sex.

A calendar, covering 1 or 2 years up to the present, is constructed on the ground, showing the seasons, months and important festivals. Several rows are made below the temporal headings, using sticks, cereal stalks, etc. – or chalk if the diagram is on a stone floor (see Table 3.6).

The livestock-keeper is asked: how many goats (s)he has in her herd; how many of these are kids and how many adults; and the sex of the adults. (S)he is then asked to select cards to represent each of the animals, and to lay these

BOX 3.1 Uses of the participatory herd history method

Disease-related mortality Discussions with groups of goat-keepers in Udaipur revealed that they perceived kid mortality from disease in the rainy season as their main problem or constraint. The herd history method was used to obtain quantitative information about the problem and to estimate mortality rates.

Reproductive performance The herd history method can provide information about the kidding interval of each breeding female (at least for small ruminants), and about abortions, stillbirths, twinning rates and peri-natal mortality of their progeny.

The herd history method is useful for collecting baseline data for subsequent use in evaluating the effect of trials – e.g. regarding the effect of feed supplementation on reproductive performance – as it enables before and after comparisons to be made. This can be a valuable supplement to data comparing the treatment and control groups (i.e. with and without comparison), particularly since some of the animals may be the same.

out in a column, at the end of the calendar, corresponding to the current point in time. To facilitate recall, each animal is referred to by its name, if they have names.

Having done this, (s)he is asked about the mother of each of the kids; and if the mother is part of the current herd, (s)he is asked to place the kid's card with that of its mother – as indicated in Table 3.6. In this diagram there are five adult (breeding) females and one adult male. Three of the females have kids that are part of the current herd, and one of these has twins: the other two adult females do not have kids in the herd.

The next step is to work backwards from the current herd, taking each adult in turn. Thus, with the doe in the top row of the diagram, the goat-keeper is asked to show on the calendar when it kidded, and to move the card for the kid to that point. (S)he is then asked whether any other kid (i.e. a twin) was born at that time, and if so what has happened to it. If there was a twin that has since left the herd another small card, of a different colour, is placed on the diagram at the time when it left the herd. The survey team makes a note of the reason why it left (e.g. death from pneumonia).

The process is then repeated for each of the other adult females, and then for any adult male. If an adult female does not have a kid in the herd the reason for this needs to be clarified – did she kid or not? If she did, what has happened to the kid? If she did not, why was this?

Tips – dos and don'ts

- When asking about the current herd, be careful not to focus exclusively on mothers and their kids: remember to ask about adult males and about adult females without kids.
- It is important to ask whether any adults have left the herd, something that becomes more likely if the calendar covers two years rather than one year. Over two years it may turn out that one of the adult females in the current herd was born to one of the others.
- Remember to ask about abortions, stillbirths and number of kids born.

Table 3.6 First stage of a participatory herd history

Summer	Rainy season	Winter	Current herd
			O o
			O o
			O
			O oo
			O
			M

O = adult female, o = kid, M = adult male.

- If the timing of births, deaths, sales, etc. is important remember to record it carefully.
- The cards symbolizing the animals should not be made of paper otherwise they may be moved by the wind (unless a stone is placed on them).
- Rows should be clearly delineated, otherwise a card may be placed in the wrong row.
- The livestock owner should be the person who manipulates the cards, NOT a member of the survey team.
- Make sure that the person you are working with is intimately familiar with the herd, otherwise they will not be able to complete the exercise. Even one knowledgeable person may struggle a little, and it sometimes helps to have two involved.
- The larger the number of animals involved, the more difficult the owner will find it to recall details about each individual. There are limits, therefore, on the size of herd for which this technique (and any other dependent on recall) will be feasible. Our experience suggests that five adult goats should be straightforward, and ten is feasible if the owner is intelligent and able to concentrate: beyond 15 may not be possible.

Participatory clutch history method

Something similar to the participatory herd history method has also been used in India for collecting information about clutch histories from poultry-keepers (Conroy et al., 2003). The fate of a particular clutch is traced on a diagram by the poultry-keeper over a 6-month period from the time when the eggs were laid, using a standardized format. The researchers used an A3 size sheet, in which all column and row headings were represented by symbols, so that illiterate people could use it. For example, all predators were represented by coloured pictures of them, and all column headings were illustrated by coloured pictures. The poultry-keeper was asked to place an appropriate number of small stones or some other material (e.g. beans) in the relevant cell. The format is shown in Table 3.7, in which the symbols have been replaced by words. In this example, out of 16 eggs laid only 12 hatched. Of these, only six reached grower age, most of them having been killed by crows; and, of these six, only 4 reached marketable age. At the time the clutch history was carried out, the two males had been sold and the two females had been retained in the flock.

Use of this method has, for example, enabled researchers to quantify mortality rates and to determine the contributions of different causes of mortality (e.g. disease, predation). The data from different clutch histories can be aggregated, enabling comparisons to be made between different categories of poultry-keepers, or between different villages, as shown in Table 3.8. In this example, the method has revealed the size of losses due to egg spoilage and mortality in young birds, and large differences in spoilage rates and causes of mortality between different types of poultry-keepers in the same village. A logical next step would be to investigate the reasons for these differences between the three types of poultry-keepers, and to find ways of reducing mortality and spoilage.

Table 3.7   Recording form for clutch histories

	Number of eggs laid	Number of eggs kept for hatching	Number of hatched eggs	Number reaching grower	Number reaching marketable age and/or weight		Currently Retained	
					Male (1.5 kg)	Female (1 kg)	M	F
→	••••••••••	•••••••••	•••••••••	••••••	••	••		••
Spoiled eggs[a]			••• infertile • dead foetus					
Disappear– reason not known				•				
Large bird of prey								
Small bird of prey								
Crow				••••				
Fox								
Cat								
Mongoose					•	•		
Dog								
Snake								
Gift								
Sale								••
Sacrifice								
Home consumption								
Disease				•				
Accident								
Others								

[a] Differentiate types of spoilage, e.g. infertile eggs or mortality of developed foetus in unhatched eggs.

Table 3.8 An overview of egg spoilage and mortality for three categories[a] of poultry-keepers in Peruganur village, Trichy District, Tamil Nadu

	Category 1	Category 2	Category 3	Overall (%)
Spoiled eggs (%)	12.1	18.5	24.8	18.2
Mortality pre-grower (%), of which[14]	26.4	17.9	24.8	23.1
■ Disease	11.9	5.7	1.7	7.0
■ Predation	12.6	11.4	21.4	14.7
Total losses [b]	37.5	36.4	49.6	41.3

[a] For a description of the three categories see Table 8.2.
[b] **i.e. spoiled eggs plus mortality.** The spoilage and mortality data are not strictly summable – they are not a percentage of 100. They have been aggregated here simply to give an overall picture of the severity of the losses, to facilitate comparisons between each group or village.

---

[14] There are other causes of mortality (mainly 'accidents'), but these are very minor compared with disease and predation. This can be seen by summing the percentages for these two causes and subtracting it from the total mortality figure, i.e. mortality due to other causes = 23.1–21.7 = 1.4%.

4 Feeding systems and resources

4.1 Spatial distribution of forage and water resources

Participatory mapping

People find it quite easy to make maps of natural resources, including sources of forage, and enjoy doing so. There is no need to show people's houses in detail, and it is important to allow enough room (on the ground) to show feed resources around the village and some distance away from it. The drawing of the map is not an end in itself – it is a tool for facilitating discussion, so once the map has been drawn it should be used as a basis for asking questions. It is quite likely that people will forget to show certain forage resources on the map, and that it will therefore need to be revised: thus, a copy of it should not be made until the discussion has been completed.

Forage walk

After the mapping it would be useful for the survey team, accompanied by one or two village members of the mapping group, to take a walk through the village that takes in some or most of the principal locations for forage resources that have been identified on the map. The walk will enable information shown on the map to be cross-checked and supplemented.

4.2 Identifying preferences for fodder tree/shrub species

Matrix scoring and ranking

This technique is useful in identifying people's preferences for different species of fodder trees or grasses, and in highlighting the advantages and disadvantages of each species. Table 4.1 is an example from Zimbabwe in which 20 beans were distributed among the different species for each criterion. Different criteria have different weights (i.e. some criteria are perceived as more important than others) and this is why the total scores do not correspond directly with the ranks.

Additional trees

Most trees are multi-purpose as far as rural people are concerned, so their preferences may be influenced by other criteria, apart from fodder-related ones. Furthermore, for project planning purposes a development agency may want to know what *additional* trees people would like to have, which may

Table 4.1 An example of matrix scoring and ranking of fodder trees

Trait/criterion	Species				
	Mupane	Mubhondo	Mupanda	Mususu	Mipwezha
Early shooting of leaves	7	4	5	2	2
Dry leaves can be eaten	1	–	–	19	–
Good taste/salty	7	4	5	2	2
High water content	–	–	13	–	7
Total score	*15*	*8*	*23*	*23*	*11*
Overall rank	1	4	3	2	5

Source: Scoones, 1994

be different from their most preferred species. They may, for example, have a relative abundance of the latter, but a shortage of another species that has a particular fodder or other value (e.g. providing fodder at the time of greatest scarcity). These issues can be explored by asking people about their preferences for additional trees/shrubs.

If they could have 50 or 100 more trees/shrubs, which species would they prefer? Why? What are their criteria? This line of discussion can be useful in **indirectly** finding out whether feed scarcity is important, by seeing whether the capacity of a species to provide forage at a particular time of the year is one of the criteria used.

4.3   Feeding systems and seasonality

Seasonal feed calendars
These can show (a) general *types* of feed or (b) *sources* of feed, and the proportions of each that are **used** in each month.[15] This kind of information can also be incorporated into a general seasonal production calendar. The advantage of this is that it makes it easier to identify possible relationships between feeding systems and other aspects of production. The potential disadvantage is that it may make the diagram rather difficult to understand – partly because percentages are allocated by column for feed types (see Table 4.2), whereas in the production calendar they are allocated by row (see Table 3.4).

---

[15]   Be careful not to confuse seasonal *availability* of forage and seasonal *use* of forage. Information about use is generally more useful.

An example of a *feed source* calendar is given in Table 4.2, in which the scheduled castes (SCs) have estimated the percentage contribution in each month of the different sources of feed.[16] These diagrams, like any others, should be discussed with the goat-keepers, and anything that is puzzling or unclear should be clarified. Footnotes can be added, giving additional information, as in this example. Alternatively, this information can be incorporated into the general text of the survey report in which the diagrams appear. It is important to bear in mind that the most appropriate and meaningful categories may vary from one village to another, or from one socio-economic group to another. Goat-keepers in Rajasthan said that they found this kind of feed diagram useful, as it enabled them to take a systematic look at how their feeding systems change over a year, and made them more aware of how significant *purchased feeds* become at certain times. They resolved to take steps to reduce the amount of purchased feed required.

Another kind of seasonal feed diagram is that which shows particular *types of forage* and the seasons or months[17] of the year when each is used: an example is given in Table 4.3. The species can be illustrated by collecting samples of their stalks, leaves, pods, etc. It is important to remember that materials for

Table 4.2 General seasonal feed utilization diagram for SCs in Indrapura, Asind Block, Bhilwara (%)

Feed sources and types	Summer				Rainy				Winter			
Community land	75	–	25ᵃ	62.5	50	85	75	62.5	62.5	37.5	50	50
Crop land (own)	–	100	25	12.5					–	25	25	25
Crop land (paid for)	–	–	12.5	–	–							
Bida ᵇ land (own)	20	–	25	12.5	50ᶜ	–			12.5	25	25	25
Bida ᵇ land (paid for)		–	12.5ᵈ	–		–	25	25				
Home supplements	5	–	–	12.5		15ᵉ		12.5	25ᶠ	12.5ᵍ		

ᵃ The principal species used at this time is *Acacia nilotica*.
ᵇ *Bida* is private 'wasteland' that is not good enough for crop production.
ᶜ They use their own *bida* land for 8–10 days before the rains start. They repair the boundary fences and during August they stop grazing on the *bida* land, and make full use of the communal land.
ᵈ This is purchased tree loppings.
ᵉ When the rain is heavy they have to cut grass for the goats.
ᶠ They give barley (which they have grown) to lactating does.
ᵍ Cotton

---

[16] The data in this table have been converted from Anas (the old Indian currency) to percentages. Villagers think of 16 Anas as 100 per cent, 8 Anas as 50 per cent, etc.

[17] A calendar based on months, rather than seasons, is preferable, as it should show whether there are any particular months within a season when scarcity is more acute.

some species may not be easily available when the calendar is being prepared: rather than omit the species from the diagram, another way should be found to represent it.[18] It is probably best to start with a general feed diagram; and then move on to individual forage species and types of supplement, either in a new diagram or by extending the first one. Table 4.4 is a hybrid calendar, in that it contains information about types of forage and sources.

Once information has been assembled about the various forage resources used during the year, this can be related to the owners' livestock production objectives and used to identify when feed scarcity occurs. A distinction should be made between overall scarcity (i.e. insufficient *quantity*) and a shortage of high *quality* feeds.

People, particularly those who are illiterate, tend to find it more difficult to draw seasonal diagrams than to draw maps. This is probably partly because the kind of diagrams usually found in the PRA literature are largely a product of western culture and concepts. However, one approach that works well is to ask people to show the seasons and major festivals (using symbols), and to draw one column for each month. Thus, if there are three seasons of equal length, there will be four columns under each season.

It is also helpful to: (a) start discussions about feeding systems with the forage resource mapping to get people thinking about this; and (b) give people time to think about how they would like to illustrate principal feeds

Table 4.3 Species-based seasonal feed calendar from Bhilwara District, Rajasthan

	Winter (November–March)	Summer (April–June)	Monsoon (July–October)
Arunjia (*Acacia leucophloea*)	✔		
Neem (*Azadirachta indica*)	✔		
Ber (*Zizyphus mauritiana*)	✔		
Cotton leaves (*Gossypium* spp.)	✔		
Desi babul (*Acacia nilotica*)		✔	
Thor (Cactus, *Opuntia* spp.)		✔ (chopped)	✔ (buds)
Bordi (dry leaves of Z. nummularia)		✔	✔
Groundnut hay		✔	
Lucerne		✔	
Khejri (*Prosopis cineraria*)		✔	✔
Fresh grass			✔
Concentrate	✔		

[18] One seasonal diagram constructed in Kirat village, Udaipur District, appeared to be showing June as the month of greatest scarcity, yet the seasonal production calendar had shown June as the time when breeding started. When the villagers were asked to explain this discrepancy it turned out that the species thought to trigger oestrus had been omitted from the diagram because there was no vegetative material available to illustrate it.

during a year – for example, by leaving preparation of a calendar until the following day.

Forage resource maps and seasonality

The issue of seasonal dimensions of feeding systems can also be explored during mapping exercises, referring to the map, as can ways of coping with scarcity (if they experience it). When referring to the dry season, it can be useful to distinguish between years of typical rainfall and drought years, as livestock-keepers may modify their feeding systems in a drought year. It is helpful to focus on specific years – for example, by asking:

- where (on the map) did you get your feed from in the last dry season (this year);
- where did you get it from in the last *severe* dry season?
- what happened to your livestock (specify which type) in the last severe dry season?

It may be worthwhile making a new map for a drought year, as people may be forced to take their animals further away from their village than they normally would, and the more distant resources may not be shown on the initial map. People who normally stay in their village all year round sometimes migrate in a drought year.

Table 4.4 A simple forage calendar

| | | Forage resources[a] | | | | | | | |
Season	Month	A	B	C	D	E	F	G	H
Dry	January	2	1			2	2	2	1
Dry	February		2			1	1	5	1
Dry	March		2			1	1	6	
Wet	April	10							
Wet	May	10							
Wet	June	10							
Wet	July	10							
Wet	August	9		1					
Wet	September	7		1	2				
Wet	October	8			2				
Dry	November	3			2	5			
Dry	December	2				5	3		

[a] Key to forage resources: A = upland pasture, B = upland pasture, burnt, C = maize leaves, D = harvested maize fields, E = harvested sorghum fields, F = harvested millet fields, G = riverine pasture, H = bean straw. Numbers 1–10 refer to the relative contribution of each forage to animal diet.
Source: Bayer and Waters-Bayer (1998)

5 Animal health

Andy Catley

5.1 Introduction

Livestock-keepers often consider disease to be an important constraint to livestock rearing. Participatory approaches to solving disease problems can include the testing of different treatments or control strategies in terms of their effectiveness, cost, ease of use and other factors. Compared with participatory research on other aspects of livestock production and health, the testing of new or alternative treatments can often produce results relatively quickly. For example, the benefits of an effective medicine for repelling flies or killing ticks will soon be apparent to farmers involved in trials.

Animal health workers have been using participatory methods for many years. In East Africa, NGOs were particularly active in developing participatory methods in the late 1980s for the design of community-based animal health worker projects (e.g. Grandin et al., 1991). Around the same time, and related to community-based approaches, there was renewed interest in indigenous animal health knowledge. In 1994, a special issue of the informal journal *RRA Notes* included five articles on participatory methods for animal health, with examples from Kenya (Grandin and Young, 1994), Afghanistan (Leyland, 1994) Somaliland (Hadrill and Yusuf, 1994), Tibet (Heffernan, 1994) and Nepal (Young et al., 1994).

This chapter discusses participatory methods for describing and analysing issues related to animal health problems. Many of these methods have already been described in previous chapters and these can easily be adapted to look at veterinary issues. Although numerous participatory methods are available to animal health researchers (Table 5.1), many studies have used only informal or semi-structured interviews. Therefore, the chapter emphasizes how different methods can be used in the same study to compare and cross-check information.

There is no standard approach to using participatory methods for animal health research, and indeed, one advantage of participatory research is its flexibility. Not all methods are suitable for every situation, and adaptation of specific methods to meet particular needs is encouraged. Also, some methods work better in some communities than in others.

Table 5.1 Some participatory methods for animal health research

Topic	Participatory methods[a]
System boundary/spatial limits of livestock population	Natural resource maps, social maps
Contact between adjacent livestock populations	Mapping, Venn diagrams
Contact with disease vectors or high risk disease areas	Mapping
History of livestock diseases in the community	Time-lines
Priority livestock diseases	Disease ranking
Differential diagnoses of diseases	Matrix scoring
Seasonal variations in diseases and exposure to vectors	Seasonal calendars
Age-specific disease incidence and mortality	Proportional piling, progeny history
Economic and social losses due to diseases	Matrix scoring, proportional piling
Analysis of control options	Matrix scoring (or ranking)
Veterinary service accessibility	Service maps, mobility maps[b]
Analysis of service providers	Preference ranking, matrix scoring
Assessing effect of treatment or control	'Before and after' scoring; sequential scoring

[a] Semi-structured interviews can provide information on all topics.
[b] Particularly useful for mobile communities as accessibility to service providers may vary.

5.2 Veterinary diagnosis and participatory research methods

One of the reasons why participatory approaches are so useful in animal health research is the similarity between participatory inquiry and conventional, modern veterinary diagnosis. When diagnosing a disease, veterinarians are taught:

- to observe the environment in which the animals are kept;
- interview the livestock-keeper (take the case history);
- physically examine sick animals; and, if appropriate,
- conduct post-mortem examinations or use additional laboratory tests.

The veterinarian combines information from each of these methods to reach a diagnosis, in a similar way to the use of triangulation in participatory inquiry. Typically, the results of one method are insufficient to confirm the problem, and it is only when information is cross-checked and combined that people feel confident about their diagnosis. Even when laboratory tests are used, professional judgement often determines the test result and the interpretation of the result. The similarity between conventional veterinary diagnosis and participatory methods is illustrated in Figure 5.1.

For researchers, it is sometimes useful to be aware of the qualitative nature of veterinary diagnosis and investigation, because conventional

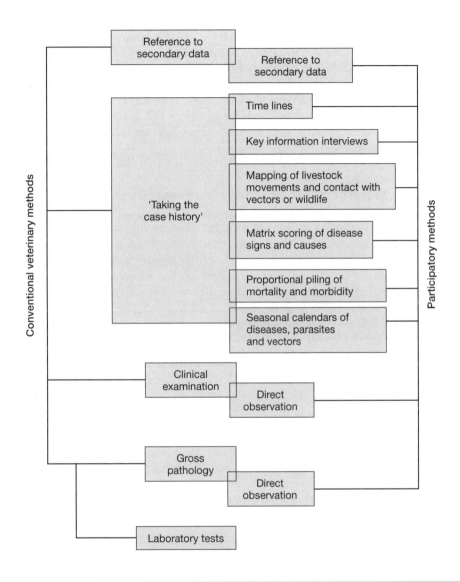

Figure 5.1 Overlaps between veterinary diagnosis and participatory inquiry

research places considerable emphasis on quantitative methods and statistical analysis. Typically, research institutions reward studies that report numbers and statistics rather than insights, narrative accounts of context, or consensus among stakeholders. Although it is often assumed that quantitative research is automatically superior to qualitative research, veterinary medicine is essentially a judgemental process and most vets probably consider themselves to be scientists.

Triangulation of qualitative data

Section 5.3 describes ways to use participatory methods in a qualitative way and triangulate methods to improve the trustworthiness of findings. Attention to triangulation is important not only because of validity issues, but also because animal health researchers often forget to do it. Much participatory research focuses on one or two methods, and typically these methods are types of informal interview. Very few animal health research projects make the most of the wide range of visualization and scoring methods used in PRA/PSA, or specify how a particular result was cross-checked using a different method.

5.3   Uses of participatory methods in research

Example 1: Participatory methods for disease diagnosis

Disease problems can be illnesses that livestock keepers are already very familiar with, but for which they lack information on the pros and cons of different modern or indigenous treatments. For example, people may know that their cattle have worms but they may not know the optimum way to use anthelmintics or the relative merits of other control options. In other situations, a disease is recognized by livestock-keepers but researchers don't know what the disease is.

In both of these situations, the starting point is to reach a common understanding of the disease in question. Livestock-keepers will usually give a disease problem a name (or names) in their own language. Researchers need to learn how to interpret these local names and understand the association between indigenous and modern disease descriptions.

Figure 5.1 shows how disease diagnosis is not based solely on the observed appearance of a disease (clinical signs) but can also use information on causes or sources of disease, seasonal and geographical variations in disease occurrence, historical disease events and the incidence and mortality of the disease. Signs of disease or parasites observed in dead animals also provide useful diagnostic information.

A comparative approach

It is advisable to encourage livestock-keepers to compare different diseases, rather than discussing only the disease that is the main topic of the research. This can be done using methods such as matrix scoring of disease signs and causes, seasonal calendars and proportional piling. This comparative approach helps to reveal differences between diseases, and to avoid exaggeration of the importance of any particular one.

Standardized component

Each method includes initial standardized procedures involving the use of counters (e.g. stones or seeds) to show relationships between the diseases and

BOX 5.1 Diagnosing an unknown wasting disease in cattle in southern Sudan

In southern Sudan, participatory methods were used to diagnose a disease in adult cattle, which local people called *liei*, that was characterized by chronic weight loss (Catley et al., 2001, 2002a). The work was done with seven groups of livestock-keepers. The methods used are described below. There is also a summary of how results were triangulated.

First, *matrix scoring* was applied to five cattle diseases, including *liei*. Initial pairwise comparison of five diseases generated indicators that were categorized as disease-signs and disease-causes. Results are presented in Figures 5.2 and 5.3, which give the median scores of the seven groups for each of the disease signs.

Key findings

- The disease *liei* is associated with chronic weight loss and loss of tail hair. The disease could be trypanosomiasis.

- *Liei* is also associated with biting flies, liver flukes, snails and flooding. The disease could be trypanosomiasis, fascioliasis, schistosomiasis, intestinal worms, or all of these diseases.

Second, *seasonal calendars* were constructed of the same five cattle diseases plus the disease vectors identified during the matrix scoring. Results are presented in Figure 5.4.

Key findings

- *Liei* occurs after exposure to Tabanids, snails and ticks, and starts in the later part of the wet season. The disease could be trypanosomiasis, fascioliasis, schistosomiasis, intestinal worms (agrees with matrix scoring results), a tick-borne disease, or all of these diseases.

Third, *mapping* was used to show areas where cattle were in contact with potential disease vectors (Figure 5.5).

Key findings

- Cattle are frequently exposed to snails in swampy areas; they are also exposed to biting flies at the beginning of the wet season (both findings agree with seasonal calendar results). Ticks not thought to be a problem. *Liei* could be trypanosomiasis, fascioliasis, schistosomiasis, intestinal worms or all of these diseases (agrees with matrix scoring and partly agrees with seasonal calendars).

Fourth, *clinical and post-mortem examination* of *liei* cases with livestock-keepers. Livestock-keepers identify and name lesions and parasites in carcases. Examination of blood for trypanosomes.

BOX 5.1 cont.

Key findings

■ All *liei* cases were heavily infected with at least two parasites (liver flukes, worms, schistosomes or trypanosomes).

The conclusion of this research was that the chronic wasting disease *liei* was single and mixed infections of various parasites. Further research was designed to determine the most efficient combinations of veterinary medicines to cure the disease.

the variables in question. If statistical analysis is required, the numbers of counters, diseases and variables should be kept constant every time a method is repeated.

Open-ended component

Each method should also include an open-ended component. Here, open and probing questions are used to cross-check the placing of counters and follow up interesting leads and ideas. A checklist of questions can be prepared for each method but this checklist does not have to be followed rigidly. In some interviews, not all issues may be covered but new, unexpected topics may emerge that warrant exploration.

Table 5.2 Triangulation of results from five methods for the diagnosis of *liei*

Method	Evidence that *liei* was:				
	Trypanosomiasis	Fascioliasis	Schistosomiasis	Haemonchosis	Tick-borne disease
Matrix scoring of disease signs	+	+	−	−	−
Matrix scoring of disease causes	+	+	+	+	−
Seasonal calendars	+	+	+	+	+
Mapping	+	+	+	+	−
Clinical examination and post-mortem examination	+	+	+	+	−

Signs	Diseases				
	Liei	Abuot pou	Jul	Jong achom	Cual
Chronic weight loss (W = 0.67**)	•••• •••• ••••			•••• •••• ••••	
Seeks shade (W = 0.88***)			•••• ••••• ••••		
Diarrhoea (W = 0.67**)	••• ••			•••• •••• ••••	
Coughing (W = 0.94***)		•••• ••••• ••••			
Reduced appetite (W = 0.38*)	•• •	•••• •••• ••••			
Loss of tail hair (W = 1.00***)	•••• ••••• ••••				
Tearing (W = 0.35*)	•••• ••••				
Swollen joints (W = 1.00***)					•••• ••••• ••••
Reduced milk (W = 0.73***)			•••• ••••• ••••		
Rough coat (W = 0.90***)			•••• ••••• ••••		
Abortion (W = 0.42**)	•• •				•••• •••• ••••

Figure 5.2 Matrix scoring of disease signs around Thiet, southern Sudan: medians

Number of informant groups = 7. W = Kendall coefficient of concordance Number of informant groups = 7. W = Kendall coefficient of concordance (*p<0.05; **p<0.01; ***p<0.001); this is a measure of agreement between the seven informant groups.

Causes or sources	Liei	Abuot pou	Jul	Jong achom	Cual
			Diseases		
Liver fluke *Daichom* (W = 0.68**)				••••• ••••• ••••• •••••	
Sick cow entering herd (W = 0.65**)		••• ••• •••			•••• ••••
Worms (W = 0.43*)				••• •••• •••	
Wet grass (W = 0.57**)	••• •••• •••			••• •••• •••	
Flooding (W = 0.35*)	••• •••• •••		•• ••	•• ••	
Biting flies *Rom* (W = 1.00***)	••••• ••••• ••••• •••••				
Ticks *Chak* (W = 1.00***)					
Snails *Chom* (W = 0.63**)	••• ••			••••• ••••• ••••• •••••	

Figure 5.3 Matrix scoring of causes or sources of cattle diseases in Thiet, southern Sudan: medians

Number of informant groups = 7. *W* = Kendall coefficient of concordance (*$p < 0.05$; **$p < 0.01$; ***$p < 0.001$); this is a measure of agreement between the seven informant groups. Actual samples of flies, ticks, liver flukes, worms and snails were used.

	Seasons			
	Mai (Feb–Apr)	Ker (May–July)	Ruil (Aug–Oct)	Rut (Nov–Jan)
Rainfall (as a proportion of total annual rainfall) (W = 0.96**)		●●●●●●●●	●●●●●●●●●●	●
Liei (W = 0.32*)	●●●●	●	●●●●●●	●●●●●●
Abuot pou (W = 0.41**)	●●●	●●●●	●●●●●●●	●●●●●●
Jul (W = 0.38*)	●●●	●●●	●●●●●●●●●●	●●●
Jong acom (W = 0.50**)		●●●●●●	●●●●●●●●●	●●●●
Rom/Tabanid sp. (W = 0.42**)	●	●●●●●●●●●	●●●●	●●●●●●
Luang/Stomoxys sp. (W = 0.38*)	●●●●●	●●●●●●	●●●●●●	●●
Dhier/mosquitoes (W = 0.85***)		●●●●●	●●●●●●●●●●●●	●●●●
Chom/snails (W = 0.83***)		●●●●●●●●●	●●●●●●●●●	
Achak/ticks (W = 0.79***)		●●●●●●●●●●	●●●●●●●	●

Figure 5.4 Summarized seasonal calendar of rainfall, cattle diseases, biting flies, ticks and snails in Thiet, southern Sudan: medians

n = 10 informant groups; W = Kendal coefficient of concordance (*p<0.05; **p<0.01; ***p<0.001).

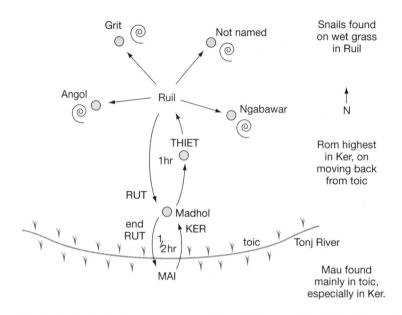

Grit

Not named

Snails found
on wet grass
in Ruil

Angol

Ruil

Ngabawar

N

THIET

1hr

Rom highest
in Ker, on
moving back
from toic

RUT

Madhol

end
RUT

KER

1/2hr

toic

Tonj River

MAI

Mau found
mainly in toic,
especially in Ker.

Figure 5.5 Seasonal movements of cattle from Madhol cattle camp, near Thiet

Map produced by seven informants in Madhol cattle camp. Arrowed lines indicate cattle movements; seasons were *mai* (February–April), *ker* (May–July), *ruil* (August–October) and *rut* (November–January); curled, circular symbols represent high exposure to snails.

Example 2: participatory methods for analysis of disease control options

Many animal health research institutes are involved in technology development, and aim to promote the uptake of new technologies. When identifying the kinds of animal health innovations that might be useful to livestock-keepers, it is important to understand how they prioritize livestock diseases and the methods they are already using to solve (or attempt to solve) these problems. Any new disease control methods have to demonstrate clear advantages over existing methods if uptake is to occur.

Another consideration is the potential role of different stakeholders in the delivery of new technology. Unless delivery mechanisms are understood, a situation can arise in which a research institute ('A') has a useful product; and livestock-keepers ('B') like the product, but there is no sustainable pathway for moving the product from A to B. For example, in an area where a tick-borne disease is important, private veterinarians or agrochemical stores might be selling acaricide to livestock-keepers. Profit from acaricide sales could account for a substantial proportion of the overall profit of the business. Now imagine that a research institute develops a new vaccine for the tick-borne disease, and assumes that the private sector will deliver this vaccine on a profit-making basis. However, although the vaccine is effective, it requires a veterinary worker to make two visits to every vaccinated animal. When the cost and inconvenience of these visits is calculated, the private operators soon realize that their profits and overall business viability would suffer if they switched from selling acaricide to selling vaccine. Consequently, the new vaccine stays on the shelf in the research institute and is never delivered.

Participatory methods can be very useful for understanding the preferences of livestock-keepers and the likelihood that a new technology is needed or will be used. Similarly, participatory methods can also be used in stakeholder analysis of different disease control options. When stakeholders include groups responsible for delivery of new technologies, delivery constraints can be anticipated.

BOX 5.2 Preferences for bovine trypanosomiasis control in Kenya

In Tana River District, Kenya, Orma pastoralist communities relied heavily on their cattle for social and economic support. The area was tsetse-infested and it was known that livestock-keepers frequently used trypanocidal drugs to prevent or treat the disease. As clinical veterinary services were being privatized in Kenya, these drugs were available from private 'Agrovet' stores. The Kenya Trypanosomiasis Research Institute (KETRI) assumed that trypanocidal drug resistance was, or could become, a problem and developed a project to establish community-based tsetse control activities, based on impregnated targets and traps.

A participatory assessment of the trypanosomiasis problem was conducted in four villages in November 2000 (Catley et al., 2002b). This research included the use of participatory methods to:

■ understand how livestock-keepers characterized and named trypanosomiasis;

■ estimate disease incidence and the importance of trypanosomiasis relative to other cattle diseases;

■ understand how livestock-keepers were controlling the disease;

■ present options to livestock-keepers for improving disease control and identify a best-bet option for further testing with KETRI.

In common with the example in Box 5.1, matrix scoring was used to characterize trypanosomiasis. Matrix scoring of disease signs and disease causes showed that Orma used the disease name *gandi* for trypanosomiasis generally, and the disease name *buku* for an acute, haemorrhagic form of the disease (presumed by the researchers to be caused by *Trypanosoma vivax*).

BOX 5.2   cont.

Estimating disease incidence and importance

A proportional piling method[19] was used to compare the incidence of *gandi* and *buku* to three other cattle diseases and healthy cattle. Cattle herds were categorized by age using Orma definitions of age groups. Taking each age group in turn, herders were asked to divide piles of stones to show proportions of healthy cattle and sick cattle, and then further divide the sick cattle to show the incidence of the five diseases plus an 'other diseases category'. Results are shown in Figures 5.6 to 5.8, and indicate that trypanosomiasis was indeed a major problem in these communities.

Existing methods for controlling trypanosomiasis

A simple matrix scoring method was used in each village to understand how livestock-keepers were already controlling trypanosomiasis. Results showed that trypanocidal drugs were an effective but high cost option that did not require collective action (Table 5.3).

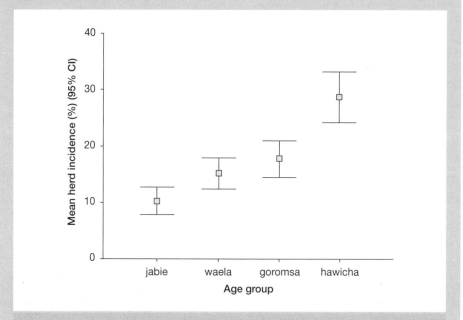

Figure 5.6   Mean herd incidence of *gandi*/trypanosomiasis in Orma cattle, 1999–2000

n = 50 herds. Age groups: *jabie* ~ 0–2 years; *waela* ~ 2–3 years; *goromsa* ~ 3–4 years; *hawicha* > 4 years.

[19]   Another example of the use of proportional piling is given in Box 2.2.

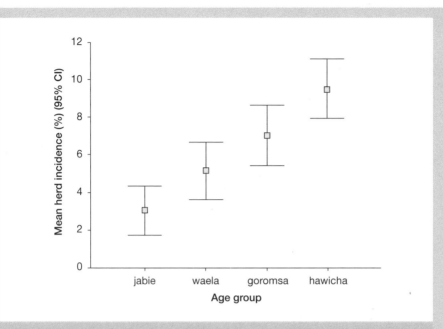

Figure 5.7 Mean herd incidence of *buku*/acute haemorrhagic trypanosomiasis in Orma cattle, 1999–2000

n = 50 herds. Age groups: *jabie* ~ 0–2 years; *waela* ~ 2–3 years; *goromsa* ~ 3–4 years; *hawicha* > 4 years

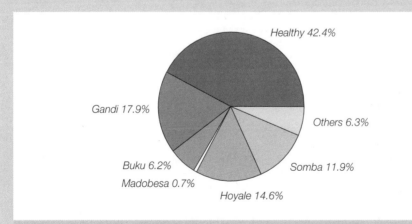

Figure 5.8 Mean herd incidence of cattle diseases relative to healthy cattle, all age groups, 1999–2000 (n = 50)

Interpretation of Orma disease names as derived from matrix scoring: *gandi*, trypanosomiasis; *buku*, acute haemorrhagic trypanosomiasis; *hoyale*, foot-and-mouth disease; *somba*, contagious bovine pleuropneumonia; *madobesa*, a rinderpest-like disease.

BOX 5.2 cont.

Table 5.3 Preference ranking of control methods for *gandi* in Gadeni, Danissa, Oda and Kipao villages

Indicator	Herbal remedy	Burning the bush[a]	Bleeding[b]	Movement[c]	Dung fires[d]	Pour on	Dips	Trypanocides from:		
								Hawkers and shops	CAHW[e]	Agrovet
Effectiveness	8.5	6.0	7.0	7.0	7.0	4.0	3.0	3.0	2.0	3.0
Low financial cost	1.0	1.0	1.0	2.0	1.0	10.0	9.0	6.0	7.0	9.0
Easily used[f]	4.0	2.0	6.0	3.0	1.0	8.0	9.0	5.0	5.0	6.0
Requires group action[g]	3.0	3.0	3.0	2.0	3.0	3.0	3.0	3.0	3.0	3.0
Individual acts alone[h]	5.0	7.0	6.0	8.0	1.0	6.0	8.0	1.0	1.0	1.0

Interpretation of ranks: 1 = highest rank; 10 = lowest rank.
[a] Bush clearance by burning was against Kenya government environmental policy.
[b] Bleeding or bloodletting involved removal of blood from the jugular vein.
[c] Cattle movement to and from the river delta to avoid flooding and tsetse.
[d] Dung fires are lit among the cattle in the kraals every evening.
[e] Community animal health workers.
[e] 'Easily used' included availability of the materials required to use the method, time and labour inputs, and the level of specialist knowledge required by the users. This specialist knowledge could be either indigenous knowledge, e.g. about a specific herbal remedy, or technical knowledge about the use of a veterinary medicine.
[f] 'Requires group action' referred to methods that could only be used when people organized themselves for collective action. This indicator was considered to be a negative indicator.
[g] 'Individual acts alone' meant that a single livestock-keeper could use the method independently of other community members, and any benefits would be received by that person alone.

Identifying a best-bet option for further research

Previous experience with trypanosomiasis control research indicated that a number of methods were effective, but few could be sustained in the long term. A stakeholder workshop was organized in which the researchers presented different control methods to stakeholders, and asked them to rank each control option against a set of 'sustainability indicators'. The stakeholders at the workshop were livestock-keepers from the four villages, KETRI staff, representatives from the Catholic Diocese of Malindi, the District Veterinary Officer and a representative from the nearby private Agrovet store.

Based on the information provided to them by KETRI, livestock-keepers ranked the four possible best-bet interventions as shown in Table 5.4. This showed that, despite KETRI's initial interest in community-based tsetse control, livestock-keepers didn't consider this method to be a sustainable option.

Table 5.4 Ranking of possible control interventions against sustainability indicators by community representatives

| Sustainability indicator | Median ranks for possible control intervention[a] | | | |
	Community -based tsetse control project	Improved use of trypanocides	Use of pour-on	Community -based dips
Community commitment to contribute:				
■ Finance	3.5	1.0	1.5	3.5
■ Labour	3.5	1.0	1.5	2.0
■ Management	3.5	1.0	1.0	2.0
Low financial cost to individual end-users	2.0	1.0	3.0	4.0
Builds on existing systems (including indigenous knowledge)	3.5	1.0	2.5	2.5
An individual can benefit by acting alone	3.5	1.0	1.0	3.0
Resistance to crises (e.g. drought, conflict)	3.5	1.0	1.0	3.0
Avoids conflict with neighbours	4.0	1.0	1.0	3.0

[a] Ranking method based on ranks: 1st = most preferred to 4th = least preferred. n = 4.

Further discussion confirmed that, apart from KETRI, none of the stakeholders considered community-based tsetse control to be a viable intervention. Based on these findings, KETRI changed their research objectives and decided to focus on further research on trypanocidal drug use, including assessments of drug resistance. This experience illustrates how researchers using participatory approaches have to be flexible and willing to change research agendas according to local analysis of problems and solutions.

Participatory research and disease modelling

A relatively new approach to improved disease control strategies combines participatory assessment with disease modelling. For example, in southern Sudan participatory methods were used to generate basic data for a rinderpest disease model (Mariner, 2001). The development of a computer model requires herd age structures and age-specific rinderpest mortality to be deduced and participatory methods such as proportional piling can be used for this purpose. Also, methods such as mapping can be used to understand contact between communities and herds, and seasonal variations in contact rates.

A model was developed to show the effect of vaccination on rinderpest presence in a given population. This model was used to predict the level of vaccination coverage required for stopping transmission of rinderpest within and between herds in southern Sudan. This research approach combines herders' expert opinions with sophisticated mathematics and conventional diagnosis to develop better disease control strategies. Furthermore, disease models can be developed with relatively small data sets provided that the reliability of the data is known.

5.4 Conclusions

Participatory research methods have proven to be valuable tools for encouraging greater involvement of livestock-keepers in defining animal health research problems and testing solutions. Numerous approaches and methods are available, and hopefully researchers will continue to use the methods creatively and avoid a reliance on interviews (which easily become questionnaires). In Kenya alone, experiences include detailed ethnoveterinary research conducted with pastoralist communities (Case study C) and the development and testing of livestock Farmer Field Schools with smallholder dairy farmers (Minjauw et al., 2002a).

A key issue for animal health researchers is the extent to which participatory methods are standardized for quantitative studies. Many participatory methods produce numbers as scores or ranks, and therefore it is relatively straightforward to standardize methods and repeat them. However, this process can easily undermine participatory research by focusing researchers' attention on the collection of numerical data. Information that cannot easily be recorded numerically is then lost. In part, wider uptake of qualitative methods within the context of participatory research depends on institutional change and support for researchers who explore alternative, non-quantitative approaches (Catley and Mariner, 2002). Issues of institutional barriers and change are discussed in sections 1.2, 7.3 and 11.4.

While qualitative approaches tend to be more adaptable, resource-friendly and accessible to livestock-keepers, the use of triangulation is often either overlooked or not reported. This means that an important measure of validity is absent from many study reports based on participatory methods. Similarly, few studies use conventional methods such as laboratory diagnosis to complement participatory assessment. More cross-checking of information by animal health professionals, and better description of the methods they have used, will increase the credibility of participatory research and will help to ensure that it becomes more widely used in animal health research and development.

6 Analysis of constraints, problems and opportunities

6.1 Preliminary identification and ranking of constraints

It is important to have a sound understanding of the production problems or constraints livestock-keepers are facing, as this will provide the basis for determining which types of interventions are needed, or what the participatory technology development (PTD) process should focus on. Various constraints are likely to become apparent through discussions of the production system, feeding system, etc., but it is still useful to have a general discussion, before any ranking of constraints is done, so that nothing is overlooked. Even for the same type of livestock, the constraints identified by livestock-keepers may vary from village to village, from one production system to another, and between men and women.

As part of the process of identifying constraints, the following question can produce some revealing answers: *if they had 100 rupees (or other local currency) to spend on more livestock, which would they purchase and why?* For example, Gujars in Rajasthan said they would spend 75 on goats and 25 on sheep. When asked to explain this, they said that the reason they preferred small ruminants (especially goats) to large ruminants was that it is too difficult to feed large ruminants in a year of low rainfall; whereas small ruminants can graze on common land.

Different types of constraint There are various types of constraints affecting livestock production, which can be classified in different ways. Be alert to these, as it is important to understand how the owner perceives the constraints, which may be different from how a livestock development worker perceives them. There are two types of animal-related categories, namely:

- limits on the *number* of animals kept (e.g. forage resources, labour for herding)
- limits on the *productivity* of the herd (e.g. disease, seasonal feed scarcity).

Another important distinction is between constraints/problems that affect the animal's productivity (which livestock scientists tend to focus on), and those that affect the owner. For example, the owner may be maintaining livestock productivity at a certain level, but incurring various costs in doing so, such as: spending money on purchased supplements; or increased fatigue caused by longer daily herding times and distances during the dry season.

Ranking constraints Once the constraints have been identified the villagers should be asked to rank them in terms of their importance. This should be done separately for different types of livestock. Examples of such rankings are given in Table 6.1: the first is the most important.

Examples of constraints Goat-keepers in India mentioned several constraints on goat production during group interviews undertaken as part of a goat research project (Conroy and Rangnekar, 2000). Apart from those given in Table 6.1, problems included theft, predators (fox, jackal, wolf) and lack of a breeding buck.

6.2   Scratching below the surface

The identification of problems, and discussions with livestock-keepers about them, are often superficial. For example, general discussions with two sub-groups in one village and another group in a second village in Bhavnagar District, Gujarat, identified water scarcity in the dry season as the main constraint or problem for goat production in all of them (Conroy and Rangnekar, 2000). However, more detailed discussions revealed that the nature of the water scarcity problem was different in each.

In the first village, one of the sub-groups was Rabari men, for whom livestock husbandry is the main enterprise and who herd their animals several kilometres each day. For them the problem was the distance they have to walk with their animals to find water in the dry season, when an important water source has dried up. The other sub-group was women belonging to scheduled castes, who keep one or two goats, mainly stall-feeding them. The problem for these women was that they have to walk 2 kilometres to the village well to fetch drinking water and bring it back home for the goats. In the other village, water scarcity was so severe that people were dependent on government tankers bringing water every day, from which they purchased it. Since the water scarcity problem is quite different in each of the three cases, the solution is also likely to be different in each case.

Table 6.1 Ranked constraints on goat production in three villages – Rabaris in Bhavnagar District, Gujarat

Rank	Kumbhan	Valukad	Hanol
1	Water scarcity – summer	Water scarcity – all year	Disease
2	Forage scarcity – summer	Forage scarcity – summer	Quantity of crop residues in late winter/summer
3	Disease	Disease	Water scarcity

Sometimes constraints exist that livestock-keepers tend not to mention. Marketing is seldom mentioned as a problem. Similarly, the availability of family labour for herding is not usually mentioned as a constraint by goat-keepers. However, a regression analysis that modelled the relationship between herd size and other variables, using data from Rajasthan, showed that the availability of household labour is one factor that is 'uniformly important in determining the herd size' (Sagar and Ahuja, 1993).

Conversely, livestock-keepers may mention first those problems that they think the survey agency is most likely to be able to help with (e.g. supply of inputs) – producing a shopping list. It should not be assumed, therefore, that the information gained from initial discussions is complete or entirely accurate. A better understanding of constraints is likely to emerge over a period of months of interaction with livestock-keepers. One tool that is useful in deepening understanding, *participatory problem tree analysis*, is described below.

Planning interventions to address a constraint may sometimes require a more detailed understanding than livestock-keepers on their own can provide. For example, they may know that disease is a serious problem at certain times, but they may not know what the disease is or what causes it: in situations like this, specific studies may need to be undertaken. The identified constraints should be reviewed from time to time as understanding of them improves.

6.3   Participatory problem tree analysis

Problem trees are a very useful diagrammatic tool for analysing problems and gaining a more in-depth understanding of their nature. They also reveal how farmers or livestock-keepers perceive problems and relationships, which may be different from how outsiders see them. They involve identifying a core problem, the factors causing it, and the effects that it has. The core problem is represented as the trunk of the tree, the causes as its roots and the effects as its branches. When explaining the technique to livestock-keepers it is helpful to emphasize the analogy, preferably by pointing to a tree or a picture of one.

The core problem may have been identified beforehand in general discussions of constraints. If not, a problem/constraints brainstorming and ranking exercise can be conducted first, and one of the highest ranked problems is then selected for more detailed analysis through use of a problem tree. An example of a problem tree is given in Figure 6.1.

Participants identify all the factors they can think of that are related to the core problem. Each of these is then symbolized on a fairly large piece of paper or card. The livestock owners then discuss the relationships between them, classifying them into causes and effects, and place the cards at the appropriate place on the ground. It is highly unlikely that these would be

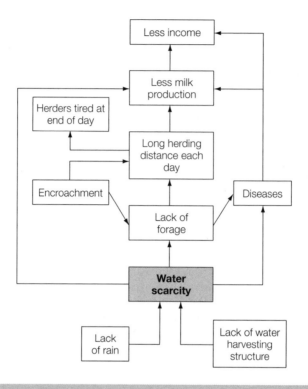

Figure 6.1   Problem tree constructed by Rabaris in Kumbhan, Gujarat, showing water scarcity as the core problem

satisfactorily identified at the first attempt, so there will be a need to move the cards around. Where a causal relationship is identified between two factors this can be indicated by placing a stick or similar object between the relevant cards.

One of the advantages of a problem tree is that it shows the **relationships** between different factors, or how livestock-keepers perceive those relationships. This is important for assessing the implications of interventions, since the fact that constraints are often inter-related means that easing one or more can lead to the alleviation or exacerbation of others.[20]

A problem tree can be converted into an objectives tree, by re-stating all of the problems as objectives, and used as a tool for planning livestock development interventions: for example, 'disease' or 'poor health' could become

---

[20]   For example, improving the supply of drinking-water during the dry season may increase animals' appetites and increase the grazing pressure on nearby pastures, resulting in scarcity of forage.

'improve health'. In the objectives tree, the cause–effect relationships become means–end relationships.

Once a basic PSA has been carried out, livestock professionals and livestock-keepers will be well placed to act upon the findings. They can do so either by implementing a livestock development programme, or by entering a phase of PTD. Part II of the book describes how to undertake PTD.

Comments on problem trees Separating the core problem from the causes and effects can be difficult – even development professionals may have problems with this. It is important, therefore, that the research team are familiar with problem tree analysis. When the livestock owners have constructed the problem tree, go through it with them, asking them to clarify the relationships – for example, ask does A cause B where they have indicated a causal relationship between the two. If they conclude, on reflection, that A does not cause B, they will need to modify the problem tree accordingly.

PART

II

Participatory
technology
development

7 When to do participatory trials

Farmer participation should not be initiated for its own sake. In many situations farmer participation in research is beneficial, but it is not always absolutely necessary. It is not simply a question of *where* the research is conducted, on-farm or on-station. The key issues are when is farmer participation likely to be (a) beneficial and (b) cost-effective? This may be influenced not just by where the research is carried out, but also by the objectives, the type of technology, the level of risk involved, and the researchers' attitude and objectives.

7.1 Types of agricultural research

Technological research practised by professional researchers may be conceived as three points on a continuum. At one end, *strategic* research pursues knowledge concentrating on understanding causality and process that has potentially global application. *Applied* research, mid-way on the continuum, involves using the process and understanding generated by strategic research, and applying these to address more specific issues, problems or opportunities with a view to making recommendations. At the other end of the continuum, *adaptive* research takes proven applied research, or good practice from elsewhere, and makes adjustments for it to work in specific situations and locations.

We should not forget that many rural people also conduct their own research, but usually in a more idiosyncratic way than do 'scientific' researchers. Having less time and resources than full-time researchers, but more local knowledge, the majority of local people are more likely to engage in an *adaptive type* of research, i.e. trying out ideas and technologies borrowed from others and seeing how they work for themselves, making adjustments along the way.

Development professionals involved in PTD often attach importance to recognizing and understanding farmers' own capacity to experiment, adapt and innovate; and treating them as equal partners in the process. This is because technologies that are suitable for one farmer or livestock-keeper may need modification before they are suitable for another (Pretty, 1995), and other farmers, rather than researchers, may be the best people to identify what modifications are required. Or there may be scope for farmers to improve a technology or use it more profitably, in ways that researchers might not think of themselves. Case study G notes that participating farmers, once their interest in fodder crops had been aroused by the researchers, developed some unique forage systems. For example, some farmers started feeding cut fodder to fish instead of cattle, because they realized it was a more profitable option.

Technology development usually needs to go through several iterations before a technology is optimized, as in Case study I, where it took several years of testing to develop a donkey plough that met farmers' needs. Research projects may come to an end before the process has been completed, in which case local innovators should ideally be able to take the process forward themselves independently (Douthwaite, 2001). Furthermore, circumstances change, and farmers and livestock-keepers need to be able to respond effectively to those changes with appropriate technological innovations: technologies that were ideal in one year may no longer be relevant 15 years later. (For further discussion about innovation processes, see Douthwaite, 2001.)

Recognition of the important role of farmers themselves (and other local people, such as blacksmiths or traditional healers) in technology development has implications for the way in which professional researchers manage their relationships with farmers and livestock-keepers. They must respect their knowledge, views and priorities, encourage them to develop a strong sense of ownership of the research, and look for ways of developing their capacity where necessary. Outsiders may be able to strengthen local technology development processes by identifying or developing mechanisms for improved sharing of information and experiences among farmers themselves, and between farmers and other relevant stakeholders (e.g. research institutes, extension workers, suppliers of inputs).

Different modes of farmer participation in local research

Location The majority of PTD is conducted where livestock-keepers or farmers live (in situ), on their own animals or land. This makes it easier for them to participate, and ensures that the research is conducted under real-life conditions experienced by the people whom the research is intended to benefit. However, there may be a few situations where it is appropriate for PTD to be conducted on-station. An example from one of the case studies is given in Box 7.1. Another example can be found in Case study C, in which formal trials were done on-station, in parallel with informal trials in villages.

Livestock researchers can conduct in situ technology development on animals, on farms or on a local site belonging to a community institution. In practice, the vast majority of research is on animals or on farms, and PTD beyond the farm is a rarity. Examples of participatory research beyond the farm include research on the development of optimum management systems for communal grazing resources; and research on ways of alleviating water

Table 7.1 Management and location of local research

Who?	Where?	
	Livestock-keepers' animals and/or land (in situ)	On-station
Designs the trial or experiment	Livestock-keepers and/or researchers	Livestock-keepers and/or researchers
Manages the trial or experiment	Livestock-keepers and/or researchers	Livestock-keepers and/or researchers
Evaluates the outcomes	Livestock-keepers and/or researchers	Livestock-keepers and/or researchers

Source: Slightly modified version of a table prepared by Simon Anderson (pers. comm.)

scarcity to reduce herding distances and times (Conroy and Rangnekar, 2000, 2003).

Management Table 7.1 shows that, irrespective of where the technology development is undertaken, management or control of the process can lie with the livestock-keepers themselves, or with the outsiders (livestock researchers or development workers), or can be joint. Even when technology development is carried out in situ the process does not necessarily involve a high degree of participation from local people.

BOX 7.1 Genetic improvement of local sheep in Chiapas, Mexico

Sheep play a major role in the livelihoods of Tzotzil families, who live in the mountains of Chiapas State, providing the raw material for their traditional woollen clothes and a significant source of income. In 1991, the University of Chiapas decided to initiate a genetic improvement programme to enable the local Chiapas sheep to produce heavier fleeces of higher quality. They built up a nucleus flock by buying ewes from the Tzotzil shepherdesses.

The weight of the fleece was a key parameter of the selection programme during the first 5 years. However, by 1996 it was realized that, due to the high correlation between fleece weight and body weight, there was an inbuilt bias towards the selection of bigger and heavier animals that would have great difficulty in meeting their nutritional requirements. This triggered the quest for better selection variables, including qualitative parameters, and the researchers recognized that the best people to identify these parameters were the experts – the Tzotzil shepherdesses and weavers. Since 1996, Tzotzil women have been responsible for the practical assessment of fleece quality, and have identified two important qualitative parameters. This became a standardized procedure within the selection programme, with fleece grading exercises being carried out at the research station every 6 months, a few days prior to the shearing of the sheep.

Source: Case study J

A valuable and widely used classification system for different types, or modes, of farmer participation in on-farm research, developed by Biggs (1989), is summarized in Table 7.2. The degree of farmer (or livestock-keeper) involvement in decision-making varies from mode to mode, and increases in the modes to the right-hand side. These four modes are really different points on a continuum. There are no clear dividing lines between them, and a project may gradually move from one mode to another during its lifetime: indeed, it is common for projects to begin in the consultative mode and to shift to the collaborative mode as researchers and farmers (or livestock-keepers) develop (a) a common understanding of experimental objectives and the best ways of achieving them and (b) a relationship based on trust.

The traditional mode, in which the researchers are dominant and farmers least involved, is the *contract* mode. The contract mode involves formal experimentation in specific on-farm situations, but the farmers' views are not actively sought by the researchers. The *consultative* mode, classically exemplified by applications of the farming systems research approach of the early to mid 1980s, includes 'diagnosing farmers' practices and problems, planning an experimental programme, testing technological alternatives in farmers' fields and developing and extending recommendations' (Tripp, 1991). In this mode, it is the researchers who provide the solutions, plan the experiments and finally recommend what is best practice.

In the *collaborative* mode, the ideas for interventions to be tested may also come from farmers or other knowledgeable people in the locality, and are the product of discussions between the researchers and farmers or livestock-keepers. In the case of the *collegiate* mode, it is the farmers themselves who play the lead role in identifying what the content of the experiments will be, and the manner in which they will be conducted. PTD roughly corresponds to the *collaborative* and *collegiate* modes, although in the early stages it may be necessary to operate in the *consultative* mode.

Table 7.2 Four different modes of farmer participation in on-farm research

	Contract	Consultative	Collaborative	Collegiate
Type of relationship	Farmers' land and services are hired or borrowed e.g. researcher contracts with farmers to provide specific types of land	There is a doctor–patient relationship. Researchers consult farmers, diagnose their problems and try to find solutions	Researchers and farmers are roughly equal partners in the research process and continuously collaborate in activities	Researchers actively encourage and support farmers' own research and experiments

Source: Biggs, 1989.

7.2   Project and institutional objectives

There are three general objectives that are often associated with PTD, namely: (i) functional, (ii) human resource development and (iii) empowerment. Different agencies attach different degrees of importance to them. For some, the primary aim is *functional*, i.e. to develop effective and adoptable technologies for poor households more efficiently. For others, particularly NGOs, the primary aim may be to *empower* poorer and weaker sections in social, economic and/or political terms. While others may give priority to enhancing the capacity of the people to diagnose problems and respond to them.

This book focuses mainly on the functional dimension of PTD, as do most of the case studies. It appears that strengthening the capacity of farmers or livestock-keepers to conduct their own research has generally not been given much emphasis in most livestock-related PTD. This objective deserves to receive more attention in future because: (a) problems and opportunities change over time; and (b) in some situations technologies may lose their effectiveness (e.g. helminths may develop resistance to anthelmintics).

Project and institutional objectives have a major bearing on which mode of farmer participation researchers should choose. Government research services are generally concerned with all of these objectives, but emphasize the first. Where this objective is given over-riding importance, a mix of the *consultative* and *collaborative* modes will generally be most appropriate. Through the application of these modes it is expected that national experts will build up the skills and experience required to conduct PTD more efficiently, and thereby address objectives two and three. Development projects, particularly those involving NGOs, may also be concerned with all three objectives, but place more emphasis on human resource development: in this case a mix of *collaborative* and *collegiate* modes is the most appropriate.

Experimental objectives and type of technology

Whether PTD is appropriate (and if it is, which mode to use) will depend partly on specific research, or experimental, objectives. Unlike the project and institutional objectives, experimental objectives are largely technical and often technology-specific. Some kinds of trial are more appropriately conducted on-station: an example of such a trial is given in Box 7.2.

There are situations in which on-farm trials are appropriate, but in which anything beyond the very limited involvement of farmers may be detrimental to the achievement of these research objectives: here the *contract* mode would be most appropriate. This applies to trials in which quantitative bio-physical information on the interaction between the technology and the environment is the primary requirement. For example, researchers might want to know the growth rate and survival rate of a tree species on a particular type of soil (different from that at the research station) under a particular set of conditions.

BOX 7.2 Determining what percentage of seeds in tree pods are digested

A goat research project (Case study E) wanted to know whether or not goats were digesting most of the seeds in *Prosopis juliflora* pods, which it was using as a supplement to address productivity constraints. The seeds are highly nutritious, but have a hard outer casing that might prevent them from being digested. If most of them were not being digested there would be a case for grinding the pods before feeding them to the goats, and the project wanted to know whether it would be worthwhile conducting an experiment in which the treatment would be ground pods.

To get the answer to this question it was necessary to quantify the number of seeds 'going into' the goats and the number of seeds 'coming out'; and to do the latter required the collection and analysis of all of the goats' faeces. This could only be done in a controlled situation where the animals were stall-fed, so the trial was conducted at the NGO's Central Research Station. The trial showed that the vast majority of the seeds were digested by the goats (which was contrary to conventional wisdom), so the project abandoned the idea of grinding the pods.

Where experimentation has more than one objective, each objective is likely to have implications for data requirements, and for the approach taken. The requirements of the different objectives can be conflicting, necessitating trade-offs between the optimal approaches (Coe, 1997). Where there are substantial conflicts it may be preferable to have separate experiments, with different degrees of farmer involvement. Suppose, for example, one objective is that given in the example above, another is to investigate how the technology performs under farmers' management conditions, and the third is to obtain farmers' assessments of the technology. In this case, one experiment (in the contract mode) is required to achieve the first objective, and a second one (in the consultative or collaborative mode) is required for the other two objectives, which are relatively compatible. The experiments may run in sequence, or in parallel, depending on the project's time-frame and resource base, and the researcher's instincts about the applicability of the technology.

Participatory research is not appropriate for all types of technology. Where the targeted livestock-keepers have limited knowledge about the research topic or the biophysical nature of the problem (e.g. viral diseases), or have little understanding of the technical solution on offer, the benefits of PTD in the more 'upstream' experimental activities are likely to be minimal. Another, related, consideration is the extent to which participating farmers would have scope for manipulating or adapting the technology being researched: livestock vaccines, for example, offer less scope for adaptation than do drugs for controlling animal parasites or diseases. However, even in the case of vaccines there may be some potential for PTD, and on-farm trials may provide valuable information on farmers' preferences for different means of administering the vaccine (see Box 7.3 for an example).

Potential problems in livestock trials

Various problems have been identified as being commonly associated with livestock trials: these are described below (Amir and Knipscheer, 1989). However, these problems do not always arise, and it may be possible to avoid them, or at least to minimize them, so that they do not invalidate or undermine the technology development process. The following chapters in this part of the book provide guidance on this.

Life cycle duration Evaluation of animal performance often requires a longer period than crop performance evaluation: it has been suggested that experiments involving the former generally last for more than a year, whereas those involving the latter are generally less than four months in duration (Amir and Knipscheer, 1989). This may be incompatible with the ceilings imposed by donors on the duration of research projects (Morton, 2001), which often have a maximum of three years; and livestock-keepers may lose interest in the experiment after a while, or animals may die during

---

BOX 7.3 The value of participatory in situ trials in the testing of vaccines to control Newcastle disease

A project working in Mozambique (Case study A) looked at different ways of administering the Newcastle disease (ND) vaccine(s) – by eye drop, oral drench or drinking-water. Although birds had to be caught by their owners to administer the vaccine by eye drop, the researchers learned from the trials that this was the method preferred by farmers because it was more effective than the drinking-water option. In one of the trials, the researchers found no apparent difference between groups that received the vaccine by eye drop once only or on two separate occasions. This was an important finding as it meant that vaccination costs to farmers could be reduced.

Similar laboratory and field trials on ND control in village chickens using live, thermostable vaccine have been conducted in Ghana and Tanzania, which also indicated that eye drop was the preferred method of application. After the field trial stage, the vaccine was used in a number of zones. In one area of Tanzania where suitable eye-droppers were not available, farmers used the tip of a feather to transfer the vaccine from the vial to the eye of the chicken. Where possible, it is always preferable to use commercial eye-droppers, in order to standardize the size of the drop being administered to chickens. However, in the case concerned, there were organizational difficulties and the farmers devised their own low-cost solution.

Source: Case study A

the trial. The monitoring periods for five trials of various kinds are given in Table 7.3 and only one is more than 12 months.

Life cycle synchronization Animal production is not synchronized (to the extent that crop production is), so it can be difficult to find enough animals in the same age category and the same production phase, and to ensure comparability between animals in treatment and control groups.

Monitoring effort Animals may need to be monitored (e.g. weighed) once or twice a month, whereas crops usually can be checked less often. This can be a problem for researchers. It can also make demands on the owner's time that (s)he may resent, particularly if (s)he does not see the need for such detailed quantitative data.

Mobility The mobility of livestock means that environment–animal interactions are difficult to describe and measure, and factors that are not included in trial treatments (non-experimental factors) are difficult to control.

Number of observation units. Animal performance in a small farm setting is measured as production per animal (whereas crop yield data are averages of a large number of plants): consequently, statistical variability of treatments between animals or animal groups tends to be greater than between, for example, fertilizer treatments.

Risk-bearing: owners reluctant to risk experimentation As animals are large and valuable, compared with crop plants, the owners may perceive controlled trials and experimental interventions on their animals as too risky, particularly where they are unfamiliar with the technology.

Inter-annual variability in livestock productivity Productivity varies considerably from year to year due to factors such as rainfall and outbreaks of disease, which may make it difficult to isolate the effect of a treatment.

Identification of experimental animals This can be a problem if they belong to herds that include non-experimental animals. The larger the herd, and the more similar the animals, the greater the potential problem.

Ensuring that the treatment is only given to experimental animals Animals belonging to the same herd often eat from the same feed container. Thus, for example, if a feed supplement is only intended for breeding does, it may be difficult to ensure that kids do not consume it too.

The author's experience suggests that a number of factors make smallstock (e.g. small ruminants, poultry) more amenable to on-farm trials than large ruminants. First, their life cycle duration is shorter, making it possible to conduct trials on an annual basis and generate results within a few months. Second, households may own several goats or chickens, which makes it easier to include a reasonable number of observation units in the trials. Third, owners are probably less averse to involving smallstock in experiments, than large ruminants, due to their relatively low unit value. However, PTD can be

Table 7.3 Examples of on-farm livestock experiments and their duration

Challenge addressed	Treatment/ technology tested	Timing of treatment	Key indicators	Monitoring period/duration of trial
Trials on goats				
Poor reproductive performance of female goats (*Case study E*)	Tree pods supplement	Daily for 10 weeks during scarcity period (mid-May to end July)	Conception and number of kids born	7–8 months, from mid-May to December
High mortality due to mange (*Case study B*)	Six treatments were used ■ 2 were commercial ■ 4 were traditional or non-conventional	One commercial drug (ivermectin) was injected twice, with a 7-day interval. The local treatments were applied 1–2 times a week for at least 4 weeks	■ Laboratory analysis of skin scrapings for mange mites and fungal infection ■ Body condition ■ Weight ■ Degree of infection ■ Reduced mortality	About 3 months. At least 1 month for treatments, and a few weeks to monitor effect of treatments
Trials on chickens				
High mortality caused by Newcastle disease (*Case study A*)	Two different vaccines were tested, each administered in various ways (e.g. eye drop, oral drench, drinking water) in different groups.	In most groups re-vaccination was carried out at 4-month intervals	Mortality rates	About 18 months, following 2–5 months of extension work and data collection. Duration was quite long, because it was necessary to wait for an out-break of the disease
Increase meat and/or egg production by chickens (*Conducted by the Western India Rainfed Farming Project*)	Four breeds of chickens new to the area (local birds as control)	Not applicable	Weight gain, production capacity, market price, adaptation to hot local environment, owners' preferences	12 months
Trial on large ruminants				
Increasing milk production by cows (*Case study D*)	Temporal re-allocation of concentrates fed to cows	All concentrates were given daily during first 12 weeks after calving, instead of usual practice of feeding smaller quantities daily for > 36 weeks	Milk yield	Treatment period was c. 12 weeks, but monitoring was carried out for 6–7 months

undertaken with large ruminants too, provided that trials are not unduly long and do not pose any significant risk to the animals.

More on risk-bearing

If a high level of risk is involved in the planned research, it will not usually be appropriate to engage a high level of farmer participation. This is particularly true early on in a project, when researchers are establishing rapport and credibility with farmers. When good rapport has been established, researchers can afford to take more risks 'publicly' because the collaborating farmers will be able to understand that, to identify a suitable technology, a number of possibilities may need to be tried out on a small scale. Early on

---

BOX 7.4 An example of livestock-keepers accepting a risky trial

In Karnataka, India, goat-keepers told researchers that high kid mortality during the rainy season was their main problem. The project conducted trials in 2001 to address the problem, which was thought to be linked to the worm burden at that time. In one trial two treatments were tested: (a) a commercial de-wormer, *Fenbendazole*, and (b) a locally available material known to have anthelminthic properties. There is evidence that mortality rates are higher for kids of does that have a heavy worm burden, so the treatments were given to does in late pregnancy and on the day of kidding. Both treatments were very effective in reducing the worm burden of the does, and hence in improving their condition. In addition, the kids of does in the treatment group grew faster than those of does in the control group.

This trial represented a potentially serious risk to the participants. The goat-keepers, who did not normally de-worm pregnant animals, were concerned that giving anthelmintics to does in late pregnancy might result in them aborting. The researchers were also concerned, and bore this factor in mind when selecting a commercial drug for use as a treatment. After a review of the literature, and discussions with animal scientists, the BAIF staff selected a drug that was considered to be least likely to cause abortion. The researchers did not pressurize the goat-keepers to participate in the trial, but took several steps to win their trust until the people saw them as friends and guides. They: visited each prospective trial participant; analysed faecal samples of goats that were sick and weak; provided or arranged veterinary assistance to them, and discussed the issues with them in several meetings. The trial only went ahead after the goat-keepers had chosen to participate despite the risk. Fortunately, abortions did not materialize. In this case, some researchers might have decided to do an on-station trial first, so that they could be more confident that the problem would not arise, provided that they had the facilities to do so.

Sources: Conroy and Thakur, 2002; Thakur et al., 2002

---

this is difficult, because farmers who have not been exposed to formal experimentation may tend to view an agricultural research trial like an extension demonstration. An example of goat-keepers collaborating in a trial that involved potential risk to their animals is given in Box 7.4.

Where the lives of people's animals are at risk anyway from the problem to be addressed by the trial, the livestock-keepers are more likely to accept the risk of a potentially effective treatment. For example, in a trial in Kenya designed to address the life-threatening disease of mange in goats, the 'farmers were willing to carry the risk of experimental failure rather than lose their animals' (Sutherland and Kang'ara, 2000; Case study B). Some goats did die, but their owners did not demand any compensation from the researchers.

7.3 Essential conditions for PTD with livestock-keepers

Institutional capacity

To implement participatory research effectively certain institutional requirements need to be met. First, researchers' organizations and their main collaborators need to have a *commitment* to PTD.

Second, an organization should have an appropriate and sufficiently broad mandate. The more narrowly focused its mandate, the less flexibility the agency has to respond to livestock-keepers' priorities. As we saw earlier (Box 1.2) this has been a problem for certain Kenyan government research organizations, whose mandates were narrow, and did not facilitate research by a single institution on all aspects demanded by client farmers. The mandate of KETRI limits it only to tsetse and trypanosomiasis research and control, while the NVRC mandate limits it to specialization in selected animal health constraints.

Even if an organization has the mandate, it is often the case that not all of the expertise required is found within it, and it may be desirable or necessary for two or more organizations to collaborate on a particular project or programme. Thus, the development of effective inter-agency working relationships (sometimes referred to as the *task network*) is often another prerequisite for PTD. National agricultural research organizations and NGOs often have complementary strengths and weaknesses, the former being stronger on technical matters than social ones, while the latter are weak on technical ones, but strong on participatory approaches (Farrington, 1998). It should be borne in mind, however, that their objectives may differ, which can give rise to complications. It is necessary to ask, therefore, whether an organization has a good track record for effective collaboration with others.

Third, research organizations (and their donors) need the *institutional ethos* to apply PTD – commitment alone is not enough. PTD needs to be undertaken in a flexible manner: a process approach (as opposed to a blueprint approach) is required. Plans, and possibly objectives, may need to be updated and revised periodically. The iterative nature of PTD may not be easily reconciled with time-bound structures and funding. Researchers need to assess whether their organizations and/or their donors are sufficiently flexible to enable them to take a 'process' rather than a 'blueprint' approach to research implementation. If they are not, it may be best not to embark on PTD. In some of the case studies the research projects had to step outside their original foci.

A flexible institutional ethos on the part of donor agencies can be very important for research projects that have a narrow focus. This was an issue for a goat research project undertaken by BAIF and NRI, whose focus was easing seasonal feed scarcity. Responding to goat-keepers' expressed priority needs, the project wanted to include experiments on anthelmintics and on water supply. The donor interpreted the project's focus loosely and accepted the researchers' case that both worm burden and water intake (Conroy and Rangnekar, 2000) are related to and interact with feed and nutritional status.

In another of the case studies (Case study F) the researchers were allowed to be flexible in their activities. They found that animal health was a priority issue for the *campesinos*. While health issues did not fall explicitly within the research team's remit, which was more to do with feed and nutrition, it was decided to respond to their questions about poultry health by holding animal health workshops in each village. The researchers recognized that this could then provide an opportunity to link the issues of animal health to problems with diet.

Involving livestock-keepers
Engendering ownership of the experiments among livestock-keepers
Creating ownership of the experiments among livestock-keepers is a vital aspect of PTD. The ownership of the experiment not only decides the success of the trial, but also helps in disseminating the experimental results for further adoption. The first step of engendering ownership of the experiment(s) is that the researchers themselves should believe in the value of the trial, and be committed to a participatory approach. They should become a role model to the people because of their actions, and because the people can see that they practise what they preach. Their sincerity and honesty should attract the people and encourage them to work together.

Once people start trusting the researchers then the task of creating ownership of the experiment among livestock-keepers themselves becomes easy. The researchers should promote the concept of self-help among the people, and ensure the involvement of livestock–keepers – particularly the women – in decision-making at every stage of the research. By cultivating the habit of respecting everybody's views, the researchers can encourage their active participation in the experiment. Besides regular meetings, researchers can also encourage a group of livestock-keepers to visit the houses of all trial participants in a week, to see the animals involved and to assess the status of the trial. All these things build up the confidence of the livestock-keepers and develop their sense of ownership of the research.

Contributions from/by livestock-keepers Subsidies can become a mechanism for securing farmers' involvement in trials and treatments that they do not really consider to be worthwhile: for this reason they should be avoided or minimized. On the other hand, there are potential problems in avoiding them altogether from the outset. First, this may make it difficult for resource-poor livestock-keepers to participate in trials, particularly where the treatment has to be purchased. Second, many rural people have a dependency mentality, having become accustomed to receiving government handouts, and hence are reluctant to pay for things themselves when they are working with development agencies.

Unless the livestock-keepers have a strong sense of ownership of the trial, and believe that it is very important and has a reasonable chance of success and profitability, they are unlikely to pay for the whole treatment themselves, particularly if it is one that they are not very familiar with. This is illustrated by the experience of a de-worming trial in Kenya, in which only about one-third of trial participants who had agreed to purchase anthelmintics actually did so; and even they did not follow the application regimes that the researchers had agreed with them, applying the treatment less often (Mulira et al., 1999).

The treatments used in the trials conducted by the BAIF/NRI goat research project were subsidized to varying degrees. The basis for this was that the technologies were new to the goat-keepers, and therefore they were taking a risk (financial and potentially to the health of their goats) in applying them. Urea molasses granules comprised the most novel of all the treatments, so a 100 per cent grant was given for this. In this kind of situation the researchers should develop a clear understanding with the livestock-keepers that the size of the subsidy will be reduced, year by year, as the goat-keepers become familiar with the technologies and see the benefits they have on their animals (assuming, that is, that they are effective).

Incentives for participants in control groups For many kinds of trials it is desirable to have a group of animals that do not receive any treatment (see section 9.4), so that comparisons can be made between the two groups to see what difference the treatment made. The non-treatment group is known as the 'control' group. If the owners of the control group animals also own the treatment group animals, motivation is not likely to be a problem. However, if they are different to those of the treatment group (see section 9.4 for a discussion of this kind of design) motivating the control group owners to participate actively in the control group can be a challenge. They may be reluctant to participate, because they do not see themselves or their animals gaining anything from their involvement in the trial.

If this situation arises, it should be pointed out to them that if the technology on trial proves to be effective they too will benefit after the trial has been completed. If that is not enough of an incentive, however, they can be offered some kind of material incentive. For example, in the BAIF/NRI project, control group goat-keepers participating in a trial focusing on milk yield were given metal drink containers, and in other trials a breeding buck was made available to both the treatment and control groups.

Another useful approach is to allocate participants to the treatment and control groups on a random basis, and in such a way that they recognize it as being random and fair. An example of this approach is given in Box 7.5. In addition, if there is a need to hire the services of a local monitor for monitoring the trial, preference can be given to someone from the control group.

Apparently, ICRAF do not carry out on-farm feeding trials comparing treatments and a control, only different treatments, partly because of the issues raised (Morton, 2001). It is generally desirable, however, to have a control group, and to find ways of motivating the members, such as those just mentioned. They are just as important to a trial as the treatment group members, so researchers should put just as much effort into developing their sense of ownership and involve them fully in group meetings, etc.

Resources

Human resources Researchers' attitudes are very important, as was illustrated by Box 1.2, as are those of extensionists. This point is also highlighted

---

BOX 7.5   Making allocation to a control group acceptable

Researchers looking into vaccination of Newcastle disease (ND) (Case study A) knew from previous studies that the survival rates for the different experimental groups (which included a control group) would vary. Consequently, experimental groups were allocated using a lottery system, in the presence of community representatives, to ensure that they knew that no favouritism had been involved with the allocation of the experimental groups. The lottery was conducted by placing pieces of paper with the different experimental groups into one tin and papers with the names of the communities in another tin. There were four groups in each trial. Representatives from each community were asked to come forward one by one to select one piece of paper from each tin. The pieces of paper were handed to the meeting facilitator and the results were read out after each representative had picked out the pieces of paper.

Compensation for farmers whose chickens had the misfortune to be allocated to experimental groups with poor results (i.e. control groups) was discussed prior to the initiation of the trials. It was decided that after the first outbreak of ND, farmers would be able to choose which administration method they would prefer to use in subsequent vaccinations. Should the project have offered monetary or other compensation, it is possible that some bias in the reporting of problems may have occurred.

in some of the case studies (e.g. Case studies G and I). They should have respect for the views and knowledge of the people with whom they intend to work. They should be prepared, for example, to traverse difficult terrain and climates, leave home early and return late, spend time in the project area, and hold interviews at times that are convenient for local people. This is particularly important when working with women. Where a major change is required in researchers' attitudes and style of working this is sometimes very difficult, and in one of the case studies (Case study I) this resulted in one staff member leaving the project/organization.

PTD requires staff skills that are often scarce. Many researchers in national agricultural research organizations may lack experience and aptitude in working with farmers in a participatory way, while many NGO staff may have little, if any, experience of research. PTD, and particularly collaborative research, poses many methodological challenges, some of which are discussed later.

It may be necessary to have staff from a number of disciplines, so that an interdisciplinary approach can be taken. The precise nature of the disciplines will depend to some extent on the constraints and opportunities that livestock-keepers identify as being most important. For example, if heavy worm burdens appear to be a serious problem, a parasitologist may be required to identify which helminths are involved and to advise on an effective treatment. Alternatively, if the focus was on improved forage production, then a forage agronomist and livestock nutritionist might be needed. However, the basic minimum should be one livestock scientist and one social scientist or agricultural economist. People from other disciplines may need to be called in from time to time, such as a statistician or a parasitologist.

Ideally, at least one member of the research team should have had some previous experience of participatory research. In addition, it is generally desirable, and sometimes essential, to have at least one woman in the team, to facilitate interaction with female livestock-keepers.

There is often a need for training of research staff in participatory research methods. To some extent it may be possible to provide 'on-the-job' training, but if funds permit short (2-day to 2-week) formal courses would be ideal. (For a valuable training manual in PTD, oriented to the collegiate mode, see Veldhuizen et al., 1997.) One of the forage case study projects (Case study G) organizes two-week courses for national counterparts. These courses also enable the project to identify and select field staff with suitable skills and attitudes, notably a willingness to accept change and learn new principles.

Financial resources The financial resources required for collaborative research are often underestimated. Monitoring and analysis may be more time-consuming than they are in more conventional research modes. With on-farm experimentation there is generally more variability in the experimental data than is the case with the contract mode, and consequently data may need to be obtained from a larger number of animals, fields, farmers, etc., if the effect of the technology being tested is to be detected. It may also be necessary to carry out more detailed monitoring of farmers' management activities to explain some of the variability in results between herds (see section 9.4). It will also take time, and hence money, to build-up an effective working relationship.

Time Research projects normally have a fixed duration, which is often no more than three years. Research scientists need to consider whether PTD can deliver/meet objectives in the time earmarked for the project, while bearing in mind the need to (a) allow for delays and complications, and (b) develop a rapport and partnership with participants. For example, if they have not worked closely with local communities already, a long lead-in time may be required to develop the necessary rapport to work effectively with them.

8 Getting started

8.1 Needs assessment

Any type of livestock research, whether participatory or not, should be based on a sound understanding of what livestock-keepers see as their priority needs – their main constraints or opportunities. In the case of PTD this is an essential foundation for the whole process, since people are unlikely to invest time and effort in research that they consider to be unimportant.

Obtaining an accurate understanding of needs and priorities can be difficult and time-consuming, and may require at least two phases of discussions with farmers. Directly asking people their most pressing problems may merely generate well-known 'shopping lists'. Problems are likely to be described in terms of a lack of an input (which the livestock-keeper hopes the project will provide): for example, where there is a high mortality rate, livestock-keepers may characterize the problem as a 'lack of veterinary medicines'. It is important to identify the underlying cause of the problem, rather than just the symptoms.

Getting farmers to rank problems or priorities, starting with the most serious or important, provides more information than simply making a list; it also reduces the risk of researchers distorting farmers' views to fit in with their own personal interests or priorities. **Part I of this book provides guidance on conducting needs assessments with livestock-keepers**. Researchers should seek to increase their understanding of what is required and what is possible as the research progresses.

Ideally, the researchers assist livestock-keepers in tackling their most pressing production problems. However, not all of these problems can be easily solved by improved technologies (although there may still be scope for influencing policies or institutions) and their research institute may not have the expertise (or resources and willingness) to address certain problems. Nevertheless, so long as the issue is a reasonably high priority for the local people, and researchers are also convinced, there is likely to be potential for fruitful collaboration.

The broader the scope of the project, and the greater the variability of the systems and situations of the target group(s), the more time and effort will be required for the needs assessment exercise.

8.2   Scheduling

The timetable for the research needs careful consideration. There are often conflicting demands regarding the pace at which research progresses. If the research project is of short duration this may encourage researchers to establish on-farm trials as quickly as possible, so that they can gather data for an extra season or year. On the other hand, it is desirable to avoid rushing, because this can undermine the participatory approach as livestock-keepers may then not be given an equal say in the design of the research, and they may not develop a sense of ownership. It may be desirable to focus on interacting with fewer farmers and villages during the first season or year, so that staff become familiar with a participatory approach. This is a time when effective relationships are developed with participants, research opportunities are identified, and the technologies to address them are agreed.

It is important that the research team members are not over-ambitious and do not spread themselves too thinly. A narrowly focused approach will be preferable where:

- resources are limited;
- staff are relatively new to PTD; or
- a lot of time needs to be invested in building up rapport with the communities.

Where the approved duration of the research is longer (say up to five years), it may be best to have an initial phase of observing livestock-keepers' own informal trials or current practices, in relation to selected issues. This helps the researchers to understand problems and potential solutions from the livestock-keepers' viewpoint, and gain deeper insight into the differing problems of individual livestock-keepers or sub-groups, and prepares them for PTD if they are new to it. Observations of this kind can also be conducted concurrently with exploratory trials, in which the researcher contributes ideas.

In many cases a preliminary needs assessment (taking a few weeks or months) is followed quickly by exploratory experiments. Through monitoring these experiments and discussion at the end of the season, the process of assessing, and re-assessing, needs continues. This works if researchers allow themselves enough time for quality interaction with farmers, carry out genuinely exploratory experiments, maintain an open mind on the problems, and do not insist on repeating the early experiments over several seasons in order to obtain 'conclusive' data.

8.3   Identifying where to work and with whom

Some general observations and guidelines about choosing samples are given in section 2.2, and should be borne in mind while reading this section. Statisticians can be a very useful source of advice and ideas on selection issues.

Selecting farming systems and zones

In determining the areas and production systems in which the participatory research will be conducted, both biophysical and socio-economic factors are relevant. Secondary data sources should be consulted, and full use made of whatever information is already available so that duplication is avoided. In many countries maps already exist that identify the various agro-ecological zones, and information on the spatial distribution of different livestock species and ethnic groups can be obtained from census data.

However, some of the information required may have to be collected by the project through short overview surveys, to enable characterization of farming and livestock systems in a way that is most relevant to the project. Initial characterization can be modified as further information is collected during the course of a project.

If a project is oriented towards a particular commodity (e.g. buffalo), it may adopt a different approach to targeting from one which is oriented to a particular area or category of farmers. It may, for example, be appropriate to choose an area that is known to be important for the livestock species concerned. In the case of a goat research project, the researchers chose to work in districts that between them represented a range of different goat production systems (see Box 8.1).

Multi-locational or multi-production system trials have a further benefit. Scientists gain a clearer picture of production variability in the on-farm

---

BOX 8.1 Selection of locations in the BAIF/NRI Goat Research Project, India

The researchers were aware that the main purposes and benefits of goat-keeping vary in India, and that production systems vary accordingly from one area and group to another. Furthermore, although some of the problems encountered may be broadly similar, the most appropriate technologies for addressing them may also vary. Thus, the project decided to work in several locations and with different social and ethnic groups (see Table 8.1).

Initially, the project was only working in Rajasthan (with small and marginal farmers) and Gujarat (with landless or near landless pastoralists). The researchers also wanted to work with landless labour households, in which one or more members were involved in agricultural wage labour. This type of goat-keeper was not very common in the initial locations, so the project expanded its coverage into Maharashtra and Karnataka, where they constituted a larger proportion of the rural population. The project also wanted to work more with women, and the researchers knew where there were landless women goat-keepers in Maharashtra.

Source: Conroy, 2003

Table 8.1 Characterization of some small ruminant production systems in various districts of semi-arid India

District (State)	Livestock type[a]	Category of owner	Production system[b]	Typical herd size	Main Product(s)[c]
Bhilwara (Rajasthan)	Goat	Small or marginal farmer	Semi-extensive, commercial	1–10	Meat
Udaipur (Rajasthan)	Goat	Small or marginal farmer (tribal)	Extensive, semi-commercial[d]	1–5	Meat
Tonk (Rajasthan)	Sheep	Better-off farmers	Extensive, commercial	20–100	Wool, meat
Bhavnagar (Gujarat)	Goat	Landless/ near landless Pastoralist[e]	Extensive, commercial	5–20	Milk
Pune (Maharashtra)	Goat	Landless agricultural labourer (women)	Liquid asset	1–2	Meat

[a] Most categories of livestock-keepers, particularly those with farms, also keep one or more large ruminants. Some landless ones, however, particularly those who are landless agricultural labourers, do not.
[b] Extensive refers to production systems that are based on grazing, with virtually no stall-feeding. Semi-extensive means that at certain times of the year there is a significant amount of stall-feeding (e.g. grains, tree fodder and/or green fodder).
[c] The animal or product is generally marketed; only a small proportion, if any, is consumed by the producer.
[d] Semi-commercial means that the sale of animals to meet contingencies (i.e. use as liquid assets) and the sale of animals as a profit-making enterprise are both important.
[e] Pastoralist is defined here as a household in which at least two-thirds of its income comes from sale of livestock and livestock products or livestock-related activities. Thus, their livestock production systems are commercial by definition.

trials (from location to location or production system to production system), so they are in a better position to judge the situations and locations (recommendation domains) in which the new technology could be successfully applied (Waters-Bayer, 1989).

Selection of research locations
Practical considerations will inevitably limit the choice of specific research locations. The further away these locations are from the researchers' base(s), and the greater the distance between the participating farmers, the greater the costs in time and fuel, and the less contact there is likely to be between participants and researchers. Trade-offs may be necessary between the extent to which the locations included are representative, and the resource costs involved. **The guiding principle mentioned in section 2.3 should be applied here, i.e. well-informed choices, based on clear criteria, are always preferable to the selection, by default, of non-representative situations.**

Where researchers or collaborating organizations have already been working with certain villages for some time, and have developed a good rapport with community members, this may be a strong reason for selecting such villages in preference to others, provided that they are reasonably representative of villages in the area concerned. This can save time and resources in that a good rapport with participants already exists, and the project may easily access valuable secondary data about livelihood systems, social and economic composition and problems and priorities.

Selection of type of livestock
In cases where a project is working in a particular geographical area, and is not tied to any particular livestock species, the researchers will need to decide which livestock species they are going to prioritize. Selection criteria that should be considered are:

1. the potential for research to address livestock-keepers' (not researchers') priority problems associated with the most important type(s) of livestock;
2. where research is likely to produce the greatest benefit, taking account of the seriousness of the problem (e.g. size of mortality rate) and the number of animals experiencing it; and
3. what kind of research is likely to provide the greatest benefit to the poorest groups.

For example, Case study B describes an area-based adaptive research project in Kenya that selected goats, rather than cattle, as the primary focus, for two reasons. First, the principal problem associated with cattle, tick-borne diseases, was considered not to be amenable to research. Second, the ownership of goats was more widespread (75 per cent of households) so more farmers, including the poor and women, stood to benefit.

Identifying participant livestock-keepers
Options for engaging participants include:

(a) volunteering (as individuals or community representatives);
(b) delegation of selection to the community;
(c) probability sampling (for a discussion of conventional approaches to sampling in agricultural projects see Casley and Kumar, 1988);
(d) guided purposive selection.

Researchers have tended to take a somewhat ad hoc approach, and/or to favour options (a) or (b), on the basis that they are more participatory than (c) and (d). However, approaches (a) and (b) tend to bias the selection, skewing participation away from the poorest. There are two reasons for this. First, within communities power is distributed unevenly and hence volunteer or community-nominated participants are often male and relatively resource-rich. Second, for many of the poorest a prolonged involvement in research activities is not attractive or feasible, as they are preoccupied with more pressing livelihood issues. PTD projects need to engage in more systematic selection strategies if they want participants to be generally representative or from particular socio-economic groups. The selection procedure needs to be discussed with the collaborators, and agreement reached on criteria and objectives (see Box 7.5 for an example).

Purposive rather than completely random selection is likely to be the most feasible approach. Purposive selection requires a prior understanding of the socio-economic composition of the village or community and inter-household relations so that farmers' views and reactions can be seen and understood in context. The research team should seek to improve its understanding of the local social structure as its work progresses.

Techniques such as wealth-ranking and social mapping, if used with skill and sensitivity, can provide the kind of information that is needed initially (see Chapter 2); and secondary data should be utilized when available. If the relevant information is not available when the initial participant selection process takes place, and volunteer or delegated sampling is used, the project should subsequently check the characteristics of the participants against those of the community as a whole. Additional participants can then be selected if necessary, to make the sample more representative of the target group.

Research objectives are also likely to influence the type of collaborator required. If the research is focused on a particular type of livestock, or a particular kind of livestock production system, then the participants will have to be people who meet these criteria, as is illustrated by the following two examples. First, in a scavenging poultry project working in Tamil Nadu's Trichy District, three categories of production system were identified (see Table 8.2), and the project was interested in comparing productivity and constraints in all three systems. Second, in a goat research project in Dharwad Karnataka, researchers particularly wanted to work with landless goat-keepers, of which they identified two types. Thus, priority was given to including them in the PTD process.

If the research is testing a new technology the project staff may decide that it is necessary to select willing risk-bearing participants with more resources (e.g. land, labour, equipment) and/or previous positive experience in technology innovation.

For programmes that run for a long time, there is a question of whether to continue collaborating with the same small group of livestock-keepers, or to

Table 8.2 Categorization of resource-poor poultry-keepers in Trichy District, Tamil Nadu

Category 1	Category 2	Category 3
Farmers – where house, agricultural land, poultry and other livestock are close together	Farmers – where house, poultry and other livestock are in one place, and agricultural land in another	Landless – who live in a colony, with poultry and livestock in the house itself

Source: Conroy et al., 2003

change every so often. Generally, this issue has to be looked at in relation to research objectives, and to the importance of maintaining rapport and relations with the community. Where empowerment is a major objective the duration of collaboration may need to be longer. In practice, it is likely to be expedient to maintain contact with some of the more interested farmers over a period of years, and also allow space for new farmers to join in as others decide to drop out or as new opportunities arise as the experimental programme expands.

Selection of experimental animals

The type of animal selected will be determined to a large extent by the nature of the trial. For example, if the experiment is focusing on weight gain in young animals the animals selected will have to be from the relevant age group, whereas if it were focusing on conception rates they would have to be mature females. Within each of these categories, however, there is scope for varying degrees of precision. This relates to the problem of inter-animal variability. In order to minimize variability the animals should be as similar as possible.

In one of the first trials conducted by the BAIF/NRI project, which focused on young goats, the age spread of the young goats was quite large, creating unnecessary variability and making the use of a standard feed supplement treatment for all of them questionable. In a similar trial the following year the age of the goats selected was more homogeneous. To minimize inter-animal variability in trials that are focusing on milk production, it may be necessary to select animals that are all of the same parity, and perhaps animals that are all at a similar point in the lactation cycle.

Another consideration is that where animals in the treatment group belong to different people from those in the control group (see section 9.4), the animals in each group should belong to many different owners. Otherwise, the prac-tices of someone owning a large number of animals could become con-founded with the comparison between treatment and control groups, or between different treatment groups. For example, in the first trial described in Case study E, 13 of the 25 goats in the treatment group were owned by one person. Thus, although the treatment group does produced more kids than those in the control group, the difference could have been due to this one goat-keeper having superior goats or feeding practices, rather than to the treatment itself.

8.4 Identifying interventions

In the early stages, the aim of the discussions with livestock-keepers is to reach agreement on the research agenda. Deciding on the research agenda is a process which should be based on an adequate understanding of: the local farming and livestock production systems, including interactions between various components and enterprises in the systems; and who is involved in, decides on and benefits from the various activities. This understanding will help to reduce a long list of possible experiments to one or two that are most useful and likely to bear fruit. While dialogue between researchers and farmers in this process is essential, dialogue with other knowledgeable researchers may also be vital, to avoid duplication and unproductive experimentation. If a consultative mode is used within a national agricultural research system setting, further discussions and consultation with other specialists on the extent of the problem and what can be done about it may be required after the needs assessment. Within a community-oriented collaborative mode, this is a joint process between the local people and the researchers.

Whatever the mode, to sustain a credible partnership with farmers and other stakeholders, the probable relevance of potential interventions needs to be gauged through careful study and widespread consultation. If researchers are convinced, but the collaborating farmers are reluctant, it may be worth organizing a farmer tour to visit an area where the proposed technology is being practised, or to a research station, before trying to introduce it in an on-farm experiment. The researcher should try and avoid the temptation to tell the local people what to do early on in the discussions. Ideas for interventions may come from any of three general sources (for examples of each, see Box 8.2):

- members of the local communities;
- other livestock-keepers or natural resource users in the region;
- researchers (and extensionists), based on their own organization's work or the general body of scientific knowledge.

Indigenous technical knowledge

In many countries there is a wealth of local knowledge about livestock production practices. During the last decade or two there have been numerous initiatives (such as that described in Case study C) to collect and record indigenous technical knowledge (ITK) to do with animal health, and sometimes to validate it. Other areas of ITK, such as feeding practices, have received less attention. ITK is an obvious starting point when considering possible interventions, and can be accessed through secondary sources[21] as well as by talking directly to local livestock-keepers about it. It would be wise to check whether there are any relevant studies available in your area or nearby.

The local people should be encouraged to develop their own ideas initially. It may be useful to discuss ways in which group members have already tried to tackle the problem previously identified, and what effect this had. Discussions should also screen ITK and previous experimentation by villagers.

---

[21] General (international) references include: Mathias et al., 1999; and Martin et al., 2001.

BOX 8.2   Sources of interventions – some examples

A. Members of the local communities

1. Case study C worked closely with 30–40 traditional livestock healers living in villages in its project area in Kenya, and recorded their ethnoveterinary practices. It then tested some of the most widely used practices, focusing primarily on methods of controlling gastro-intestinal parasites in sheep.

2. In Case study B, also in Kenya, mange had been identified by goat-keepers as a major problem. Farmers considered commercial products for treating it to be too expensive, and had started looking for locally available alternatives. The project staff sought to identify alternatives by holding a number of group discussions and by visiting local herbalists, and came up with a list of eight local concoctions already being tried by farmers. The list was further screened through discussion with farmers, and a trial was designed comparing three of the local treatments with two of the recommended commercial ones and a herbal treatment of Neem solution.

B. Other livestock-keepers or key informants in the region

3. In a goat de-worming trial in Dharwad, Karnataka, the idea for the treatment came from the practice of another ethnic group from a nearby area, who keep buffaloes (see Box 7.4). The treatment was the trichomes (hairs) from the pods of a leguminous creeper, mixed with jaggery, a lukewarm sugary solution.

C. Researchers or extensionists

Many ideas for interventions are suggested by researchers or extensionists, based on research that has been conducted 'on-station' (in the field or the laboratory) and has shown a particular technology to be effective in addressing a constraint or opportunity.

4. Case study A describes village trials on two vaccines that had previously been developed 'on-station', to combat Newcastle disease in poultry.

5. In Case study D a trial involving the feeding of concentrates to dairy cattle was carried out on station. This showed that milk production could be increased at no extra cost to the farmer, and so researchers then proposed on-farm trials to farmers based on the findings of the on-station trial.

Often there are recognized specialists within or near a community, and it may be worth identifying these and inviting them to join in discussions, or making visits to them later for more in-depth discussions.

Understanding the nature of the problem

This issue is discussed in Part I, where tools for determining priority needs are described. Understanding the nature of a problem correctly requires researchers to know what the objectives of the livestock-keepers are.

Sometimes the livestock-keepers (or the researchers) may not know, or be sure of, the nature of the problem; but they may have an informed hunch as to the cause. In these situations it is essential for both parties to discuss and explain their ideas and hypotheses before selecting treatments. One common problem that is sometimes poorly understood by goat-keepers is that of high worm burdens, which can result in high mortality rates in kids due to a combination of factors. A high worm burden in the mother may lead to a dramatic reduction in milk production, thus weakening the kid; and if the kid itself then becomes infected it will have a poor chance of survival (Peacock, 1996). However, the goat-keepers may not realize that helminths are causing the death of their kids, nor understand the life cycle of helminths and their effect on the goat's physiology. If so, the researchers will need to educate the livestock-keepers on 'the underlying principles of the technology effect' (Mason et al., 1999).

This is similar to the situation with integrated pest management of crops, where 'farmer field schools' have been developed as an educational tool (Ooi, 1998). The International Livestock Research Institute is researching how the farmer field schools approach can be applied to animal husbandry (Minjauw et al., 2002b). The high importance livestock-keepers attach to visible problems may also mean that they prefer to take a curative approach (i.e. respond to the problem when it appears) rather than a preventative one. This was found to be the case in one de-worming experiment on cattle and sheep (Mulira et al., 1999).

Determining the size of the treatment

This should be based on a combination of technical and cost factors. For example, the quantity of a supplement or a drug should obviously be related to the size of the animal. However, the cost of the treatment should also be taken into account (see next section). Livestock scientists may be inclined to choose the quantity that will have the biggest physical effect, but that is not necessarily the most profitable size of treatment. Furthermore, poor livestock-keepers are usually very short of cash, and therefore have to ration what they have among different items of expenditure; thus, they may not be prepared to incur the full cost of what the scientist considers to be the ideal quantity. If enough animals are available for the trial it may be possible to test two or more different quantities of a treatment.

Screening technologies for profitability

It can be useful to make a simple appraisal of the likely profitability of the proposed treatment, particularly those that involve the purchase of an input. If the treatment has been clearly defined the cost is usually easy to calculate and predict. The size of the benefits is uncertain, of course, but comparing potential benefits with a range of 'guestimates' of the benefits will give some indication of whether the technology concerned is worth investigating. (See Table 8.3 for an example.) If the expected benefits are about the same as the predicted costs it would be advisable to reconsider the proposed trial. This test can be a useful check on ideas coming from researchers with a technical background, who may not be used to thinking in terms of profitability.

There are several different tools for analysing the profitability of treatments or interventions. They have differing degrees of sophistication and slightly different uses, and each has its advantages and disadvantages. The ones described here are among the simplest available, and should be adequate for most types of on-farm trials. For information about other techniques the reader is referred to Amir and Knipscheer (1989) and to standard textbooks on agricultural economics.

Partial-budget analysis is a simple method for estimating the profitability of a treatment, which involves the tabulation of expected gains (benefits) and losses (costs) due to a relatively minor change in farming methods. (The term partial indicates that the change only occurs in one component of the farm.) It is widely used to determine the profitability of a single intervention. Table 8.3 contains an example of a partial budget analysis related to Case study E. It assumes that the goat-keepers' primary objective is to maximize the number of kids produced, so that they can either be sold or retained to maintain or increase the herd size. The value attributed to a kid under the

Table 8.3 Estimated profitability of tree pods as a supplement to increase kidding rates (Indian rupees)

1. Cautious assumptions	2. Optimistic assumptions
Cost	
Price of pods = Rs 3/kg	Price of pods = Rs 2.5/kg
Cost of pods treatment per doe =	Cost of pods treatment per doe =
Rs 3 × 0.25 kg/day × 70 days =	Rs 2.5 × 0.25 kg/day × 70 days =
Rs 52.5	Rs 43.75
1A. Cost of pods treatment for 10 does =	2A. Cost of pods treatment for 10
Rs 525	does = Rs 437.5
Benefit	
Extra 3.5 kids per 10 does	Extra 4.5 kids per 10 does
Value of 1 kid = Rs 300	Value of 1 kid = Rs 500
1B. Value of extra 3.5 kids = Rs 1050	2B. Value of extra 4.5 kids = Rs 2250
Profit	
Net benefit (profit) per 10 does = Rs 525	*Net benefit (profit) per 10 does =*
(1B – 1A)	*Rs 1812.5 (2B – 2A)*
Break-even point	
Minimum extra kids needed to break even	Minimum extra kids needed to break
= 1.75 (525/300)	even = 0.875 (437.5/500)
Benefit:cost ratio	
2:1 (1B:1A)	5.14:1 (2B:2A)

cautious assumptions is the value it would fetch if sold shortly after birth; whereas that under optimistic assumptions is the price it would fetch at about 6 months of age (say Rs 800), minus the cost of rearing it during that 6 months (say Rs 300).

Sometimes it is more appropriate to develop partial budgets for a whole herd than for a single animal, as in this example. Profitability has been estimated per ten does, rather than per doe, because the treatment does not affect every individual: some does will produce more kids than they would have without the treatment (e.g. one instead of none, or twins instead of one), but others will be unaffected. The analysis shows that the treatment should be profitable, even on the basis of cautious assumptions.

Costs of items that are not traded can be difficult to quantify. In the earlier example, there is a small market for tree pods, so the market price has been used in the analysis. However, the goat-keepers were collecting the pods themselves, so it would have been more appropriate to estimate the labour cost of doing so, but since there is no wage payment involved, determining the labour cost is not entirely straightforward. To do this it would have been necessary to estimate the *opportunity cost* of labour; that is, the cost of collecting the pods would be equivalent to the value of the best employment alternative that the goat-keeper had foregone so that (s)he could collect them.

For example, if (s)he had had to give up 2 days of wage employment at a rate of Rs 40 per day, then the labour cost of collecting them would be Rs 80. In rural areas, the opportunity cost of labour tends to vary considerably over the course of a year: it depends partly on how much work is available, with wage rates being higher during busy periods. As it happens, the pods are collected at a time of the year when there is little work available, so the opportunity cost would be quite low in this case. If there were no alternative work available, then the opportunity cost would be zero.

Break-even analysis In partial budgets there are always a few key factors that affect the balance of gains and losses. Break-even analysis determines the level at which the gains and losses are equal: this level is known as the break-even point. Generally, break-even analysis is done by manipulating the most uncertain key factor. When used in association with partial budgeting it can be used as a measure of risk, indicating at what value of a critical factor a new technology is expected to no longer be profitable to a farmer.

Break-even analysis can be applied to the tree pods example, where the number of additional kids is considered to be the most uncertain factor. Thus, the researcher (and livestock-keeper) wants to know, given the estimated costs of the treatment, what is the minimum number of extra kids required to enable the owner to break even. The results are given in Table 8.3.

Benefit:cost ratio is simply the ratio of benefits to costs. It is normally calculated in financial analyses that take account of the flows of costs and benefits over many years (the duration of the activity – e.g. a commercial poultry unit), and that discount future costs and benefits. Thus, in a financial analysis it would be the ratio of discounted benefits to discounted costs. For simple technologies that have fairly immediate effects there is no need to do a discounted cash flow, but it can still be very useful to calculate benefit:cost ratios. They show how much extra benefit the livestock-keeper is likely to get for each unit of cost incurred – in other words they give an indication of the likely size of the return for a given level of investment.

If farmers behave rationally then they will be most likely to adopt those technologies with the highest returns, all other things being equal. The benefit:cost ratios have been calculated for the tree pods technology in Table 8.3. However, where significant cash expenditure is involved, particularly in 'one go', they may not be able to access enough money to pay for all of the input; or they may avoid spending money if they believe that there is a high degree of risk involved.

Standardizing the treatment

For trials that are seeking to quantify the size of the benefit brought about by a particular treatment it is important to standardize that treatment across all the animals in the treatment group. (This will not be an objective in some trials, such as the forage trials in Case study G, which may be more interested in seeing how the livestock-keepers modify a treatment developed by researchers.) For trials in which the treatments are feed supplements it is desirable to provide participants with a measure (e.g. a beaker) that corresponds with the quantity of the treatment.

For treatments that are more complicated, such as those requiring the processing or mixing of ingredients, it may be necessary for the researcher to provide the treatment. For example, in a trial to address mange in goats (see Case study B), the local concoctions were supplied and prepared by the researcher.

8.5   When to experiment

Sometimes it is necessary to consider whether an experiment is required. If you know of a technology that has proved effective in similar situations elsewhere, it may be appropriate to introduce it without following a rigorous process of experimental planning, implementation and evaluation. While everything new to an area may be seen, in certain senses, as an experiment by farmers, not everything new may need a formal experimental design. Through discussion with farmers, especially any with some experience of laying out trials, it may be possible to classify those interventions which require a formal experimental design, and others which can be introduced or tested in a less formal and less resource-intensive way.

9 Designing trials and experiments

9.1 Identifying experimental hypotheses

Once a treatment has been chosen for a formal experiment, it needs to be formulated in terms of a precise hypothesis. It is important to involve the livestock-keepers in the process, and it need not be difficult to do so. The format (from Veldhuizen et al., 1997) illustrated by the following example can be used.

If... I give a de-wormer to my does in late pregnancy and at time of kidding

Then... Their kids are less likely to die young

Because ... 1. Their mothers will produce more milk and thereby make them stronger

  2. Their mothers will not transmit worms to them through their faeces.

Veldhuizen et al. (1997) stress the importance of hypothesis formulation in the context of the collegiate mode as follows:

'This is a crucial step in the dialogue between farmers and outsiders. It helps the researchers and collaborators to define more precisely what they want to try out and why, and enables them to analyse more clearly the results of the trial. It is a planning, monitoring and evaluation tool. It helps both parties to understand each other's logic better. It provides an opportunity to check the reasons for the problem and prevents jumping to conclusions about possible solutions.'

9.2 How many livestock-keepers and animals should be involved?

Where statistical analysis of experimental data is envisaged, it is strongly recommended that researchers consult a statistician to help them address this question. In considering the question, it is necessary to bear in mind a number of factors.

1. The cost and logistics of meeting participants and collecting data.
2. The quality of interactions with participants versus the quantity.

3. The time required to process and analyse monitoring data.
4. The minimum number of sample units (fields, animals) required to be able to draw general conclusions and for statistical analysis (if required).

Trade-offs may be required between factors 1, 2 and 3, on the one hand, and the fourth factor. Poor judgement may lead to serious errors of one kind or another. Too few sample units (factor 4) may mean that the sample is not representative or that firm conclusions cannot be drawn from the data. Too many sample units, on the other hand, may mean that the researchers are overwhelmed by the amount of data that they need to collect and analyse, and that this results in errors of recording, coding, data entry or processing. In addition, limited interaction with livestock-keepers may result in them not identifying strongly with the trials, and not understanding or correctly following the trial design. Further discussion of these issues, and conflicting views, can be found in Casley and Kumar, 1988; and Chambers, 1997. The issue of minimum sample size, with particular reference to statistical tests, is discussed further in Box 9.1.

BOX 9.1 Sample size and statistical analysis

Where statistical analysis is planned, the minimum number of sampling units (farms, animals) should, in principle, be based on the number required to show a certain difference (e.g. in yields) between different treatments, or between treatments and controls, at a given (e.g. 80 per cent) confidence level and significance level. (For further details, see, for example, Casley and Kumar, 1988.) The margin of error (comprising both sampling and non-sampling error) also needs to be taken into account. Sampling error depends partly on the 'population' sampled: if there is wide variation in the universe, sampling error will be high for a given sample size and design. In other words, higher variability requires more replication for the detection of differences between control and treatment groups. Thus, it is desirable to have some information, early on, of the degree of variation in the universe. An estimate of the likely amount of variability among the animals (e.g. in terms of milk yield) can often be obtained from previous experiments or relevant literature.

It is not only sampling error that needs to be taken into consideration when determining sample size. Other practical matters also need to be considered. For example, if the minimum number of sampling units required is deemed to be high, this could create problems in terms of finding a village with enough suitable animals to conduct the trial. There is then a risk that field staff may be forced to select a village with which the research team has not yet established a good rapport, making it difficult to get the villagers' co-operation.

One general guideline is that it is best to avoid being over-ambitious to begin with – mistakes in small trials are less costly than mistakes in large trials. Where statistical analysis is not involved, there are no hard and fast rules for determining sample size. One suggestion, however, is that in the initial phase, if fieldworkers are learning to work in a participatory mode with farmers, the number of experimenting farmers per fieldworker should be limited to, for example, a maximum of 2–3 villages with 5–8 experimenting farmers in each (Veldhuizen et al., 1997).

One factor that should be taken into account when determining the number of animals required is the probability of some animals leaving the herd during the course of the trial – due to sale or death, for example. For smallstock this could be as high as 50 per cent for a trial lasting 6 months or more. The necessary number of animals should be added to the minimum to allow for this. Researchers can, of course, try to persuade livestock owners not to sell their animals until the trial has finished, but in a participatory trial this possibility cannot be ruled out.

With livestock types or in regions where serious epidemics occur quite often (e.g. Newcastle disease in poultry) it could be advisable to work in a few villages that are not very close to each other. Then, even if most animals die from the disease in one village, animals in another village may be unaffected. In other words, don't put all your eggs in one basket. Generally, however, this is not a problem, and it is not mentioned in any of the case studies. In dryland regions, another problem (experienced by the project described in Case study E), is that departures can be particularly high in a drought year, when livestock kept as liquid assets may have to be sold.

9.3 How many treatments?

Since farmers' situations may differ considerably, it may be desirable to test several interventions through experimentation. However, more interventions will generally mean that more participants and resources are needed, if statistical analysis is to be done. Thus, there may have to be trade-offs. From the point of view of data analysis, it is better to collect meaningful data on a few experiments, or on one experiment with a modest number (1–2) of treatments, than inadequate data on a larger number. However, from the individual farmer's point of view, it may be preferable to have a large number of simple (i.e. 'with and without' or 'before and after' type treatments – see next section) experiments which carry fairly low risk and may be superimposed on existing farming practices. (An example of a six-treatment trial is given in Case study B.) There is room for negotiation between researchers and livestock-keepers on this topic.

9.4 Experimental design

Experiments seek to test hypotheses by comparing treatments: there must, therefore, be some basis for comparison. In principle, the animals on which the treatment or intervention is to be tested can be compared:

■ *before and after* the intervention; or
■ with animals on which the treatment was not tested (a *with and with-out* comparison); or
■ with animals on which a different treatment was tested.

Each method has its advantages and disadvantages, which are discussed in the following sections. Which is more appropriate may depend to some extent on the nature of the experiment.

The 'before and after' method

The *before and after* method can be used in such a way that the comparison is made for the same animal. When this method is used it is some-times the case that 'a sequence of experimental treatments is randomly allocated to each farm animal, and there are several different treatment sequences' (Statistical Services Centre, 2000). Each animal is given a treatment for a fixed period of time, and then changes over to another treatment. For example, a cow's milk yield can be measured before feed supplement 'X' is given and after, and then before and after feed supplement 'Y', and so on; and the effect of each supplement can be determined in this way.

When used in this way the before and after method has the major **advantage** of excluding inter-animal (and inter-farm) variation as a factor influencing the parameter being measured: this kind of variation is usually larger than within-animal variation, at least in the short term (Statistical Services Centre, 2000). If, instead, the comparison had been made between one group of four cows that were receiving the supplement and another group that were not, differences between the two groups could have been influenced by several other factors, such as general differences in diet between them or differences in the stage of lactation or parity. However, this method also has potential **disadvantages.**

First, any changes that occur may be influenced by extraneous factors that have changed over time, such as rainfall or forage availability, and these could be more important than the effect of the treatment. It is not well suited, therefore, to experiments lasting several months, in which the before and after data are from different years or different seasons. An example of inter-annual differences is given in Box 9.2. **Inter-seasonal variations** may also be marked, for example growth rates or milk yields between dry seasons and rainy seasons.

Second, 'before and after' experiments have more scope for 'going wrong'. For instance, if treatment periods are long, or there are too many of

BOX 9.2 The influence of inter-annual differences: an example

The BAIF/NRI project's work in semi-arid regions of India has identified situations in which inter-annual variations in rainfall can have a significant impact on livestock. This is particularly so in relation to mortality rates of young goats in the rainy season. This was a major problem in some places, so the project introduced treatments intended to reduce mortality. Mortality rates were 25–50 per cent in the baseline year, which had 'normal rainfall', but fell off dramatically (to say 5 per cent) the following year, when rainfall was low. Fortunately, the project had used the '*with and without*' method, and the researchers knew that there was little mortality in the control group, and hence that the reduced mortality rate was not due to the treatment. In this case, use of the 'before and after' method to determine the efficacy of the treatment could have been highly misleading, falsely attributing the improvement to the treatment.[22]

Another factor suggested by goat-keepers to explain the inter-annual difference in mortality rates was that they had increased their application of disease-control measures, following the discussions with the project team the previous year, which had raised their awareness of the problem and the need to address it.

Source: Conroy, 2002

them, the whole trial becomes too long and the farmer may lose interest and fail to complete the trial.

Third, this kind of experiment can also have carryover (or residual) effects. This is when a treatment given in an earlier period still has some effect in a later period when a different treatment is being given. This could be a problem with lactation experiments, if one treatment is started shortly after another one has finished.

Another example of the 'before and after' method can be found in Case study B. Here, the researchers and farmers tested various mange control methods simultaneously and compared them with each other. In this case the method worked well, for two reasons. First, effective treatments had an almost immediate effect; and second, because the researchers and farmers knew that mange does not normally disappear without treatment. For both of these reasons they could be confident that the disappearance of the mange was due to the control method, and not to some extraneous factor.

---

[22] A good researcher would have noted the difference in rainfall and would have realized that this non-experimental factor could have had a significant influence. Nevertheless, (s)he would not have known which factor was more important and the trial would have had to be repeated.

'With and without' experiments

The disadvantage of this method is that inter-animal variability can be high, and this can make it difficult, if not impossible, to separate out the effect of the treatment. When this method is used, therefore, steps should be taken to minimize this kind of variability.

Inter-animal variability arises from two sources: (a) the genetic make-up of the animals and their ages; and (b) environmental factors, including the owner's animal husbandry practices (e.g. housing, feeding systems). It is important, therefore, that animals in the different groups being compared are of similar breeds and ages, and that the environmental conditions experienced by the groups are broadly similar. Some differences in the latter may be unavoidable, however, in which case they should be noted and referred to when the results of the experiment are being interpreted and discussed. (This matter is discussed further in section 10.1.)

If environmental conditions between different experimental groups are substantially different, it may not be possible to draw any meaningful conclusions from the experimental results, and valuable time and resources will have been wasted. An example of different environmental conditions between groups undermining an experiment is given in Box 9.3.

BOX 9.3   Example of non-experimental differences between treatment and control groups

In one of the BAIF/NRI project trials, testing the effect of feed supplementation on the health and growth rates of young goats, the control group goats were on average of similar weight to those in the treatment group at the end of the experiment. The researchers needed to know why this was – did it mean that the treatment was ineffective?

The control group participants were from a different hamlet to those in the treatment group, and investigations revealed that this had confounded the trial results. The two groups used different grazing areas, and the one used by the control group members was superior to that used by the treatment group. (It was only after the trial that the project staff discovered this.) In planning the trials the project team had concluded that the treatment and control groups should be in the same village, partly to avoid this kind of problem.

A second factor identified by the investigations was that people in the control group were generally better off than those in the treatment group, so when they saw the young goats of the latter group growing faster than their own they regarded this as socially unacceptable and started giving the supplement to their own goats.

Source: Conroy, 2002

With and without animals – within same herd or between herds?

If the 'with and without' design is the one selected, the next decision is whether animals in the different groups should be from different herds or the same herds. In other words, should control group animals belong to the same livestock-keepers who are testing the new technology, or to different livestock-keepers; and if there are two treatments, should they be applied to animals in the same herd? In many cases the answer to this question may be determined by the normal size of the herds: where herds are very small, and tend not to contain two comparable animals, the inter-herd option will have to be used. But where herds are large enough, which of these options is preferable?

A potentially major **disadvantage** of the different herd option is that there may be differences between the practices and circumstances of livestock-keepers in the two groups (as illustrated in Box 9.3), and these may confound the influence of the treatment. The experience of the project described in Box 9.3 highlights the need to ensure that households in the treatment and control groups are similar, so that differences in non-experimental variables are minimized. On the other hand, this approach means that animals in the different groups are kept apart, which can be **an advantage** (see below).

The converse applies when using animals from the same herd. Having animals from different groups kept together can present problems, particularly where the treatment is some kind of feed, and particularly where all of the animals in the herd normally feed from the same container. Animals in the control group may get access to the treatment, or animals in one treatment group may eat feed intended for animals in another treatment group. In addition, if the owner sees animals in the treatment group benefiting from the treatment, (s)he may be tempted to divert some to animals in the control group.[23] This problem can also arise in the between-herd method, but in that situation the owner in the control group would have to obtain the treatment him/herself.

In de-worming experiments there could also be inter-animal interactions. If worm eggs are eliminated from animals in the treatment group(s), this might lead to a decrease in the worm burden of animals in the control groups, since one source of infestation would have been removed, i.e. the faeces of other animals in the herd.

9.5 Conclusions

The *before and after* method is not well-suited to experiments lasting several months, in which the before and after data are from different years or different seasons. The *with and without* method would be preferable in this

---

[23] This is a common problem, according to Amir and Knipscheer. They give the example of a farmer administering anti-helminthic drugs to his/her control animals after observing the benefits for the treatment animals (Amir and Knipscheer, 1989).

kind of situation. When the before and after method is used in experiments of short duration (say 2–3 weeks), it is important to leave a sufficiently long gap between treatments to ensure that there are no carryover effects from one treatment period to the next.

For trials of longer duration than a few weeks *with and without* comparisons are likely to be more reliable than *before and after,* provided that proper care is taken to minimize inter-animal variations. It is easier to achieve this, and avoid bias, by having animals from different groups within each herd, rather than making a 'between-herds' comparison. However, the 'within-herd' approach can be problematic for certain types of treatments, particularly those involving feed supplementation. Nevertheless, it can work if the owner understands and agrees with the purpose of the trial design; and if there is a good rapport between the researchers and the livestock-keepers, and frequent visits by the researchers.

We have seen that both *with and without* comparisons and *before and after* ones have their potential weaknesses. When experiments are being conducted using the *with and without* design it can be useful to collect baseline data as well so that a *before and after* comparison can be made, provided that this can be done at a reasonably low cost (see section 10.2). The two sets of data can then be cross-checked with each other.

Some trials have two or more treatment groups, but do not have a 'no treatment' group, the comparison being between the different treatments. This approach is commonly used in trials on new animal health treatments, particularly those drawing on EVK, when the new treatment is compared with an established commercial one whose efficacy has been thoroughly studied already. In such trials the established treatment is used as a control. However, the example in Box 9.2 illustrates why it is often important to have a 'no treatment' control group too.

Most of the above discussion and conclusions was concerned with trials that are seeking, among other things, to ascertain the biophysical effect of a particular technology or treatment. In order to isolate the effect of the technology the variability in other (non-experimental) factors needs to be either minimized or understood in such a way that it can be taken into account. However, there are two other types of trials in which isolating the effect of the technology is less important, i.e. trials that are primarily concerned with ascertaining livestock-keepers' attitudes to a new technology; and trials designed to test the suitability and efficacy of a technology under a range of conditions.

Whatever the nature of the trials, experimental design issues should be discussed with participants before any trials are initiated. A series of meetings may be required: these are sometimes referred to as Farmer Experimental Design Workshops (Reintjes et al., 1992; Veldhuizen et al., 1997). Researchers may need to remind themselves that the design is as much the livestock-keepers' as their own.

10 Monitoring and evaluation of experiments

Monitoring is a vital part of any participatory experiment and resources should always be made available for it to be undertaken effectively. Without adequate data collection and management the value of a trial will be greatly diminished. Monitoring of participatory trials usually requires a combination of qualitative and quantitative information.

10.1 What data, why and how often?

The type of data that needs to be collected will depend very much on the nature of the experiment. If it is a trial to test the acceptability of a technically proven technology to farmers, then it may be enough to record their views at the end of the trial period. On the other hand, if the experiment is to determine whether a previously untested treatment increases conception rates significantly, more quantitative data will be required.

Data requirements are also partly dependent on whom the research team wish to influence when they have the results of the research, or who the 'target groups' are. If the 'target groups' are only participating livestock-keepers and others in the locality, it may not be necessary to collect any data at all. The participants may consider their direct observations to be sufficient, and others from the area may find the participants' views convincing and an adequate basis for adopting the technology themselves. On the other hand, some detailed documentation of results will be required if the target groups include extension agencies, researchers, academic journals or livestock-keepers in distant places.

What data?
When determining what type of data is required it is important to take account of how the data will be analysed to produce useful and meaningful results. The type of data may be either qualitative (e.g. body condition[24]) or quantitative (usually biophysical). *Qualitative* data are often needed to *explain*

---

[24] However, even something like this can be quantitative, if livestock-keepers are asked to score their animals' condition, say on a scale of 1 to 5.

what has been happening: for example, why farmers applied a certain level of input at a certain time, or (in a relatively unstructured trial) why some farmers applied one treatment while others applied a different one. The type of data to be collected should ideally be *agreed* between the researchers and the livestock-keepers before the experiment commences. To some extent this will follow from the nature of the hypothesis.[25]

Biophysical trial data Important indicators of the efficacy of treatments should be incorporated into the monitoring system. For example, in a trial comparing tree forage supplements for dairy cows, the criteria selected by farmers were: milk output, feed intake and condition of the animal (Mason et al., 1999). In another trial, this time on worm control methods, the indicators were: state of animal's coat, size of appetite, body condition, and presence or absence of diarrhoea (Mulira et al., 1999).

As indicated by the above examples, some indicators can be measured in an 'objective' way (e.g. milk output, weight), while others (e.g. body condition, shininess of coat) are relatively subjective. For indicators that can be measured relatively objectively consideration should also be given to the unit of measurement, bearing in mind that the livestock-keepers may have their own units and may not be familiar with metric and scientific units. This is illustrated by Case study J, in which the Tzotzil shepherdesses had their own way of measuring the quality of a sheep's fleece (see Box 10.3).

Collecting data to explain variation In on-farm experiments it is not only treatments that affect animal performance, but non-experimental variables (NEVs) as well. In participatory experiments NEVs are often not controlled or standardized, so if we are interested in exploring the causes of farm-to-farm or animal-to-animal variation it is necessary to monitor the NEVs (e.g. characteristics of the farm, farmer or animal, including farmer management practices) that might affect the performance parameters that the trial will be monitoring. Therefore, it is important to identify what ancillary data need to be collected before (baseline) and during the trial. These data will be used in the subsequent analysis in three different ways (Statistical Services Centre, 2000):

- to explain some between and/or within animal variation, and thus improve precision in respect of important objectives;
- to explore the behaviour of different groups of animals or farms, as identified by the objectives of the study; and
- to help to explain unexpected findings that emerge in the analysis.

An example of this approach is given in Box 10.1.

Process data Depending on the nature of the trial, researchers might also want to record data that are not directly related to the treatment and its

---

[25] For example, for the hypothesis described in section 9.1, obvious indicators to be monitored are: the quantity of milk produced, kid mortality rates and growth rates, and the presence or not of worms in the kids (e.g. through faecal egg counts).

BOX 10.1   Improving the efficacy of concentrate usage

This case study describes a researcher-designed trial. Based on the results of an on-station trial, the researchers hypothesized that by temporally re-allocating the total amount of concentrates typically fed to a dairy cow by smallholders, without increasing the total, cumulative milk production would be significantly increased. The on-station trial had shown that if all concentrates were fed during the first 3 months, instead of being spread out at a fairly constant daily rate over many months, milk production increased.

The trial was unusual for a supplementation trial (and application of the technology potentially more sustainable), in that the researchers did not provide any free inputs to the farmers. They did, however, arrange with the collaborating dairy co-operative that, during the first 3 months after calving, its members would be able to obtain larger quantities of concentrates than usual on credit.

The trial was also noteworthy (and participatory) in that smallholders were given discretion as to the extent to which they followed the recommended 'treatment'. In this respect the trial represented an interesting departure from the conventional approach of testing well defined biological treatments under conditions where (a) underlying variation is either minimized or taken account of; and (b) changes in application of the 'treatments' by farmers are often strongly discouraged and results discounted when they occur. The researchers were interested in knowing how farmers modified the recommended treatment. Rather than control for underlying variability, the study attempted instead to record the variability (e.g. level of education of farmers, access to off-farm income) and use this to explain results, because data gathered in this way are more likely to be translatable into information useful to farmers as it allows farmer circumstances to be taken into account. There were no treatment and control groups as such.

Source: Case study D

effects. For example, it may be helpful to collect data that provide some indication of the nature of livestock-keepers' involvement in the technology development process or their relationship with the researchers (particularly where empowerment is a major objective), such as:

- How many people have been attending group meetings?
- Who attends and who does not (e.g. men versus women, rich versus poor)?
- How many suggestions for treatments have come from livestock-keepers, as compared with researchers?
- How many participants have made modifications to treatments suggested by researchers?
- Are livestock-keepers maintaining their own monitoring records?
- Are livestock-keepers processing or summarizing monitoring data in any way?

How frequently and for how long?

Frequency This needs to be carefully considered, because the process of collecting monitoring data can be quite time-consuming for the owners, if they have to be present while the data are collected or are to be involved in collecting the data themselves. Researchers and livestock-keepers may have different views on the amount of data required or the frequency with which it needs to be collected. It is important for researchers to listen to people's views: compromise may be necessary. The principle of optimal ignorance, which is one of the fundamental tenets of PRA, is equally applicable here – which is that one should only collect the data that one knows one needs, and should not worry about being ignorant about things that one does not need to know.

Duration The duration of the monitoring period will depend on the nature of the trial. Table 7.3 gives monitoring periods for several different kinds of trial, which range from three to 18 months. Basically, the monitoring period should be long enough for data to be collected that show whether or not the treatment had the hypothesized effect. Where there is also good reason to expect the treatment to have a side-effect, it may also be worthwhile to extend the monitoring period to see whether the side-effect materializes. For example, in de-worming trials undertaken by the BAIF/NRI project the researchers monitored how long a period passed before the does conceived again; and they found that the kidding interval of does that had been in the treatment group was shorter than that of those in the control group.

10.2 Collecting baseline data

A common weakness of PTD is that researchers often do not collect adequate baseline data to enable a comparison to be made between before and after situations. The participant farmers may not see the need for this, as they may think it is enough to hold the information in their memories. For the researcher, however, baseline information can greatly increase confidence that the intervention or treatment has made the difference that participants say it has.

Once the foci of the experiments and the hypotheses have been identified the type of baseline data needed for comparisons will be apparent. At this point researchers and participants can decide how useful such data would be and with what ease and accuracy (recall errors could be a problem) they could be obtained. The participatory herd history method, which facilitates recall and reduces the likelihood of any misunderstandings between the researchers and the livestock-keepers, can be useful here (see section 3.3).

10.3 Who monitors and how?

In the collaborative research mode both the researchers and the participating livestock-keepers play a role in monitoring. It is important that the livestock-keepers participate fully in the monitoring (and evaluation),[26] so that their sense of ownership of the technology development process is maintained, and so that they can contribute fully to identifying, and possibly explaining, observed changes. Where participants are illiterate, or where measurements of biophysical data are somewhat complicated, one or two literate local people (perhaps older schoolchildren) in each village can be trained to carry out the monitoring and maintain records of the data. It is important, however, that they share and discuss the information collected with the participating livestock-keepers. Both parties (livestock-keepers and researchers) could keep records of the same data. For example, if livestock weight is one of the variables being monitored the participants may keep records in their homes on their own recording cards or in school exercise books, and the researchers (or local monitors) might record the same data themselves.

Data recording by illiterate livestock-keepers

Farmers can be assisted in designing simple formats (sheets or notebooks) for recording the information periodically. Where many community members are illiterate extra thought may need to be given to devising record sheets, etc. that are intelligible to them. Various PTD programmes have given calendars to farmers to note important events: symbols can be used where necessary. In some cases, schoolchildren interview the other family members involved in the experiments at fixed intervals, and do the recording (Veldhuizen et al., 1997).

However, the livestock-keepers may not always see any need to quantify or record changes in their animals, and may be content to rely on their observations and their recall (as in Case study E). If this situation arises their views should be respected.

10.4 Processing monitoring data

Every effort should be made to speed up the collection and analysis of data. This helps to reduce errors and speeds up the dissemination of results back to the farmers. It is important to be clear at the outset which members of the research team are expected to analyse the monitoring data, and in what ways. Field staff may not be used to analysing data, and may assume that this is only done by senior members of the team. It is desirable, however, that field staff undertake at least preliminary inspection and analysis of the data, so

---

[26] For further information about participatory monitoring and evaluation, see Rietbergen-McCracken and Narayan, 1998.

that they know what is happening to the trial animals. Where it is possible to computerize the data locally this will facilitate analysis.

In the BAIF/NRI project there was in a few cases a time lag of weeks or months before the data collected by the field staff were entered into a computer and analysed by the researchers. Livestock-keepers, on the other hand, are doing real-time monitoring, observing changes in their animals week by week, if not day by day. Thus, when joint monitoring meetings took place the field staff were not always aware of important trends, and hence they were not able to make the most of the meetings and to investigate certain issues promptly (see Box 10.2).

This problem is not insuperable, however. Field staff can be trained to enter data into computers, or to calculate simple descriptive statistics (e.g. means) using calculators. They can also be trained to convert data into media that are amenable to visual inspection, such as graphs or histograms, which can be highly informative (Casley and Kumar, 1988).

10.5 Physically distinguishing animals to be monitored

Where there are several animals in a herd it may be necessary to identify the experimental animals in some way and, where necessary, to distinguish between those in different groups. There are various ways in which this can be done, including: painting horns, dyeing the hide or feathers, tagging and ringing (for poultry). Livestock-keepers may have strong views on the acceptability or otherwise of different options, so it is important to discuss this matter with them before making a decision. There may be a local technique that can be adopted or adapted. In India, livestock-keepers paint their animals during some festivals as a mark of love. Hence, painting of horns with different colours for different groups can be an appropriate technique for identification of animals in the trial.

BOX 10.2 Issues raised by inspection of monitoring data in a goat research project

Examples of issues only identified after completion of trials include:

- convergence in the weights of kids in the treatment and control groups, due to various factors including (a) control group members starting to apply the treatment and (b) treatment group members starting to give the treatment to the whole herd, including non-experimental animals; and

- some goats producing more milk in the dry season after construction of a water trough, while others' milk production is unaffected.

Source: Conroy, 2002

Members of the family who own the herd will probably have no difficulty identifying individual animals. In some countries or ethnic groups, there is a widespread practice of giving a name to each animal, and every family member is well acquainted with these names. The names may be based on the colour of the animals, their behaviour, season of birth, place of birth/purchase, identification mark, etc. In India, owners also sometimes give the name of a god, goddess or river to their animals. The PTD team should ensure the participation of all the family members during identification of animals for trials, to avoid confusion. The name and identification marks of each animal should be recorded in the monitoring notebooks of the researchers and participants, so that they can be easily identified by any of the team members.

10.6 Methods for measuring treatments and performance indicators

Measuring treatments

Whenever a trial is conducted on livestock, whether it is PTD or a researcher-managed trial, accurate measurement of treatments is important. For example, to assess the effect of feed supplementation or de-worming, it is essential to feed or drench the animals, respectively, with the recommended quantity of input as per the trial protocol. At the research station, where facilities are available, it is easy to measure such inputs every day; but it can be difficult to measure them in the field. In PTD, it may not be possible to use the exact quantity of input, but a high degree of accuracy can be achieved by developing local methods to measure inputs that are convenient for the livestock-keepers, as is illustrated by the following examples.

First, if you wanted to provide a supplement of 200 g of sorghum + horse gram mix, or 250 g of *Prosopis juliflora* pods, to goats, it would be impractical to weigh the materials every day, as this requires more time as well as a weighing facility. To overcome this problem, local measures should be developed to feed the recommended quantity of supplement. Such issues should be discussed in a group meeting before the initiation of the trial. In the meeting, the appropriate quantity of supplement should be weighed on a balance in front of all partners and family members. Subsequently, it should be measured with some kind of local measure (container). Generally, in Indian villages every house has a measure (called a *sher*) that is in daily use to measure grains or flour. Once the capacity of the measure (sher) is made known to all partners, there is no need to weigh the input every day.

Second, in the de-worming trial described in Box 7.4, 20 mg of trichomes (hairs) of *Mucuna pruriens* pod are applied per kg of body weight. A local plastic spoon was selected by the PTD team to measure the recommended quantity of trichomes to drench the animals. The team established that one level plastic spoon of 4.5 g capacity contains 500 mg of trichomes, while one two-finger pinch of trichomes weighs about 100 mg.

In other situations more approximate measures may need to be adopted or may be adequate. For example, in Case study E, to measure 250 g of *Prosopis juliflora* pods, the Karnataka-based researchers developed measures like two handfuls (of an adult man).

Where the research is drawing on indigenous knowledge, the livestock-keepers may already have their own ways of measuring the relevant parameters. In this kind of situation the onus is on the researchers to understand the local methods and measurement units, and to consider using them instead of, or in conjunction with, 'western' methods or units. An example of this is given in Box 10.3.

Measuring performance parameters

Weighing animals The weight of animals is an important performance indicator in many types of trial. It reflects the growth and health of animals, and also their value. It is important that animals are weighed carefully,

---

BOX 10.3 Assessing fleeces of Chiapas sheep

Tzotzil shepherdesses assess the characteristics of the fleeces every six months at the research station where the nucleus flock is kept. The combination of key words exchanged among the women while performing the assessment of fleece quality of an animal allowed the sheep scientists to assign a compounded quality grade going from 1 (poor) to 4 (excellent), integrating both staple length and textile aptitude. Grades would be included in the databases for statistical analyses.

The single most important criterion used by the shepherdesses is staple length. Although most of them are illiterate, they have developed an efficient quantitative method of measuring the staples using a series of distances that can be established with the fingers of their hands They use from one to four horizontally stacked fingers for the shorter distances, and they calculate the larger ones measuring from the tip of their thumb to the tip of their index or their middle finger.

To validate the empirical method, this series of finger distances was measured with a ruler and plotted on a graph, and they were highly correlated, which means that each woman has an integrated ruler in her hands. This measuring system is also used by Tzotzil women in other household and agricultural activities; it is a convenient tool for them, very useful and efficient. Direct measuring of the different finger distances in different women at a given time, and in one of them over a period of eight consecutive shearing seasons (four years), showed that they are highly repeatable and thus a trustworthy selection tool under village conditions.

Source: Case study J

particularly if they are pregnant: owners may not like to see their animals becoming scared or uncomfortable.

Weighing non-pregnant animals is not at all difficult, but weighing female small ruminants that are in an advanced stage of pregnancy is more risky, if they are not handled carefully. One type of weighing system for small ruminants is a small wooden platform attached to a spring balance, where the animal is lifted up onto the platform for weighing. The disadvantage of this system is that animals will not stand calmly, because of shaking. It is also difficult to carry the wooden platform from house to house, because of its weight. A better alternative is a piece of rectangular gunny bag cloth with four holes at appropriate distance, with rope attached to each of the four corners so that it can be hung from the weighing balance. Using this system, the small ruminants can be weighed comfortably.

Measuring milk yield In countries or areas where standard measures based on metric units are not widely used by local people to measure milk yield, it may be preferable to use any local measure that people are accustomed to, like a tumbler, to measure the quantity of milk.

10.7 Evaluation: assessing the effect of interventions

Meetings or workshops need to be held at which the outcome of the experiment can be jointly assessed by both farmers and researchers. The results of the experiment are systematically described and discussed according to the criteria defined during earlier group meetings. The original objectives of the experiment, and the criteria for success, are reviewed. However, there should also be flexibility in the topics covered, so that participants feel comfortable about raising any unanticipated results or influences on the trials.

Qualitative assessment

For certain types of trials, assessments may be based partly or entirely on participants' opinions, and these in turn may be based on subjective criteria, such as taste, feel, shininess of coat, etc. For example, people's preferences for different breeds (e.g. of poultry or goats) are often based on the animals' appearance (e.g. colour, shape) as much as any quantifiable production parameters. Where participants' own judgements are the main consideration, their willingness or otherwise to 'adopt' the technology that has been tested will be the main indicator of its efficacy. In Case study F researchers carried out an ex-post evaluation, nearly two years after completion of the research project, in which a major focus was the extent to which the different technologies had been adopted and were continuing to be used.

Participants may not need any quantitative data to persuade them of the merits of the treatment. For example, in a trial to address mange in goats the visual results were so impressive, and farmers were so enthusiastic, that it was not necessary to wait for statistical analysis before reaching a conclusion on the efficacy of the treatments (Case study B).

Based on quantitative data collected by trained monitors, trials conducted by a BAIF and NRI project provided clear evidence that selective supplementation with tree pods resulted in does producing significantly more kids (through higher conception rates and higher twinning rates) than they would otherwise have done (see Case study E). It would have been a mistake, however, to rely on quantitative data alone in evaluating these trials, as these could give a misleading picture: participants' views are also of paramount importance. For example, goat-keepers sometimes prefer to have one kid rather than twins, because (a) one kid may have a better chance of survival, and/or (b) some milk may then be available for consumption by the owner's family. They could, therefore, regard twins as a disbenefit rather than a benefit, but this point would not be captured by quantitative data, and hence the results could easily be interpreted in a biased and incomplete way.

Quantitative assessment

If hypotheses were formulated, and relevant variables monitored, some quantitative summary data should be available that can provide a basis for the joint assessment: such as, the percentage of farmers who rated a technology highly, or the average performance of a technology according to some objective criterion or parameter. For example, in an agroforestry project, data were collected on where farmers planted selected species, their preferred uses of different species, their opinions about the effect of the species on crop yields (positive, negative or no effect) and their mean ratings of the species against various criteria (Coe, 1997).

Participants' assessments can be quantified in various ways, for example, through scoring and ranking exercises. Matrix ranking is useful in that it also shows the criteria on which the rankings are based. The results obtained by each participant need to be noted against each of the main criteria, distinguishing between the different treatments. The results of all the experimenters can be summarized by calculating averages; simple tables may provide an effective way of presenting this information (Veldhuizen et al., 1997). An example of matrix scoring is given in Table 10.1. Nevertheless, the presentation of summary data by researchers to illiterate livestock-keepers in an intelligible form can be a major challenge.

Individual participants may be aware of quantitative data about their own animals, but researchers have seldom involved them in assembling aggregate data for all participants. Usually, researchers aggregate the data and analyse it on their own, and then present a summary to the participants. This puts the participants at an immediate disadvantage. In addition, summary data are usually presented in numerals and words, which makes it impossible for illiterate people to understand them.

Table 10.1 Farmer evaluation of fodder trees using matrix scoring[a]

Fodder tree species	Creamy milk	Milk output	Health of animal	Ease of collecting leaves	Ease of marketing milk	Palatability
Calliandra	13	9	9	12	12	12
Sesbania	6	7	7	3	6	7
Grevillia	1	4	4	5	2	1

[a] This table aggregates separate scores of male and female groups: the differences between the groups were minor. Each group had ten counters to allocate between the three tree species against each criterion.

Source: Adapted from Mason et al., 1999.

Profitability analysis The methods that were described earlier in Chapter 8 can be used again to see whether the original profitability analysis has been confirmed, and to see how different treatments compare with each other.

Statistical analysis

There is often scope for some statistical analysis of data in PTD. With *farmer-designed* trials quantitative assessment data may be in the form of scores or yes/no answers: for example, did a farmer adopt the technology or not? With *researcher-designed trials* quantitative data may include: continuous (parametric) biophysical data, such as milk yields or growth rates; non-parametric data, such as the numbers of animals that did or did not die, or that did or did not conceive; and categorical data such as scores or ranks.

Meaningful statistical analysis and interpretation of *biophysical data* is sometimes problematic in participatory research, particularly in the collaborative and collegiate modes, due to high levels of variability. However, the problem may not be as acute as some observers have suggested, particularly with advances in computing power and the development of more user-friendly software for statistical analysis.

Where local staff do not have access to a computer, or do not know how to use one for data analysis, they should be encouraged to do simple forms of analysis using a calculator. For example, in a feed-related trial they could estimate mean weights over time, for both trial and control groups. They could then plot a graph manually to show changes over time. Graphical representations of experimental data are generally easier and quicker to interpret – for an example, see Box 10.4.

BOX 10.4   Graphical presentation

The bar graph below clearly highlights the important differences in conceptions for treatment and control groups, in trials conducted in 1998 and 1999, in which *Prosopis juliflora* pods were given as a supplement to female goats (see Case study E for details).

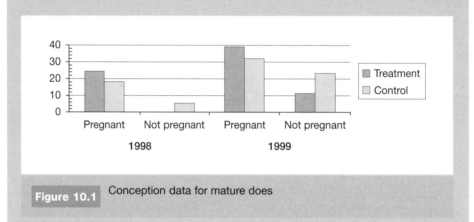

Figure 10.1   Conception data for mature does

11 Achieving wider impact

Projects or programmes that adopt a participatory approach to technology development with resource-poor farmers tend to be more resource-intensive than those involving on-station research and the consultative mode (see Table 7.2), and to have higher unit costs per farm household. A number of factors contribute to this. First, the technology development process is slow, as it usually requires considerable time to be spent on developing the capacity of project staff and farmers or livestock-keepers, and building up a positive rapport between them, before it can function effectively.

Second, it requires a multi-disciplinary team, and a few organizations may need to be involved as often no one organization possesses all of the necessary skills and expertise. This in itself can be costly, and it also slows down the technology development process, because staff from the different organizations need to get to know each other, and the organizations themselves need to sort out how they are going to relate and to develop a *modus operandi.*

Third, points one and two mean that the research is only undertaken with a relatively small number of farmers or livestock-keepers, and hence the size of the benefits generated (assuming the project does develop effective technologies) is small relative to the high unit costs (per household or village) involved. Fourth, it has also been argued that even if there were serious efforts to disseminate the technologies, the spread effect would be limited, because the farming and livelihood systems of resource-poor farmers and livestock-keepers are so varied and complex that no one technology is likely to be appropriate for a really large number of them (Jiggins, 1989; Okali et al., 1994).

The obvious counter-argument[27] to the above points is that conventional research processes themselves have a poor track record in developing technologies that are suitable for adoption by resource-poor farmers and livestock-keepers (see Chapter 1) – and that is why many researchers have advocated PTD as an alternative approach. However, this counter-argument does not entirely address the points raised. It could still be argued that both approaches are rather ineffective at developing technologies suitable for adoption by a large number of resource-poor people, and that the costs of both of them outweigh their benefits. Neither governments nor donor

---

[27] Another counter-argument is that PTD develops the capacity of farmers to innovate themselves, and therefore has more long-lasting benefits than conventional agricultural R&D.

agencies are obliged to fund agricultural/livestock R&D, nor are they obliged to give priority to resource-poor farmers. Indeed, there has been a reduction in donor funding for agricultural R&D precisely because of dissatisfaction with its apparently limited impact.

The concerns over the efficacy of PTD deserve to be taken seriously. Agencies involved in PTD, if they are genuinely interested in poverty reduction, should in any case be asking themselves how they are going to maximize the benefits from the technologies they have developed with livestock-keepers, by disseminating them as widely as possible. In addition, if their experience confirms that PTD can be more effective than conventional technology development processes, they should be seeking to promote the more widespread adoption of this approach.

This chapter looks at how PTD projects can maximize their wider impact. There are various ways that they can do so. They can extend their impact *spatially* (sometimes described as horizontally[28]) by encouraging other development agencies operating outside of their immediate project area to promote the uptake of the technologies they have developed (see section 11.1 below); and by promoting the effective use of PTD by sharing their experiences with other agencies, including the benefits they have seen arising from its use (see section 11.4). They can also extend (i.e. sustain) their impact *temporally* by: strengthening the capacity of livestock-keepers to experiment (section 11.2); and by institutionalizing PTD within the project's lead organizations (section 11.3). Finally, section 11.5 looks at ways of improving the enabling environment for participatory research.

Box 11.1 contains an example of how one project, described in Case study C, has sought to have a wider impact in various ways.

11.1 Disseminating technologies developed by the PTD project or programme[29]

Organizations should develop a dissemination plan for projects or programmes before the implementation phase, as this may influence the choice of collaborating organizations and 'target' agencies. For example, if an NGO project decides to focus on ethnoveterinary methods to control diseases in small ruminants it may choose to invite a national or state/province level veterinary or small ruminant research institute to be a

---

[28] Horizontal scaling up is used here to mean geographical spread and expansion to more people and communities within the same sector or stakeholder group.

[29] This section covers issues that are not specific to livestock research and development. Much has been written about them, and for additional information readers are referred to the following publications: Norman et al., 1995 for farming systems research's philosophy and methods; Norrish et al., 2001; Gündel et al, 2001; Reijntjes et al., 1992 for PTD in general; and Veldhuizen et al., 1997).

BOX 11.1 Achieving wider impact – the case of ethnoveterinary knowledge in Kenya

ITDG East Africa has been implementing a participatory project on ethnoveterinary knowledge (EVK) validation since 1996. The project has been working directly with about 30 ethnoveterinary practitioners. Each of them represents about 100 households, so it is estimated that about 3000 households have benefited directly from the project, and many others indirectly. This project has made a substantial impact through the following activities.

Collaborative partnerships The project has been undertaken from the outset in partnership with pastoralists, local healers, local veterinary officers, other local development organizations and formal research organizations. This broad coalition has helped to widen the project's reach.

Local healers contributed their knowledge to the researchers, and participated in the trials. The project organized several 'healers' workshops', which enabled healers, pastoralists and scientists to share their knowledge. Some of the healers also participated in informal trials, which involved monitoring of their work.

The scientific partner organizations are the University of Nairobi, Kenya Agricultural Research Institute (KARI) and the International Livestock Research Institute. Their involvement has contributed to at least one of them (KARI) initiating related research elsewhere in the country. KARI has prioritized EVK as one of the research themes in its programme, and has commissioned scientists in a number of its regional offices to undertake the research.

Capacity building has taken place in each of the main stakeholder groups (healers, vets, scientists). The 30 traditional *healers* have been trained as community-based animal health workers. They have also been facilitated to form and register healers' associations in five districts to strengthen their capacity to advocate and promote their practice in Kenya. *Veterinary practitioners* have been trained in EVK, which has helped to change their attitudes to it. However, one lesson learned is that it would have been better to involve more local vets and livestock extension workers in the research, to encourage better adoption of the results and approach.

Supply of raw materials A study was undertaken of the status of the plants involved in the validated remedies. EVK drug stores have been established in Samburu, as have community-based herbal gardens and shops.

Extension materials Information about effective EVK practices, particularly for the control of internal parasites, has been widely disseminated, both through training and publications. The project published a *Community-based Animal Healthcare Training Manual*, which incorporated the project's baseline information. It also published a two-volume book on socio-economic aspects

BOX 11.1 cont.

of the practices used, including who holds the knowledge and how it is shared. It has also produced leaflets on the project that were distributed to various organizations and individuals.

Policy The project facilitated the formation of the Kenya Working Group on Medicinal and Aromatic Plant Species. Through this group, a national strategy on research and development of these plants has been developed. The project has also been promoting appropriate intellectual property rights (IPRs) regimes that recognize practitioners' IPRs.

Source: Case study C

collaborator, so that it can draw on the institute's expertise and facilities in conducting post mortems and identifying diseases. The plan should then be revised periodically as the work progresses: for example, after needs assessment work has identified priority issues, and thereafter perhaps once a year.

Collaborating organizations are those that are directly involved in implementation, while target agencies are those that the project intends to encourage to promote the technologies. Some collaborating organizations may also be target organizations. Indeed, this is desirable, as an organization that has been fully involved in implementation is more likely to be an effective target organization, as it will have a thorough knowledge of the work, and also a sense of ownership of the findings and recommendations.

A dissemination plan needs to identify how the project will get its messages to target organizations, to act on or promote the recommendations. Project budgets should include a reasonable allocation (e.g. 10 per cent) for dissemination activities. A general weakness of conventional agricultural and livestock research, and also of PTD projects, has been inadequate attention to dissemination from an early stage.

Determining the size and nature of the recommendation domain
In general PTD projects have arguably not given enough consideration to the question of how widely the technologies they develop can be disseminated. Where the lead agency is an NGO it may only be concerned with adoption of technologies by resource-poor people in its project area, such as a few dozen or hundred villages in a particular district. It may be the case, however, that the project has developed a technology that has a much wider relevance, and could be beneficial to, for example, tens of thousands of other livestock-keepers. A serious attempt should be made, therefore, to identify who and where those livestock-keepers are.

The concept of the 'recommendation domain' (RD), which was by developed by the Farming Systems Research and Extension community, is valuable here. It enables agricultural and livestock researchers to be relatively precise in targeting those farmers or livestock-keepers for whom any particular technological recommendation is likely to be appropriate and adoptable.

An RD has been defined as: 'a group of farmers ... [who] have similar circumstances, resources, problems, and [hence] solutions to these problems' (Norman et al., 1995).

Differences between RDs may be due to:

- agro-ecological differences affecting the production environment (e.g. soils, climate, topography); or
- differences in farmers' (or livestock-keepers') resource endowments (e.g. farm size, labour, capital) and circumstances (e.g. land tenure, access to markets).

Four factors that may determine the size of the RD for targeting the dissemination of a successful technology are:

1. the number of households involved in producing the relevant commodity (e.g. maize or scavenging poultry) or with a similar problem (e.g. soil erosion);
2. how widespread the production constraint or opportunity[30] is;
3. the resources (land, labour and money) available to the farmer or livestock-keeping household producing the commodity; and
4. the likely availability of the inputs needed (in the case of technologies based on locally available materials, the geographical distribution of the local material).

Information about these four factors can be obtained from a combination of primary (project surveys) and secondary (census data, other projects' reports and scientific papers) sources. However, there may be significant gaps, particularly regarding the production constraint. Tables 11.1–11.3 illustrate how the four factors mentioned above can be taken into account in estimating RDs. They contain very preliminary estimates of the RDs for five technologies.

The nature and size of the RD is partly shaped in the early stages by a project's or organization's client group (e.g. poor livestock-keepers in semi-arid regions of country/province X). However, as the term is used here, an RD can only be fully defined once a recommendation has been developed. Domain sizes vary considerably, and 'have ranged from a few thousand farmers to several tens of thousands, or more' (Harrington and Tripp, 1984). They

---

[30] Opportunities often arise where product markets (e.g. for milk) are better developed. Good transport systems can link livestock producers to urban areas, where the demand for milk and meat is often relatively high, and where prices are often higher. Good market prices for products may justify the adoption of input technologies (e.g. certain fodders) that would not have been financially attractive otherwise.

should not be too small, otherwise the benefits of a new technology developed for a specific domain may be less than the corresponding research costs.

The definition of the RD may affect the choice of target organizations. For example, if the project concludes that one or more of its recommendations are relevant outside of the districts where it has an operational presence or mandate, it may identify a relevant organization that works in another location within the RD to promote the recommendation in that area.

RDs for technologies suitable for the resource-poor

Some people have argued that the RDs for resource-poor farmers or livestock-keepers living in complex and diverse environments are likely to be small: in other words, the number of farmers in any group will be small, because there is a high degree of heterogeneity in their circumstances, farming systems and problems. The point has been made as follows:

> '... micro differences are often significant enough to limit diffusion among otherwise apparently homogeneous populations ... especially in varied and unstable environments' (Jiggins, 1989).

An extreme version of this view is that, in complex, diverse and risk-prone environments, 'the "recommendation domain" is, for all intents and purposes, reduced to the scale of a particular field or farm' (Okali et al., 1994).

While this point may be true for some types of technology (e.g. the suitability of a particular type of plough is strongly affected by soil conditions and topography), it may not be true of all technologies. Maurya (1989) gave examples of crop varieties that had spread rapidly and widely in India from farmer to farmer, without government support. One of these, the paddy variety *Mahsuri*, was eventually used in six different states and became the third most popular variety in the country. Clearly, it has a very large RD, with millions of adopters. Even if only 10 per cent of the adopters were RPFs, this would still be 100 000 farmers or more. It may be that other types of technology also have large RDs, including ones that are suitable for RPFs.

Although the estimates in Tables 11.1–11.4 are sketchy, they do contain *prima facie* evidence that the RDs for three of these technologies, all of which are based on locally available materials, could involve tens or hundreds of thousands of resource-poor livestock-keepers in each case. There is some uncertainty as to how widespread the constraints are: some constraints (e.g. low conception rates in the dry season) are less visible than others (e.g. mange). In addition, regarding example 5, the opportunity cost of labour could vary significantly from one part of India to another. In example 5, the technology has been adapted to address a different problem, and hence, in effect, the RD has been extended.

Table 11.4 contains specific assumptions, based on the information in Table 11.3, and on some guesses where information is lacking. Based on different sets of assumptions for Bhilwara, Rajasthan and India, it shows the sizes of the recommendation domains for each. For example,

Bhilwara RD = 70 000 $\times$ 75% $\times$ 75% $\times$ 25% = 9843.75

The assumptions used are more conservative as the geographical unit increases in size, because the degree of uncertainty is also increasing and there is a growing likelihood that conditions (regarding the prevalence of the constraint, and the labour situation) may differ from those in the original project district.

Table 11.5 contains comparable information for another technology, this time to control mange. The specific assumptions in it are based on the information in Table 11.2, and some guesses where information is lacking.

Promoting use of the technology in the RD

Through development agencies Once the domain has been mapped out, the next step is to identify agencies that are working on livestock development within the domain; and then to develop a strategy for reaching them effectively. In the case of relatively small PTD projects, with limited

Table 11.1 Information required to estimate recommendation domains – examples 1 and 2

Production constraint:	High kid mortality in the rainy season due to gastro-intestinal parasites in does and their kids
Main sources of information:	Conroy and Thakur, 2002; Conroy et al. 2002; Thakur et al., 2002
Initial location:	Dharwad district, Karnataka, India
1. **How widespread is the commodity?**	A survey in 1997 found that there were 64 639 goats in Dharwad district; and there were 3 838 000 in Karnataka in 1990 (livestock census). A project survey suggests that average herd size in the project villages is 4–5. There are about 120 million goats in India, which are kept by about 12–30 million families.
2. **How widespread is constraint in original project location and country?**	Project surveys only covered 6 villages in 2 locations about 70 km apart. There is a need for further analysis, based on surveys, talking to key informants, analysis of secondary information, etc. (Also see point 6 below.) The level of annual rainfall may have a strong influence on the importance of the constraint. Variations in the timing of the principal kidding season may also determine whether the constraint exists in particular areas or groups of livestock-keepers, i.e. where few kids are born during the rainy season there may not be a mortality problem.
RECOMMENDED TECHNOLOGY	1. DRENCHING WITH TRICHOMES OF *MUCUNA PRURIENS* PODS AND JAGGERY 2. DRENCHING WITH FENBENDAZOLE

Table 11.1 cont.

3. **Farmer resources required for adoption**	This technology does not require private land or cash. The only resource involved in utilizing it is the labour required to harvest and process the pods. This is very little. The pods occur in bunches and only 4–5 bunches are needed to meet the requirements of goat-keepers with small herds. In Karnataka, pods are harvested in late February and in March.	This technology requires cash. The price of purchasing enough of the drug to treat one animal would be Rs 6 (3 rupees per dose) for a goat weighing 20 kg. The market for drugs to control the helminths of sheep and goats is relatively small, which suggests that price is a serious deterrent.
4 (a). **Availability of raw materials in project country**	*Mucuna pruriens* may only be found in particular agro-ecological zones (e.g. within a certain range of annual rainfall, perhaps 600–1500 mm p.a.). Data on its distribution are lacking, but it is known to be present in parts of Orissa, and Rajasthan, as well as Karnataka.	Fenbendazole is produced by numerous companies and is widely distributed in major rural centres in India. It tends not to be available in relatively remote areas.
4 (b). **Accessibility of raw materials in project country**	In India *M. pruriens* is commonly found growing uncultivated by roadsides, in forest areas and on private land, making it accessible to everyone in these areas. It would not be accessible outside of areas where it grows, unless the material could be *purchased* at low cost by goat-keepers in such areas.	At these centres it is accessible to anyone who can afford to purchase it commercially (see below).
5. **Any evidence of technology's adaptability?**	The technology is used by buffalo-keepers, which gave researchers the idea of using it on goats. It could, therefore, be effective in de-worming large ruminants, with appropriate modifications to dose rates.	Fenbendazole has a broad spectrum of activity in cattle, buffalo and sheep as well as goats (www.vetcareindia.com).
6 (a). **Constraint relevant outside original project location?**	Nematode infestations of does and their kids are 'one of the main causes of death among kids' in the tropics (Peacock, 1996).	
6 (b). **Technology relevant outside original project location?**	*M. pruriens* is also found in Mexico, the Caribbean and Nigeria (Kiff et al., 1996).	Fenbendazole is used in many tropical countries.

Table 11.2 Information required to estimate recommendation domains – examples 3 and 4

Production constraint:	Sarcoptic mange
Main sources of information:	Case study B
Initial location:	Tharaka-Nithi and Mbeere Districts, Kenya

1. How widespread is the commodity?	At least 75% of the 50 000 households in the project districts, and in other mange-endemic areas, keep goats. There are around 344 195 goats in the project districts, so average herd size is about 9. There are about 10 million goats in Kenya. About 20% of Kenya's human population of 31 million live in arids and semi-arid land (ASAL) areas, and about 80% of meat goats are found in ASAL areas.
2. How widespread is constraint in original project location or country?	Project survey found that mange is the second most important cause of mortality in goats in the district. The survey covered four sub-locations in Tharaka district and four in Mbeere district. Mange occurs in most ASALs of Kenya, including Kajiado, Kitui, Makueni, Machakos, Mwingi and Narok.

RECOMMENDED TECHNOLOGY	3. TAMARIND FRUIT PASTE MIXED WITH OILY PASTE OF CRUSHED ROASTED CASTOR OIL SEED IN EQUAL QUANTITIES	4. IVERMECTIN, AN INJECTABLE DRUG THAT IS COMMERCIALLY AVAILABLE. INJECTION IS REPEATED 7 DAYS AFTER THE INITIAL DOSE: EACH DOSE IS 1 ML
3. Farmer resources required for adoption	This technology does not require land or cash, unless the fruit is purchased. The only resource required to utilize it is the labour required to harvest and process the raw materials. Nevertheless, it would be important to check whether the harvesting time coincides with a seasonal labour peak.	Ivermectin is 'quite expensive' (Peacock, 1996). In the project area, a 50-ml bottle of Ivomec cost about Ksh 5000 (equivalent to US$62), and was enough to treat 25 mature goats. A farmer would have had to sell 4–6 healthy goats to save 25 sick goats, which was not seen as attractive, and it was difficult to sell a goat from a sick flock even if it was healthy.
4 (a). Availability of raw materials in project country	*Tamarindus indica* is quite widespread in areas where the trials were conducted, and in much of semi-arid Kenya. It was less common in a second area, Gategi, leading livestock-keepers to plant it there. The fruit is also sold in local markets, where it is cheap in season. Castor (*Ricinus comunis*) is also widespread.	Ivermectin is available in towns in the project districts, under the trade name Ivomec®.
4 (b). Accessibility of raw materials in project country	Both ingredients are reasonably accessible (even to RPFs), particularly castor, which is a weed in some places.	At these centres Ivomec is accessible to anyone who is prepared to purchase it commercially (see below).

Table 11.2 cont.

RECOMMENDED TECHNOLOGY	3. TAMARIND FRUIT PASTE cont.	4. IVERMECTIN, cont.
5. Any evidence of technology's adaptability?	Sheep and calves were also infected with mange, and were treated effectively by the project.	Technology is effective in treating other ruminants.
6 (a). Constraint relevant outside original project location?	Sarcoptic mange is by far the most important mange of goats in the tropics, and in some systems it can be the most important cause of death (Peacock, 1996). 10% of Kenya's ASAL area is mange-endemic.	
6 (b). Technology relevant outside original project location?	*Tamarindus indica* is found in many semi-arid regions of SSA and India. Castor grows in a very wide range of environments in the tropics (Peacock, 1996).	Ivermectin is used in many tropical countries.

resources, the presence of potential target organization(s) with the capacity to disseminate findings on a larger scale could be a criterion for selecting the area in which the project is going to work. If communication is established with target organizations early on in the project, and then sustained over time, the likelihood of them taking an interest in the project's findings will be greatly enhanced. In the case of larger projects (or programmes) it may be possible for certain target organizations to be active collaborators in the project.

Livestock development agencies can be reached through several media, including:

- Published materials for researchers (reports, articles, etc.);
- Published materials for field staff/extensionists (technical bulletins, picture books, posters, etc.);
- Conferences, workshops, and livestock/agricultural shows;
- Tailor-made meetings or workshops, specifically for dissemination purposes;
- Electronic media (websites and email); and
- Radio and television.

It is important to be clear which organizations, professional communities, types of livestock-keepers, etc. the project is seeking to reach, and to then make sure that the most appropriate media for each target group are included in the dissemination plan. Although this may seem to be an obvious point, it is surprising how often this is not done in a systematic way.

Table 11.3 Information required to estimate recommendation domains – example 5

Production constraint:	Low conception rates in goats in the dry season (March–June inclusive)
Main sources of information:	Case study E
Initial location:	Bhilwara District, Rajasthan, India

1. **How widespread is the commodity?**

In 1997, there were about 16.9 million goats in Rajasthan and 700 000 in Bhilwara (livestock census). Average herd size, excluding kids, is about 10 (Sagar and Ahuja, 1993), so number of households owning goats may be about 1.7 million and 70 000 for the state and district respectively. There are 120 million goats in India as a whole (livestock census), kept by about 12–30 million households (author's guesstimate). It is not known how many live in areas where *Prosopis juliflora* is found, but goat ownership does tend to be higher in dryland regions.

2. **How widespread is constraint in original location or country**

Bhilwara district is semi-arid, with a mean annual rainfall of 700 mm. Project survey covering 6 villages in the district identified feed scarcity as a constraint in all of them. In 5 villages scarcity in dry season was specified, and in some June was identified as the worst month. The latter part of the dry season is the preferred breeding season, as kids are then born after the rainy season, when there is less disease but plenty of forage. Trials in 4 villages all resulted in higher conception rates.

Other districts In similar surveys in three other semi-arid districts (one each in Rajasthan, Gujarat and Karnataka), goat-keepers also identified this constraint as a serious one. In a fourth district (in Madhya Pradesh) it was not seen as a constraint.

General observation The surveys suggest that feed scarcity in the dry season is a constraint where access to browsable material on private lands and common lands near the village is limited, i.e. there is a lack of forests and/or shrubs to which goat-keepers have usufructary rights. It may also decrease in importance as mean annual rainfall increases. Seasonal migration with animals may overcome the problem, but this is only practised by a minority of agropastoralists, mainly those who have large flocks/herds of small ruminants.

It is not known how widespread the preference for breeding in the dry season is. More villages need to be surveyed and secondary data analysed to answer this question.

RECOMMENDED TECHNOLOGY

5. SUPPLEMENTATION WITH 250 G/DAY OF *PROSOPIS JULIFLORA* PODS FOR 10 WEEKS AROUND THE DESIRED TIME OF BREEDING

3. **Farmer resources required for adoption**

This technology does not require land or cash. The only resource required to utilize it is the labour needed to harvest and process the pods. Nevertheless, it would be important to check whether the harvesting time coincides with a seasonal labour peak. If it does, this could deter people from using the technology. In Bhilwara district, harvesting occurs when demand for labour is low.

4 (a). **Availability of raw materials in project country**

P. juliflora is the most dominant and widespread tree species in India's arid and semi-arid regions, supplying 75% of fuelwood needs in these regions (Tewari et al., 2000). It is also widespread in sub-humid regions. In four states of India

141

Table 11.3 cont.

	(Andhra Pradesh, Gujarat, Maharashtra and Rajasthan) at least 20% of the land area is arid/semi-arid.
4 (b). Accessibility of raw materials in project country	*P. juliflora* is commonly found growing uncultivated by roadsides, and on common lands, making it accessible to most households in arid/semi-arid India.
5. Any evidence of technology's adaptability?	In Karnataka, the pods have been used as a supplement for does around the time of kidding. This improved the health of pregnant does and increased their milk production, and hence their kids were healthier and grew faster. In this case, because the tree pods are being stored for use in the rainy season, pest damage appears to be a greater threat, and the technology has been adapted through the introduction of fumigation.
6 (a). Constraint relevant outside original project location?	The technology's original use and point 5 above suggest that it may be effective in addressing a number of constraints on goat productivity outside the original location.
6 (b). Technology relevant outside original project location?	*P. juliflora* is a native of Venezuela and Colombia. It is an exotic weed in parts of Sudan, Eritrea, Iraq, Pakistan, Australia, South Africa and the Caribbean (Pasiecznik et al., 2001). It is also found in north-east Brazil, where its pods are used as an ingredient in commercial cattle feed.

Directly to livestock-keepers Livestock-keepers are, of course, the ultimate target group. Farmer-to-farmer extension tends to be highly effective, because the extensionist (the farmer or livestock-keeper involved in PTD) has a high degree of credibility with his or her peer group arising from the fact that he/she has actually used the technology, understands their situation and can speak from first-hand experience. Arranging visits to project villages during, or immediately after, trials can be very effective, as the visiting livestock-keepers can then see the technology being applied and/or see the benefits derived from using it.

Table 11.4 Assumptions used in estimating the size of the recommendation domain for *Prosopis juliflora* pods

Assumptions	Bhilwara	Rajasthan	India
No. of goat-owning households	70 000	1 700 000	20 000 000
% whose goats are experiencing constraint	75	25	15
% having labour to collect pods	75	50	25
% having access to *P. juliflora* pods	25	10	15
Result			
Size of domain (no. of households)	9843.75	21 250	112 500

Table 11.5 Assumptions used in estimating the size of the recommendation domain for treating mange with castor and tamarind paste

Assumptions	Tharaka-Nithi District	Kenya	East Africa
No. of goat-owning households	75% of 50 000	40% of 6 million	40% of 15 million
% whose goats are at risk of experiencing constraint[a]	80	50	50
% having labour to collect and process castor and *Tamarindus indica*	60	60	60
% having access to treatment materials	50	30	30
Result			
Size of domain (no. of households)	9000	216 000	540 000

[a] While less than 10 per cent may be badly affected at any one time, the risk of getting infected over a period of 3–5 years is high.

Farmer-to-farmer extension is constrained by the fact that it is a very resource-intensive process, and hence can only reach a limited number of farmers or livestock-keepers. Thus, other methods (such as videos, slide shows and posters) with the capacity to reach a much larger number of potential users also need to be utilized.

Conventional extension services are under-resourced (in terms of staff, financial resources and/or equipment/drugs) in many, if not most, less-developed countries (LDCs), and hence have been failing to reach a large proportion of livestock-keepers, especially the poorest. This situation contributed to the interest in community-based animal healthcare during the 1980s and 1990s, and the training of 'paravets' or community-based animal health workers (CAHWs).[31] Where PTD is being undertaken as part of a livestock development programme it would be desirable for CAHWs, or other kinds of community-based livestock specialists, to be closely involved in the technology development process and subsequently in the dissemination of recommendations.

---

[31] For an overview of the current status of community-based animal healthcare see issue 45 of *PLA Notes*, October 2002.

11.2 Building livestock-keepers' capacity for participation[32]

This section deals briefly with the question of institutionalizing the research capacity of farmers. Farmers have been doing their own research for many years, and will continue to do so, with or without support from development agencies. What then is meant by building or institutionalizing farmers' research capacity? The idea here is that, through project inputs, organizational arrangements can be established to facilitate better interaction between researchers and farmers. This should help to ensure that: (a) researchers have a better understanding of farmers' (or livestock-keepers') production systems and priority concerns, and that (if necessary) this re-orients their research programmes accordingly; and (b) livestock-keepers are able to draw on researchers' knowledge more effectively. In a number of projects, farmer research groups have been effectively used for performing these functions. Groups formed may be empowering, but the main aim is to enliven and sustain the flow of interactions (mainly information exchange) between researchers and farmers, and also between farmers themselves (Sutherland and Martin, 1999).

From the point of view of pragmatic research efficiency, and not wasting farmers' time, farmer research groups do not need to be 'sustainable', but need only exist as long as they are performing a useful function in the research process – useful, that is, to both the farmers and the researchers participating. However, because formation of effective groups can be resource-intensive, higher returns to establishment may be achieved if the groups facilitate dialogue between formal sector researchers and farmers on a semi-permanent basis. In some villages there may be *existing* groups with which researchers can work, rather than establishing new groups. A few tips for those wanting to work with farmer/livestock-keeper research groups are provided in Box 11.2.

11.3 Sustaining and promoting PTD within lead R&D agencies

Conventional natural resources organizations tend to be categorized as concerned *either* with research *or* development, and are given corresponding mandates. Since PTD straddles this artificial division it does not fit easily into most existing organizations, and this jeopardizes its chances of becoming institutionalized within them. Research organizations may see it as a marginal adjunct to their mainstream research agenda; while extension or development agencies may see it as peripheral to their central mandates and as less important than development work *per se*. Nevertheless, there have been positive developments in many countries. One example is the Kenyan NARS, where old barriers (see Box 1.2) are being

---

[32] This sub-section and the following one draw heavily on two references, which should be consulted for further information: Sutherland and Martin, 1999; and Sutherland et al., 2001.

BOX 11.2 Tips for starting and managing farmer research groups

1. Starting groups

- Study the past history of farmer group formation and existing group structure and norms

- Select representative villages/communities with reference to zonation

- Evaluate existing groups and select those with potential

- Conduct awareness-raising through PRA, public relations activities, technology marketing, participatory planning

- In the above, define image of outsiders through clear presentations

- Provide guidelines for farmer research group (FRG) composition and establishment (e.g. secret ballot for electing group leaders)

- Use well-established FRGs to help establish new FRGs in other areas

2. Managing the working relationship

- Monitor representativeness of group members

- Provide training for transformation to empower groups and researchers

- Conduct regular reviews of research priorities/results

- Support of village information systems – linking farmer groups

- Stimulate farmer to farmer in-season visits

- Experiential learning by researchers in linking with farmer groups

- Establish co-ordinated information management mechanism on the research side to reduce conflicting images and messages being presented to FRGs by different researchers

- Discuss processes (biological and ecological) as well as products with farmers

- Discuss ideas of experimentation with farmers

- Listen, discuss and resolve conflicts arising within the group

- Work with a limited number of communities/groups and encourage farmers to make group size self-regulating through their own mechanisms

- Invite FRG representatives for workshops and ensure FRGs a role in the research planning process

Source: Sutherland and Martin, 1999

removed, and where various initiatives to promote participatory research have borne fruit (see Box 11.3).

Careful consideration needs to be given to where PTD initiatives should be located institutionally. On the one hand, locating them in conventional, hierarchical mainstream organizations may mean that progress is slow and difficult at first: on the other hand, locating them in a small and progressive organization (or as a free-standing unit within a larger organization) may seriously reduce the chances of PTD becoming institutionalized within mainstream structures or organizations. Thus, when PTD projects or programmes are being designed it is desirable to conduct an institutional assessment of the potential host organizations (see Box 11.4 for guidance on this).

Much PTD work has been funded on a project basis by particular donors, and there is a risk, therefore, that when the project ends the use of a participatory approach to technology development by the organization(s) concerned will also end or quickly fade away. Sustaining and promoting the use of PTD requires commitment from senior management, and the retention and nurturing of a critical mass of expertise among the staff. The danger is that staff who have been trained in, and worked on, PTD will gradually either:

- move on to new jobs elsewhere (as mentioned in Box 1.2); or
- be transferred to a different type of job within the organization; or
- be transferred to a different location where their line manager is not receptive to PTD; or
- continue in the same post but without the financial and other support needed to sustain their involvement in PTD.

These threats to the sustained use of PTD highlight the importance of having a strong commitment from one or more senior managers. If that is not present at the outset of a project it is something that the senior project staff should cultivate during the course of the project. Box 11.5 lists some tactics for working within a hierarchical management structure, in ways intended to gently challenge and change part of it.

11.4 Promoting PTD outside lead R&D agencies

Three types of factor may be discouraging other organizations from getting involved in PTD, namely:

- lack of skills and relevant experience;
- negative attitudes towards PTD; and
- an unsupportive working environment.

Organizations that have been successfully involved in PTD can help to overcome the *first* factor by providing short training courses for staff from other organizations (e.g. the Kenya EVK project provided training in EVK to

BOX 11.3 Institutionalizing participatory research in Kenyan government research institutes

Both KETRI and KARI established **socio-economics units** under the leadership of senior and experienced officers to enhance the incorporation of participatory approaches in the biophysical research programmes. Both institutes also established **competitive research funds** that encouraged applicants to demonstrate farmer-led demand for the proposed research activities, and these enhanced the incorporation of participatory approaches (PAs) in animal health research.

In addition, **appraisal procedures** for scientists in the institutes were revised to recognize and award reports and publications based on participatory studies. Participatory approaches are now integrated in institutional missions and visions, including project monitoring and evaluation processes.

KARI has initiated the Agricultural Technology and Information Response Initiative (ATIRI) to improve the transfer of appropriate agricultural technologies to end-users. ATIRI aims to *improve the ability of farmers to make demands on agricultural service providers* and to enhance the effectiveness of intermediary organizations and farmers' groups in meeting the knowledge needs of their clients and members. Through ATIRI, KARI will strengthen its capacity to respond more efficiently to these demands through provision of information on improved technologies and by increasingly focusing its research on problems and opportunities identified by farmers.

KARI and KETRI are currently working in partnership with NGOs, CBOs, individual farmers and development partners using PAs, in order to enhance *multi-institutional networking* and information sharing among stakeholders.

Although there are still some problems, participatory approaches are now widely accepted tools for conducting applied research in the Kenyan NARS. The attitudes previously held by scientists that communities had little to offer in technology development and dissemination have changed and they have learnt that communities have a wealth of knowledge which can be used to enhance research outputs. As a result of using PAs, scientists have been able to develop rapport with the clientele, making it easier for farmers to adopt the technologies resulting from research. There is an increasing interest among stakeholders (including policy makers and implementers, researchers, NGOs, CBOs and individual farmers) in using PAs to enhance poverty reduction in farming communities. There is increased targeting, especially in applied research projects, of the resource-poor as partners rather than subjects. There has also been development of strong linkages among stakeholders using PAs. Some communities have been empowered through capacity building activities to ensure that they participate effectively in proper record keeping, follow-up and scheduling of research activities.

Source: Okuthe et al., 2002

BOX 11.4 Strategies for location

An institutional assessment can be undertaken to determine the suitability of different organizations to play the lead role in participatory projects or programmes. It should:

- Provide a clear understanding of the organization's policy, including commitment and understanding from senior management, on implementing participatory client-oriented approaches.

- Review the past experience of the institution with participatory approaches and evaluate the current institutional capacity (and resources) for participatory research.

- Design a programme within the policy of the host institution, building on past positive experiences of participatory research – if possible involving some of the same staff. If necessary build appropriate training into the project design.

- Weigh the relative importance of institution capacity building versus production of technical results. As a rule of thumb, there should be confidence that building capacity in participatory research will improve the applicability and uptake of technical results – if there is doubt that this will be the case, then very carefully consider the amount of emphasis placed on participation in the programme.

- If more than one institution is critical to achieving a successful outcome, consider options for partnership in implementation.

Source: Sutherland and Martin, 1999

veterinary practitioners); or just by inviting them to the project area and briefing them on the work that has been done and the methods used. By publicizing their successes they can also help to counter the *second* factor. With NGOs lack of research and scientific skills may be the main constraint, whereas with government researchers it is more likely to be lack of social skills or inappropriate attitudes (e.g. a sense of superiority and a belief that scientists have little to learn from farmers). The third factor is discussed in the next section.

> **BOX 11.5** Tactics for using participatory approaches within hierarchical management cultures
>
> ■ Respect established modes of communication and meeting procedures from the start of the project.
>
> ■ Invite management to observe or officiate at meetings and events that use alternative and more participatory methods.
>
> ■ Include in the budget training for management in participatory approaches.
>
> ■ Spend time explaining new approaches and involving management in planning and decision making.
>
> ■ Keep management fully informed of all activities.
>
> ■ Form a programme steering committee which includes the key management representatives one is hoping to influence.
>
> *Source:* Sutherland and Martin, 1999

11.5 Improving the enabling environment

The public sector working environment

Changing the working environment so that it supports participatory research rather than hindering it is a major challenge, particularly in government agencies, whose rules and norms may be determined outside the agency itself. Thus, it is only larger initiatives that might have the capacity to influence it. As we saw in Chapter 1,[33] non-supportive factors include:

■ lack of *incentives* (or even perceived disincentives) for this kind of work; and

■ lack of *resources*, including funds to cover the travel and subsistence costs of fieldwork.

The experience of the Kenyan NARS (see Box 11.3) includes the following initiatives to address the two above-mentioned constraints:

■ *Incentives:* changes in appraisal procedures so that staff are rewarded for undertaking participatory work instead of being penalized.

■ *Resources:* the establishment of competitive research funds specifically for demand-led participatory research.

---

[33] See also Part 4 of Chambers et al., 1989; Chambers, 1997; Sutherland and Martin, 1999; and Sutherland et al., 2001.

Policy and legislation

Policy and legal issues do not always affect PTD directly, and hence may not need to be addressed in some projects. However, the Kenyan EVK project (Box 11.1) is one that has become directly involved in these issues. It has played a decisive role in the development of a national strategy on research and development of medicinal and aromatic plant species. It has also been promoting appropriate intellectual property rights (IPRs) regimes that recognize practitioners (e.g. healers') IPRs.

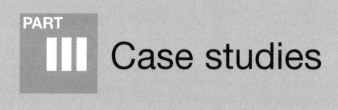

PART

III Case studies

12 Case study A: Learning about the control of Newcastle disease with village chicken farmers in Mozambique

Robyn Alders, Filomena dos Anjos, Brigitte Bagnol, Raúl Fringe, Quintino Lobo, Belmira Mata and Mary Young

SOME INTERESTING ASPECTS OF THIS CASE STUDY

Development and testing of vaccines is sometimes seen as a process confined to research stations. This case study shows the importance and value of testing vaccines with poultry-keepers in the field.

The project it describes looked at different ways of administering the ND vaccine(s) – by eye drop, oral drench or drinking-water. It found that one administration method (by eye drop) was more effective than others, and that, despite the fact that it was more labour-intensive, farmers preferred it. Another benefit of the field trials was that the researchers found that administering the vaccine by eye drop once was as effective as administering it on two separate occasions, which meant that vaccination costs to farmers could be reduced.

Similar laboratory and field trials have been conducted in Ghana and Tanzania, which also indicated that eye drop was the preferred method of application. After the field trial stage, the vaccine was used in a number of zones. In one area of Tanzania where suitable eye-droppers were not available, farmers devised their own low-cost solution, using the tip of a feather to transfer the vaccine from the vial to the eye of the chicken.

Selection of farmers for different experimental groups is often not done in a random or systematic way in PTD trials, which raises the possibility of there being differences between farmers in the different groups that could distort the research findings. In addition, allocating livestock-keepers to a control group, as opposed to a treatment group, can be difficult, as people naturally want their own animals to experience the benefit of the treatment. From a statistical point of view selection should ideally be done randomly, but this is rarely the case, and some people believe that random selection is inherently non-participatory. In this case study selection was done on a random basis, and in a way that was apparently acceptable to farmers. Experimental groups were allocated using a lottery system, in the presence of community representatives, to ensure that they knew that no favouritism had been involved with the allocation of the experimental groups. The lottery was conducted by placing pieces of paper with the different experimental groups into one tin and papers with the names of the communities in another tin.

12.1 Background

In many parts of Africa, the majority of the population is rural-based and involved in agricultural production. In sub-Saharan Africa, most of the smallholder sector production is done by women and up to one-third of rural households are headed by women. In addition, female farmers work longer hours than male farmers but have fewer assets (the chicken being a welcome exception in many cases), lower income and almost no access to credit and technical support. Raising village chickens plays a vital role in many poor rural households, and is usually a female activity. Agricultural extension services are frequently weak and deal mostly with crop and ruminant production, and not chicken production. The extension staff are usually male, who mostly contact male farmers.

One of the major constraints to production of village chickens is Newcastle disease (ND). Potential losses are so high as to make vaccination mandatory. Since 1984, the Australian Centre for International Agricultural Research (ACIAR) has been supporting collaborative research on the control of ND in village chickens in South-east Asia and sub-Saharan Africa.

While the development of thermostable ND vaccines has made it possible to get viable vaccine into rural areas, the vaccines themselves have not been sufficient to guarantee sustainable ND control. Attention to social, economic and organizational issues is vital to ensure the improvement of village poultry production and hence poverty alleviation and improved household food security. While the importance of good extension was recognized from the outset, it was only in the 1990s, with the introduction of the technology to

Africa, that effective farmer participation was emphasized as a key component in sustainable ND control.

The challenge has been to develop ND control strategies for rural areas (in collaboration with government services, NGOs, private operators and male and female farmers) that are reliable, low-cost and sustainable. Participatory technology development approaches have facilitated this process and were used in ACIAR-funded projects in both Mozambique and Tanzania.

12.2 Overview of ND control activities to date

Investigations into the control of ND in South-east Asia and Africa have involved:

- laboratory testing of thermostable live ND vaccines NDV4-HR and I-2;
- field testing and wider use of these vaccines;
- the development of appropriate extension material; and
- Attention to cost recovery and cost minimization issues.

The laboratory tests enabled local researchers to verify the efficacy of the live thermostable ND vaccines against challenge by local ND virus strains. In both Mozambique and Tanzania, field extension workers were invited to visit the laboratory to observe the trials and to refresh their knowledge of the clinical and post-mortem signs of ND.

12.3 ND control activities in Mozambique

The field testing of the live thermostable NDV4-HR and I-2 vaccines was a long and involved process. In Mozambique, two field trial sites with active agricultural extension networks were selected in co-ordination with government livestock and extension services.

The importance of community involvement and regular follow-up meetings was highlighted during the implementation of two field trials with NDV4-HR and I-2 vaccines. The ways of interacting with the communities differed slightly between the trial sites with noticeable consequences. The effects of the different lengths of time taken for pre-trial extension activities in the communities, criteria for selection of community assistants, calibre of local government extension workers and length of the trials all impacted on the quality of the results.

Following satisfactory laboratory trials, field trials with the thermostable live ND vaccines NDV4-HR and I-2 were done over a 2-year period to identify the most cost-effective ways of administering the vaccine in rural areas. Extension activities with communities and training of community assistants commenced prior to the initiation of the trials. These activities consisted of community meetings, baseline data collection and training of community assistants in record keeping.

The vaccine field trial protocols and initial baseline surveys were developed in collaboration with the Village Chicken Working Group, consisting of representatives from government agencies concerned with livestock production and rural extension. The trials aimed to determine the best route of administration of the vaccine (whether eye drop, drinking-water or oral drench), and the protection afforded by the vaccine against natural field challenge by local virulent strains of ND virus.

In order to conduct scientifically valid vaccine field trials and, at the same time, learn about farmers' concerns and interpretations, it was necessary to invest a considerable amount of time in getting to know the communities and their poultry husbandry practices. It was important: (a) to have an idea of the number of birds in a particular area, and the willingness of their owners to participate in the trials to ensure adequate numbers of birds per experimental group; and (b) for farmers to accept that the allocation of routes of administration needed to be done on a random basis. We also needed to know what farmers did with their birds in order to devise a code for recording the status of birds in participating households. Approximately 50 chickens were tagged per experimental group and the status of these birds was monitored on a two-weekly basis by community assistants. Farmers were at liberty to do as they wished with their tagged birds: the researchers wanted to find out what normally happens under village conditions.

Farmers whose only livestock are chickens are generally resource-poor and have had little contact with government veterinary services. In many cases, their contact with western approaches to human medicine has also been limited. Consequently, farmers' understanding of preventive veterinary medicine based on the use of vaccines is often rudimentary at best. This is certainly the case in Mozambique where farmers are often wary of the notion of vaccinating chickens, particularly when their children rarely receive such treatment. Participation levels in the first vaccination campaign were not high and vaccinators had to chase up farmers. During the second campaign, four months after the first vaccination, researchers were pleasantly surprised to find farmers waiting with their birds. Farmers indicated that this time they had faith that the researchers would deliver on their commitment to vaccinate the birds. The increased participation was probably also because of farmers becoming assured that the vaccine did not actually kill the birds.

Subsequent to the trials, a flip chart about ND control was developed and it is presented to farmers by either community vaccinators or extension workers. The idea of ND being caused by a virus, and being prevented by vaccination, is presented by making an analogy with training soldiers (the vaccine) to fight an invisible enemy (the virus) and defend their land (the chicken).

In the NDV4-HR vaccine trial site, five months were devoted to extension activities and collection of data on village chicken production and husbandry. In the I-2 vaccine trial site, only two months were given to these start-up activities. The time given to pre-vaccination extension activities was less in the I-2 vaccine trial site mainly because of time constraints and the need to implement the trial during the life of the project. During the pre-trial period, discussions were held with village chicken farmers to ensure that they understood the nature and importance of the trials (specific attention was given to the fact that a trial is different to a vaccination campaign) and to determine their willingness to participate.

From previous studies, researchers knew that the survival rates for the different experimental groups would vary. Consequently, experimental groups were allocated using a lottery system, in the presence of community representatives to ensure that they knew that no favouritism had been involved with the allocation of the experimental groups. The lottery was conducted by placing pieces of paper with the different experimental groups into one tin and papers with the names of the communities in another tin. There were four groups in each trial. Representatives from each community were asked to come forward one by one to select one piece of paper from each tin. The pieces of paper were handed to the meeting facilitator and the results were read out after each representative had picked out the pieces of paper.

Compensation for farmers whose chickens had the misfortune to be allocated to experimental groups with poor results (i.e. control groups) was discussed prior to the initiation of the trials. It was decided that after the first outbreak of ND, farmers would be able to choose which administration method they would prefer to use in subsequent vaccinations. Should the project have offered monetary or other compensation, it is possible that some bias in the reporting of problems may have occurred.

Assistants were selected from each community. Their role was to administer the baseline questionnaire, and monitor and record the number of chickens and the fate of individually numbered chickens in vaccinated and control groups over the trial period. In the NDV4-HR trial area, one community representative who demonstrated ongoing interest in trial activities during the pre-trial period and who possessed basic literacy skills was selected from each experimental group area. All assistants at this site were mature males. Payment for services rendered by the community assistant commenced at the start of the trial and was minimal. In the second trial area, following an example of similar work done in Sri Lanka, young women (18–20 years of age) just out of high school were selected by project staff to act as community assistants. Selection was based largely on their performance in a literacy and numeracy test. Once again, payment for services rendered by these women commenced at the start of the trial and was minimal.

In each trial area, overall organization of the community was done by the local secretary of the ruling political party. In some parts of Mozambique, such issues are dealt with by party representatives rather than traditional leaders.

The NDV4-HR vaccine trial consisted of four treatment groups each containing approximately 500 birds. Groups received vaccine via eye drop, oral drench or drinking-water, and the control group was mock-vaccinated, i.e. vaccination was simulated using a live ND vaccine that had been heat-inactivated, rendering it inactive. This was important to ensure that each group of farmers had the same expectations, removing bias in the reporting of problems with their birds. One drop of vaccine was administered to each bird every four months over a 12-month period. The I-2 vaccine trial also consisted of four treatment groups. The first group received vaccine via eye drop, one drop every four months. The second group also received the vaccine via eye drop, but the initial vaccination consisted of one drop of vaccine given on two occasions at an interval of 2–3 weeks. The third group also received an initial vaccination consisting of one drop of vaccine given on two occasions at an interval of 2–3 weeks, but vaccine was administered via drinking-water. The fourth group was the control and received a mock vaccination. Revaccination was done at four-month intervals.

Community assistants recorded numbers of birds per household and the status of individually marked birds at two-weekly intervals. Project staff visited the sites each month and held a meeting with community representatives prior to commencing work in the field.

At each trial site a natural outbreak of ND occurred and this was verified by the isolation of the ND virus from birds that succumbed to the disease within the trial areas.

Extension

Communication with farmers was an integral part of the field trials and helped researchers to develop an understanding and appreciation of farmers' knowledge and priorities. In the preparation of extension material, special attention was paid to the perceptions and sensitivities of the village chicken owners. The different needs and capabilities of men and women were considered constantly. This enabled the development of material that addressed their concerns in a manner that also facilitated their comprehension. Women often have more difficulty than men in interpreting communication material, especially printed materials, because of their lack of schooling.

This approach resulted in the development of a comprehensive extension package on how to implement ND control activities successfully. The current extension package includes the following components, the oral ones in four or five languages:

- an ND vaccination song;
- a radio drama and a question and answer programme;.
- a pamphlet for front-line extension staff and literate farmers;

- a poster that can be used to advertise the next ND vaccination campaign;
- a drama piece;
- an ND field manual that provides information to veterinarians on ND and its control;
- a flip chart with clear, largely self-explanatory line drawings and a simple accompanying narrative.

12.4 Results and discussion of Mozambican field trials

Both vaccines, when administered via eye drop every four months, yielded approximately 80 per cent protection in the field. It was expected that eye drop administration would provide the best results, but it was important to see if any of the other methods could provide adequate protection in the field according to farmers' criteria. In veterinary epidemiology, it is generally considered that protection rates of 60–70 per cent are adequate to prevent the spread of disease in large populations of animals. However, 60 per cent protection is generally not acceptable to a farmer who owns small numbers of birds. Most farmers who own around ten village chickens say that they expect to see at least eight of their ten birds surviving an outbreak to convince them that the vaccination has been effective.

In the I-2 trial, no apparent difference was noted between groups that received the vaccine by eye drop once only or on two separate occasions. This was an important finding as it meant that vaccination costs to farmers could be reduced.[34]

In each trial, vaccination via eye drop provoked a greater immune response (haemagglutination inhibition (HI) titre) than vaccination by other routes; and more birds vaccinated via eye drop survived field outbreaks of ND. The average immune response of each group was communicated to farmers using visual means. A stone or leaf was used to represent one unit (log to base 2). For example, one month after vaccination with NDV4-HR, the immune response for the different experimental groups was demonstrated by drawing on the ground with a stick to create rows for each group and indicating the level of protection by the number of stones:

Eye drop: ● ● ● ● ● ● ●
Oral drench: ● ● ● ●
Drinking-water: ● ● ● ●
Control: ● ● ●

---

[34] In the commercial sector, a booster vaccination is recommended to ensure that the birds mount an adequate immune response. With scavenging village chickens, it may be that circulating field strains of the ND virus are acting as booster or vice versa.

Although birds had to be caught by their owners to administer the vaccine by eye drop, this was the method preferred by farmers because of its efficacy. Farmers in the eye drop group saw their bird numbers increase considerably and ND outbreaks did not have a major impact in their area. It was observed that farmers from other experimental groups started to transfer their birds to the eye drop treatment area during the first outbreak. The introduced birds were carrying virulent ND virus and the HI titre of tagged birds in the eye drop group rose dramatically. From a cost-benefit point of view, the eye drop method has the added advantage that the vaccine can be administered less frequently than other routes and so is less expensive to farmers.

Survival rates of birds were not demonstrated visually as the number of birds in each area could be seen as you walked through the villages. Farmers discussed this among themselves and so the need for facilitation from the project was limited on this subject.

Community involvement increased in proportion to the amount of time given to extension activities prior to the commencement of the trials and the degree of community involvement in the selection of the local assistants. In each trial, community participation increased most in those groups where the vaccine was given by eye drop. It was assumed that this increase was due to the increased number of birds in the area. In other groups, survival rate after natural challenge was lower, and in the case of the control group, many farmers lost interest altogether. No matter how much emphasis was given to the fact that a trial rather than a vaccination campaign was being conducted, many farmers simply wanted to see their birds survive. Unfortunately, it was not possible for different routes of administration to be used on birds held by the same household. The vaccines used contain live virus that are capable of spreading from vaccinated birds to unvaccinated birds in close contact. So even if different administration routes were used, birds housed together in the same chicken house would have ended up with similar HI titres.

The NDV4-HR vaccine trial proceeded with minimal difficulties. On the whole, the government extension worker and community assistants fulfilled their tasks admirably. The attempt to involve young women as community assistants in the I-2 vaccine field trial was not a success. They had little interest in serving the community, lacked responsibility and were unhappy with the amount paid for their services. In addition, they had a low profile within the community. This situation was compounded by the inadequate support provided to the women by the local extension worker. Subsequent field work in other areas has found that mature women with an interest in village chicken production make very good community ND vaccinators.

While valid scientific results concerning the efficacy of the vaccines were obtained from both sites, the amount of useful information gained about farmers' perceptions was greater in the NDV4-HR vaccine trial site where interaction with the community had been greater.

12.5 ND control activities in Tanzania and Ghana

Similar laboratory and field trials on ND control in village chickens using live thermostable vaccine have been conducted in Ghana and Tanzania that also indicated that eye drop was the preferred method of application. After the field trial stage, the NDV4-HR vaccine was used in a number of zones. In one area of Tanzania where suitable eye-droppers were not available, farmers used the tip of a feather to transfer the vaccine from the vial to the eye of the chicken. Where possible, it is always preferable to use eye-droppers to standardize the size of the drop being administered to chickens. However, in the case concerned, there were organizational difficulties and the farmers devised their own low-cost solution.

Researchers from Tanzania shared the idea of using feather applicators with colleagues from Ghana where it was incorporated into trials. The trials showed that 80 per cent of birds vaccinated with I-2 ND vaccine using the feather applicator survived the challenge of a virulent ND virus, compared with 100 per cent using a standard eye-dropper: all birds in the control group died of ND.

12.6 Conclusions

Government veterinary and extension services in many countries are unable to provide cost-effective services, such as routine vaccinations, to smallholders. More and more, persons from the local community selected by the community complement the work of government departments. If the control of ND by vaccination in rural areas is to be sustainable, the co-operation and active participation of the communities is essential. The lessons learnt to date should be taken into account when planning field activities.

- Sufficient time must be given to participatory planning and monitoring with the communities and their leaders. This is crucial for the success of any field initiative. Ongoing active participation and the taking of initiatives are indicators that the community is involved and interested in the work.
- Special attention must be given to the geographical location of trial sites to ensure that areas are accessible throughout the year and that, should a disease outbreak occur in one trial area, it is likely to affect all trial sites at more or less the same time.
- The experience and reliability of field staff in areas selected for the implementation of pilot activities is crucial.
- Mature, responsible, community-minded assistants and vaccinators must be selected by the community.
- Assistants and/or vaccinators must receive adequate training, monitoring and refresher courses to guarantee the sustainability of any external programme.

- Community assistants and vaccinators should be seen as an extension of the government veterinary services network and should be supervised by local government staff.
- The manner in which assistants are to be compensated for the time given to their ND control trials must be negotiated and agreed upon from the outset. The level of compensation should match the community's ability to provide support to vaccinators once project activities wind down.
- The collection of baseline data from those responsible for village chicken production (in most cases, this will be women farmers) is crucial. Reliable baseline data are needed to monitor and evaluate the impact of the various experimental interventions. A simple baseline questionnaire (that recorded among other things, livestock numbers, poultry husbandry practices and ethnoveterinary knowledge) was conducted as a collaborative exercise between researchers and community assistants.

It is hoped that the further development of participatory monitoring and evaluation mechanisms will enable farmers to be actively involved in the way ND control activities are implemented in their areas. As participatory methodologies are not always automatically gender-sensitive, particular attention is required to ensure that the participatory methodologies used enable women to participate in an effective manner given their special mandate regarding the raising of village chickens. Facilitating the participation of women requires a multi-pronged approach and includes:

- The use of local languages and non-formal communication methods in meetings.
- Holding the meetings close to where women are working and at a time when it is possible for them to participate.
- The inclusion of female extension workers or facilitators; or training male extension workers in practical methodologies that will enable them to interact effectively with women.
- Ensuring, as much as possible, that the women's families, including their husbands, are in agreement with the proposed activities, i.e. even if the idea is to work with women, the whole family should be invited to the initial meetings. Community leaders should also be informed and aware of the importance of encouraging the participation of women in village poultry activities.
- Working with male and female farmers in separate groups to ensure that women's ideas are heard and responded to.

The implementation of an effective ND control programme in countries such as Mozambique has resulted in increased chicken numbers, increased household purchasing power, increased home consumption of chicken products and increased decision-making power for women. Despite the need to control ND in village chickens, it has been difficult to achieve a sustainable control programme. Experience has shown that a sustainable ND control programme is composed of four essential components:

- an appropriate vaccine and vaccine technology;
- effective extension materials and participatory methodologies that target veterinary and extension staff as well as community vaccinators and farmers;
- simple participatory evaluation and monitoring systems of both technical and socio-economic indicators;
- and economic sustainability based on the commercialization of the vaccine and vaccination services and the marketing of surplus chickens and eggs.

Acknowledgements

This overview is the product of many years of collaboration with colleagues interested in village chicken research and development and village chicken farmers from many parts of the world.

Support provided by the Australian Centre for International Agricultural Research (ACIAR) to assist the authors to conduct research into the control of Newcastle disease in village chickens is gratefully acknowledged.

13 Case study B: Participatory development of mange treatment technology in Kenya

John N. Kang'ara

SOME INTERESTING ASPECTS OF THIS CASE STUDY

This case study is interesting because it combines the use of local technical knowledge with a scientific approach to trial design and with statistical analysis of the results. It compares local and commercial treatments of mange, which can cause high mortality in goats. The former were supplied and prepared by one of the researchers, in order to ensure standardization.

Statistical analysis of the data was undertaken, which demonstrated that two of the treatments based on local technical knowledge were significantly more effective than the other treatments, including a commercial one. Taking a scientific approach to the research meant that the results of the trials could be presented with confidence to livestock professionals involved in extension and research.

Another positive feature is that there was full involvement of livestock and veterinary extension officers throughout the project. This provided ownership of and commitment to the new technology, and made the veterinary officers less sceptical about local remedies.

13.1 Historical background to DAREP

The technology was developed under the Dryland Applied Research and Extension Project (DAREP) which was located at the Kenya Agricultural Research Institute's (KARI's) Regional Research Centre Embu (RRC-Embu) between 1993 and 1996. DAREP was a collaborative project between KARI, Kenya Forestry Research Institute (KEFRI), Ministry of Agriculture Livestock Development and Marketing and Natural Resources Institute (NRI). The project was funded by the Kenya Government and the Overseas Development Administration (ODA) through NRI's Agronomy and Cropping Systems Programme. It was an offshoot of the former Embu, Meru and Isiolo arid and semi-arid lands programme (EMI ASAL Programme) and the Dryland Applied Research Project (DARP) which was co-ordinated by the then Ministry of Agriculture. The EMI Project had both development and applied research mandates reflecting the need to gain understanding of the many problems of the ASAL. EMI had four components, i.e. a goat and sheep project based at Marimanti, forestry covering the three districts in EMI mandate, Isiolo range water development and dryland farming soil and water conservation.

DAREP took over the activities of DARP in July 1993 and remained active until March 1997. DAREP expanded the EMI technical mandate, adding on livestock and agro-forestry components, and expanding the dryland cropping to include tools and tillage and soil and water conservation. The project was charged with responsibility for developing and evaluating sustainable agricultural technologies and participatory research methodologies. Participatory farming systems methodologies were evolved to strengthen linkages between farmers, extensionists and researchers. In this system all stakeholders (i.e. farmers, extension personnel from the Ministry of Agriculture and Livestock Development and the NGOs) were involved from problem diagnosis through to evaluation and dissemination. The collaborating extension agent also had a hand in the modification and scaling up of the technology to farming communities outside our mandate area.

The main DAREP goal was to improve the quality of life of smallholder farming families in the semi-arid areas of Mbeere, Isiolo and Tharaka-Nithi Districts through development and dissemination of sustainable agricultural technologies and participatory research methodologies.

13.2 Livestock production and constraints in the ASAL community of Tharaka and Mbeere

Livestock plays a very important role in the welfare of the households and agricultural development in general in the arid and semi-arid lands (ASAL) of eastern province in Kenya, where Tharaka and Mbeere districts are located. The functions of livestock in ASAL areas include: provision of food, income generation, food security, dowry, manure, prestige and store for wealth. Livestock makes it possible for people to survive and eke a living in the dry harsh environment. Most of the households (over 75 per cent) keep goats as they are prolific and are easily converted into cash or exchanged for cattle. Therefore, most young married couples start with goats before acquiring cattle, which require a heavy initial capital investment (Devendra and Burns, 1983). DAREP decided to concentrate on goats, because improving goat production would benefit the majority of the rural households, even the poor who own one to six goats.

Two diagnostic surveys were conducted by multi-disciplinary teams, composed of 23 individual scientists in Tharaka-Nithi in November 1993 and 32 individual scientists in Mbeere in May 1994. They found the major livestock problem, as perceived by the farmer, to be diseases (DAREP 1994a, 1994b). The disciplines represented included agronomists, breeders, entomologists, soil and water specialists, foresters, socio-economists, socio-anthropologists, livestock nutritionists and veterinarians. Nutrition was viewed as a problem only in the event of drought. The seasonal dry periods were not viewed as a problem because the animals are usually taken far away from home to the traditional dry season grazing areas. However, where dry season grazing areas are no longer accessible, as is happening in some parts, nutrition is a major problem.

The farmers' perception was different from mine. Being a livestock nutritionist, I was inclined to view nutrition as most constraining. Smallholders' animals are characterized by slow growth and small size, but on-station research has shown that these animals, when subjected to good nutrition, gain weight fast and have good finish to qualify for any elite market. Their perception also differed from that of the EMI livestock specialist, as was evident from how EMI prioritized interventions for improving livestock in ASAL. EMI, through its goat and sheep project, emphasized breed improvement and therefore brought in exotic Toggenburg dairy goats and the Galla goat from north-eastern Kenya, which were large and likely to grow faster and these were crossed with the local goats. For sheep EMI introduced the Dorper breed to upgrade the local Red Masai sheep.

The importance of diseases emanates from the fact that some diseases quickly result in death of the animals. Loss of an animal through death, theft or predation by wild animals directly reduces the household wealth and welfare, and risks the food security. Therefore, goat diseases that have a cure, or those that are associated with low mortality, are not considered to be a problem even if they weaken the animals.

The survey found the main health problems resulting in death of goats, in order of importance, to be contagious caprine pleuropneumonia (CCPP), mange, helminthosis, 'Nduru (suspected to be heart water disease) and fleas in kids . Mange is caused by mites that cause severe dermatitis: this may or may not be itchy, depending on whether it is burrowing or surface type. The majority of mites found in Mbeere and Tharaka were the burrowing type, which causes severe irritation, and the animal spends most of its time scratching on stationary objects instead of browsing. Of the four diseases mentioned above, mange was most dreaded by farmers, for three reasons.

First, once a goat is infected, the parasites spread rapidly to the rest of the animals, wiping out almost 90 per cent of the flock within a year if not treated. In most cases mange attack is followed by secondary infection of bacteria or fungus (Mugera et al., 1979).

Second, usually the livestock owners slaughter and eat meat from most sick animals if they suspect the animal may not survive, and also sell their skins. However, in a mange case, farmers count total loss since the skin is not saleable and meat is not consumable.

Third, most farmers did not know the cure, and even those who knew did not use the conventional mange treatment drugs as they were very expensive for the ordinary small-scale farmer.

The commercial treatments include: dipping with acaricide at double the strength of tick control, once or twice per week for a minimum of four weeks; and the injectable ivermectin repeated seven days after the initial dose. A 50-ml bottle of Ivomec® (a trade name for Ivermectin), is adequate for 25 mature goats and costs about Ksh 5000 (equivalent to US $62). Considering the current market prices of goats in that area, this was not cost-effective because the farmer had to sell 4–6 healthy goats to save 25 sick goats. This was not sustainable considering the existing economic situation which was bad and probably not feasible because the herd was already infected and nobody would want to buy a goat from a sick flock even if it was healthy. Based on these facts, there was a need to find inexpensive alternative methods for mange control which were appropriate to the rural poor.

The project's objectives were:

1. to determine the efficacy of indigenous methods of mange treatment; and
2. to document and popularize any cheap effective mange control methods that were identified.

13.3 The technology development process

This was approached in three steps:

- a survey on existing indigenous livestock disease remedies;
- a pilot trial to filter and reduce the long list to a few reasonable treatments; and
- a trial to evaluate the efficacy of the most promising ones.

Survey on indigenous remedies for livestock diseases

A focused survey on livestock diseases, with particular emphasis on mange and worm control, was conducted late in 1994 to gather the indigenous local knowledge on their treatment and control. This was conducted in public meetings convened by the area chief and by contacting some individual knowledgeable farmers. During the meetings, individuals (whom we referred to as expert) who had any form of treatment or control methods and skills narrated their methods in the meeting (or later privately if they were reluctant to do so in public). This took time as some felt like they were disclosing business secrets while others felt that they would be considered as backward. With time we developed friendly relationships and assured them that the results of the research would be documented so that we could conserve and multiply some of those botanicals if they were under threat of extinction through cultivation and over-exploitation. I informed them that failure to document them may lead to a loss of God-given knowledge which was meant to benefit the community. Even if they passed the knowledge to their children, it was risky to entrust it to a few individuals in this era of high HIV/AIDs prevalence.

Pilot trial

Over ten concoctions that could treat mange were identified and filtered in a pilot trial with few animals (41 sick goats) to find out if they were working. This was done in conjunction with an expert herbalist who identified the plants or plant part to be used, the method of preparation and administration. Those preparations that showed no effect at all on mange were dropped. The expert farmers (originators of the treatments) were incorporated during the pilot trial so that they could identify the plant and parts to be used, how to prepare or process the drug, the dosage and administration of the drug. Four of these concoctions which looked reasonable, and were mentioned in most areas as being effective, were tested alongside the commercial drugs. Some of the discarded ones involved using parts of wild animals, including snakes, and this could obviously conflict with the wildlife conservation laws.

Screening for efficacy

Four indigenous mange treatment methods were tested alongside the conventional drugs on the infected goats. This trial was conducted in the affected farms because mange is highly contagious and therefore, it was advisable to restrict the infected animals within the affected flock. The trial farmer selection was not difficult because most farmers were in desperate need of saving their animals from this menace, hence they were willing to co-operate.

Treatments The conventional drugs on test were:

1) Dipping with an organophosphorous acaricide (Supa dip⁄) at the recommended rate for mange control (i.e. twice the rate used for tick control) in a half drum cut longitudinally.
2) Ivermectin (Ivomec®) injectible. This was injected subcutaneously at 1 ml per dose and repeated after 7 days.

The traditional and/or non-conventional treatment methods tested were:

1) Tamarind (*Tamarindus indica*) fruit paste mixed with oily paste of crushed roasted castor oil seed (*Ricinus comunis*), mixed 1:1 by weight.
2) Old engine oil plus Mwarwa (*Albezia anthelmintica*).
3) Old engine oil plus moth balls and salt.
4) Neem (*Azadirachta indica*) extract (a suspension of ground neem seed).

The infected animals were ear-tagged, given a name by the farmer for identification (just in case they lost their ear-tags in the thickets), and allocated randomly to different treatments. The farmer and the field assistant, who was a local school leaver hired by DAREP, each kept the record of goat number and names for each different treatment, any activity carried out and anything that happened to the animal. The traditional treatment methods were smeared once or twice per week depending on severity of infection. This was repeated for at least four weeks. There were more than 15 animals in each treatment but their treatments were initiated at different times as more herds got infected. Farmers knew what each animal was being treated with and participated in the application of all the treatments (except Ivomec injection), although the concoctions were prepared by the researcher, to ensure standardization.

Data recorded were:

1) Initial and final body condition (score) 1, 2, ... 5 from bad to best.
2) Initial and final weight.
3) Degree of infection (intensity) score 1, 2 ... 5 from clean to severe.
4) Parts of the body affected.

Skin scrapings or biopsy were taken and sent to the veterinary laboratory at Karatina to confirm the presence of mange and other micro-organisms. The collected data were subjected to analysis of variance, and means were compared using the Genstat version 5 release 3.1 of 1993.

Results and discussion

Laboratory results showed no mange mites in 60 per cent of the samples taken from sick animals, but these animals had massive fungal growth. The rest had: (a) mange mites (*Sarcoptes scabei* var. caprae) and fungal attack; or (b) both *S. scabei* and *Psoroptes cuniculi* plus fungal attack. The massive fungal attack was attributed to secondary infection by opportunist fungi after infection by mange mites. Lack of mites in the samples could be due to the difficulties in sample collection for mange, as the mite digs deep into the dermis; only those samples where skin biopsies were taken showed mange mites, not the scrapings.

The efficacy of the concoctions as treatment for mange was depicted by the reduction in intensity of infection, after their application on sick animals (Table 13.1). The degree of intensity was measured by visual scoring from 1 to 5, with a score of 5 indicating a very good healing response and a score of 1 being no response to treatment. Castor oil plus tamarind fruit paste, and old engine oil plus Mwarwa had significantly ($p < 0.05$) greater reduction in intensity of infection after 4 weeks of initial treatment than the Ivomec and the Neem suspension. The fast healing and good body condition observed from treating sick animals with a combination of castor oil and tamarind was attributed to two factors: (a) inhibitive effect of tamarind paste (which is acidic in nature) on opportunistic fungi; and (b) an almost immediate cessation of severe irritation associated with mange infection thus allowing more time for grazing. The laboratory analysis indicated that fungi constituted the

Table 13.1 The mean change in intensity of mange infection after treatment

Treatment	Mean intensity reduction	Standard error
Ivomec	2.631	0.202
Supadip	2.811	0.327
Castor seed oil + tamarind	3.230	0.239
Old engine oil + Mwarwa	3.688	0.401
Old engine oil + moth balls + salt	2.946	0.503
Neem suspension	2.338	0.247

majority of micro-organisms causing the secondary infection on the mange-infected skin. The differences in reduction of infection intensity between the rest of the treatments were not significant.

The body conditions (Table 13.2) were not significantly different between treatments. The higher body weight change for Ivomec (Table 13.3) could be explained by the fact that Ivomec is systemic and acts on all parasites including worms (helminths), while the rest only worked on the skin. A number of animals died after treatment with Ivomec (4) and engine oil plus moth balls (3), which could not be explained.

Table 13.2 The mean change in body condition after treatment

Treatment	Mean body score change	Standard error
Ivomec	0.808	0.206
Supadip	0.840	0.328
Castor seed oil + tamarind	1.258	0.253
Old engine oil + Mwarwa	1.154	0.422
Old engine oil + moth balls + salt	0.940	0.437
Neem suspension	0.747	0.253

Table 13.3 The mean change in body weight 4 weeks after treatment

Treatment	Mean weight (kg) change	Standard error
Ivomec	2.350	0.268
Supadip	1.407	0.434
Castor seed oil + tamarind	1.980	0.317
Old engine oil + Mwarwa	1.746	0.531
Old engine oil + moth balls + salt	1.988	0.666
Neem suspension	1.647	0.328

Overall, the local treatments were better than commercial drugs when one considers: the aforementioned deaths, the cost of treating mange using the commercial drugs, and the ease of obtaining the materials for the different treatments. Although goats treated with old engine oil healed within four weeks, the hair took longer to grow. The farmers and the field assistant also complained that it tended to heat their hands on a hot sunny day as they applied it to the animal.

Most indigenous concoctions worked, although their rate of healing differed. The environmental effect of old engine oil is not certain considering that it may have traces of lead (a heavy metal), which could be injurious to animals. Also the fact that it is not readily available in ASALs due to lack of garages and the noted slow body hair recovery after its use made us hesitant to recommend it. Castor oil seeds were commonly planted by farmers and tamarind grew wild in these areas and were therefore recommended, because they were cheap, readily available and effective.

Effort to refine crude castor oil The processing of castor oil seed for use in treatment left it in crude form. This crude form was as dark as old engine oil since it was first fried on a pan. To the young farmers, especially women, it looked messy. It was then decided to refine it and try it alongside the crude form. The efficacy was greatly reduced by refining. Therefore it was resolved to recommend the crude form, as after all it was cheaper to process it.

13.4 Dissemination of technology

Gategi farmers residing about 100 km from the nearest trial site also reported an outbreak of mange in their area. Our previous experience with farmers indicated that, when a farmer demonstrated a technology which had worked well in his/her farm to other farmers, the technology was adopted by the other farmers with enthusiasm. Therefore a farmer to farmer teaching tour was organized for them by DAREP in August 1995 to visit the trial farmers at Kaamwa, Kamanyaki and Chiakariga to learn from them how they had been treating goats with mange infection. Most of the teaching and demonstrations on treatment methods were conducted by the host farmer. The questions were answered by the farmers but were assisted by the researcher (who was the tour organizer) or the veterinarian when the farmer could not answer the questions.

By the end of the tour, Gategi farmers were fully convinced that the local concoctions were effective, less expensive, user-friendly and available locally. However, one of the ingredients, tamarind fruit, is seasonal; and by the time of the tour the tamarinds were off season and were therefore relatively expensive. This implied that tamarind needed preservation. The Gategi farmers bought their own castor seed and tamarind fruit and treated their animals without our assistance. They also taught their neighbours the new skills and used them to treat their animals. By the beginning of October 1995, five out of the six flocks treated by farmers who participated in the tour were clean. The sixth flock had not healed because the owner used sunflower oil instead of castor oil. The pace at which the technology was adopted is commendable. The success generated demand for tamarind tree seedlings by Gategi farmers and these were supplied by the project agroforester from the DAREP Mutonga nursery at a price of Ksh 2.00 each. These were planted in Gategi and they now serve as food and medicine in the area.

Demonstrations on mange treatment using castor oil and tamarind were conducted in farmers' open days held every 6 months at all DAREP sites. The farmers who attended the field days in the seven DAREP sites numbered about 300 on average with the highest number reported in Kaamwa, Gategi and Kathwana sites, where over 600 farmers and school parties attended. Mange demonstrations were done in two seasons, the long rain and short rains of 1995, i.e. when the technology was ready for dissemination, and about 3500 farmers were reached through these field days. Other farmers reached directly by this technology were the 16 involved in the trial (10 from Tharaka District and 6 from Mbeere District), and a further 12 farmers from Gategi (a location in Mbeere District) with infected animals who, after a study tour to the trial farmers, also passed on this technology to an estimated 40 other farmers in the Gategi locality. The study tour was organized after an outbreak of mange in Gategi was reported to the researcher.

Taking a scientific approach to the research meant that the results of the trials could be presented with confidence to livestock professionals involved in extension and research. In 1998 the Government of Kenya, DFID and the Netherlands Government funded the production of a brochure (1000 copies) on the mange treatment technology using our recommendations. The brochure has a farmer-friendly simple language, and is used by farmers and extension agents in Tharaka and Mbeere. These brochures were distributed to extension agents in ASAL areas. However, mobility by the extension agents from dry areas to high potential areas (where mange is not endemic) is very high and therefore this needs another supply.

Due to DAREP and other projects and initiatives, participatory technology development has been institutionalized in our research centre and many other KARI centres in practically all disciplines.

Linkages with other agencies

During the diagnostic surveys and the research planning of various components, experts from other KARI centres, KEFRI, the extension services and universities were invited. I recruited two veterinarians, Dr J.N. Kamau and Dr J.N. Njiru of Mbeere and Tharaka respectively, as collaborators. Both of them were involved in the mange and worms trials, and in the diagnostic survey. The extension agents of the ministry responsible for agriculture and livestock development were involved in the survey and planning, including identification of the area with affected animals where eventually on-farm trials were conducted. The two veterinarians accompanied and assisted us during the application of treatment as their schedule allowed them. They also organized farmers to attend the seasonal field days that were conducted by DAREP and the tours to DAREP on-station and on-farm experimental sites. They also became agents in identifying farmers with other ethnoveterinary knowledge needing further investigation.

13.5 Concluding observations

Problems encountered and lessons learned
The researchers gained the following knowledge and insights from the research.

- Goats are sold for cash almost every market day. Sometimes farmers need to sell their animal even if they are involved in a trial. Some goat owners may sell them before the conclusion of the trial thus affecting results. Fortunately, the trial had over 118 animals from different flocks and therefore sound conclusions could still be drawn.
- Farmers were initially slow to release their indigenous local knowledge and this took some persuasion. One has to be patient and friendly before they start talking freely without suspicion.
- We still have a few people who believe that use of herbal medicines, even if they are effective, is against Christian ethics or is a sign of backwardness.

Factors contributing to project success
The following factors contributed to project success.

- The farmers/livestock-keepers were involved in diagnosis, prioritization, experimentation and dissemination.
- They also managed the animals in the trials since they were their own.
- The ingredients were cheap and easily available in their area.
- It was demand-driven.

Luck was also on our side in that one of the flocks we started treatment with during the pilot trial was situated right in Chiakariga market. The flock was badly affected such that the owner Mr Moses Ngoci had lost hope for them, as they were dying one by one and he was no longer taking them home to the boma at night. His goats were sleeping outside the shops in the market and nobody could be bothered with them. They were therefore a public eyesore. After one month of trial the animals' condition was so good that many people who saw them wanted theirs treated too. Unfortunately, a few days later a number of them were stolen and the owner had to take the remaining goats back home to the boma for the night.

We involved the two area Veterinary Officers in the exercise and, although they were sceptical initially, they came to have confidence in the indigenous knowledge. Many veterinary officers in Kenya do not value EVK and actually they discourage its use because they would like all disease cases referred to them for treatment at a price. Recently some vets have started appreciating the efficacy of EVK practices, but the Kenya Veterinary Association (KVA) has still not supported it yet.

Case study C: Participatory validation of medicinal plants for livestock diseases of pastoralists in Kenya

Jacob Wanyama

SOME INTERESTING ASPECTS OF THIS CASE STUDY

This case study describes a project that has been working to validate, improve and promote the use of effective ethnoveterinary knowledge (EVK) and practices, and to influence the attitudes towards EVK of veterinary professionals. ITDG East Africa has been implementing a participatory project on EVK validation since 1996, which has, for example, validated three ethnoveterinary remedies for internal parasites in sheep.

An important aspect of this project is that it has been strong on dissemination, and has made a substantial impact through the following activities: collaborative partnerships, capacity building (e.g. EVK practices included in animal health training programmes), extension materials and policy work. The project has been working directly with about 30 ethnoveterinary practitioners (local healers). Each of them represents about 100 households, so it is estimated that about 3000 households have benefited directly from the project, and many others indirectly. The project facilitated the formation of the Kenya Working Group on Medicinal and Aromatic Plant Species, through which a national strategy on research and development of these plants has been developed. The project has also been promoting appropriate intellectual property rights regimes that recognize practitioners' IPRs.

14.1 Background and approach

Traditional animal healthcare systems, otherwise known as ethnoveterinary knowledge (EVK) and practices, play an important role in complementing modern approaches in the control of diseases in Kenya. Indeed, livestock-keepers throughout the world have utilized traditional animal healthcare techniques for centuries, albeit through trial and error (McCorkle et al., 1996). In Kenya, Samburu and Turkana pastoralists depend on livestock for their livelihood. Since livestock disease poses the greatest challenge to livestock-keeping, these communities have accumulated a lot of experience in dealing with these diseases (Wanyama, 1997). These traditional animal healthcare practices include the use of medicinal plants in addition to surgical techniques and management practices.

In a survey carried out by the Intermediate Technology Development Group (ITDG) in Samburu District, it was found that the Samburu and Turkana community use up to 50 plant-based preparations to treat livestock diseases in the area. Of these, 13 plant-based treatments were cited as most frequently used (Wanyama, 1997).

Despite the important role that these practices play in ensuring livestock health, there is lack of information on their validity and use. Without such information, development professionals are hesitant to integrate these practices into conventional animal healthcare programmes (ITDG and IIRR, 1996).

This case study presents the process and results of participatory research that ITDG-EA is using to validate and promote the use of medicinal plants among pastoralists of Samburu District Kenya. It shows how, by using participatory approaches, effective medicinal plants used among Samburu and Turkana pastoralists were identified, selected and subjected to field trials for validation.

Participatory research is a process, which incorporates systematic inquiry with collaboration of those affected by the issue being studied for the purpose of education and taking action (North American Research Group, 1998). This approach ensures that the community is an equal and active partner with other stakeholders involved in the study. In this case the knowledge and expertise of all collaborators are considered complementary. The process relies heavily on participatory rural appraisal tools. These are a set of tools that use multi-disciplinary teams to develop and facilitate the local communities to carry out a systematic overview of their own village systems, and plan, implement and evaluate their own projects.

Aims and objectives
The research and development project described in this chapter is part of ITDG-EA's Ethnoveterinary Research and Development Project. The main objectives of this project are:

- to find out the level of understanding and use of traditional remedies among pastoralists of Samburu District;

■ to identify and validate treatments that the pastoralists are confident worked and determine whether these treatments can be improved and recommended;

■ to convince conventional animal health practitioners that traditional animal healthcare and more specifically medicinal plants are valid and safe;

■ to encourage adoption of participatory research approaches by research and development institutions.

Approach

The participatory research approach has been implemented in two phases, i.e. identification of best bet and validation.

Identification of best bets This was carried out during the baseline data collection. The process was used to identify the main animal health problems in the project area as well as to select and identify ethnoveterinary treatments which are most likely to be effective, otherwise referred to as screening and selection of best bets. Using participatory rural appraisal tools, animal health was identified by the Samburu and Turkana pastoralists as one of the main constraints to livestock production in the study area. It was also noted that despite attempts by development organizations to facilitate availability of veterinary drugs and skills, most pastoralists still found it difficult to access conventional animal health services and instead still relied on traditional alternatives.

As a result of these findings, a methodology and analytical approach was used to identify and analyse the most confidently used traditional treatments. Using this approach, a list of commonly occurring livestock diseases was generated with the local community. The communities were also asked to select among themselves men and women whom they knew had more knowledge of traditional animal healthcare. Through ranking, selected by traditional experts, the ten diseases most confidently treated using traditional remedies were identified. Through detailed one-on-one interviews with the selected key informants, detailed information on the traditional remedies used to treat the ten most confidently treated diseases was collected and analysed. The information collected included: ingredients used, methods of preparation and administration. On analysis, it was found out that most of the remedies are plant-based.

In addition to the technical information, a study of the socio-economic aspects of the practices was carried out. This was aimed at finding out who holds the knowledge and how it is shared and used. The information collected was published in a two-volume book (Wanyama, 1997).

14.2 Validation

Literature review
The baseline information on confidently used ethnoveterinary remedies indicated that most remedies are of plant origin. Over 100 plant species were identified as being effective in treating more than 10 livestock diseases (Wanyama, 1997). In order to initiate a process of validation of these plant-based remedies, it was necessary that these plants were correctly identified botanically and a comprehensive literature review carried out on them to determine their documented uses in animal and veterinary medicines as well as their propagation. Through consultancy, samples of 45 plants species were collected with the participation of the local traditional animal healthcare practitioners and taken to the National Museums of Kenya and identified botanically. Based on this two comprehensive literature reviews were carried out on documented evidence of use that are related to ethnobotany, ethnoveterinary and ethnomedicine as well as phytochemical substances known to be active against diseases and their pharmacological effects (Kaburia, 1998; Khayota, 1998).

Experts workshops
A number of workshops involving healers and other stakeholders were organized. The objectives of these workshops were to provide an opportunity for sharing and learning between the healers as well as between healers and conventional experts. These workshops involved sessions during which healers presented their knowledge to the rest of the participants. This facilitated the validation of each healer's knowledge and remedies through commonality in methods of use. In one such workshop, a number of healers and conventional animal health experts participated in an intensive participatory workshop during which EVK was described, validated and compiled into a manual (ITDG and IIRR, 1996). The results of these workshops formed the basis on which remedies to be validated scientifically were selected.

Field trials
This phase involved two approaches, namely formal and informal field trials. The trials were aimed at testing EVK remedies, which had already been identified by pastoralists as confidently used. Both trials were carried out in the field. However, a formal trial was based on a scientific research protocol developed and agreed upon by all the stakeholders and carried out on controlled research animals. An informal trial was based on continuous monitoring of the success and failures of the practising healers on treating common livestock diseases for a certain period of time. In both cases, however, healers took an active role in the preparation, administration and monitoring of the trials. The trials involved a sequence of steps as described below.

Preparation for the trials

During this step, all the stakeholders were analysed, identified and prepared to take part in the trials. The capacity of healers and field staff to fully participate in the trials was built through training workshops at Baragoi and the University of Nairobi. The healers' training workshops also involved strategic planning sessions for the research process. In addition, 10 research-oriented healers were identified to take part in the trials through analysis of the healer's bio data.

Through consultative meetings with collaborating research institutions, a research protocol, which took into account the different strengths of the stakeholders, was developed jointly (Gathuma et al., 2004). To ensure the protection of communities' intellectual property rights (IPRs), a formal collaboration through a memorandum of understanding (MoU) was established with all the stakeholders. Based on the research protocol, the necessary equipment and tools were put in place. These included research animals, holding pens and field laboratory.

Implementation of the trials

In the formal trials, the trials were carried out at field research stations. The sites, which were selected by all the stakeholders, were Baragoi and Nyiro in Samburu District. The trials involved the participation of healers in collection, preparation and application of the remedies. The healers also participated in the taking of certain parameters and the overall monitoring of the trial process. Researchers from the University of Nairobi and International Livestock Research Institute provided technical backstopping. The purpose was to validate the remedies under normal field conditions. In the first phase of the trials, three plant-based remedies used by Samburu and Turkana healers to control worms in animals and humans were tested on local sheep. The trial design involved 52 worm-infested sheep of indigenous origin, aged 6–10 months, both male and female. The animals were allocated at random to five experimental groups of 10–11 animals each using age, weight, sex, origin and level of infestation as the grouping factors. Three of the groups received the three local treatments. The other two groups were a positive control group (which was given a commercial de-wormer – Albendazol™) and a negative control group that did not receive any treatment. The data have been analysed to identify the gaps in efficacy, dosage rates preparation and application and were submitted for publication in a scientific journal (Gathuma et al., 2004).

The informal trial involved monitoring the success and failure of the healers' practice for an extended period of time. Field monitors collected data on these trials on a regular basis. The data were then analysed to establish the number of cases each healer attended to and the results. Although comprehensive analysis has yet to be done, the results will help to identify effective treatments and help to corroborate the results from the formal trials.

Results and discussion

Identification of best bets From the baseline survey, it was found out that the Samburu and Turkana have a wealth of knowledge on livestock diseases and how to treat them using traditional remedies. This knowledge is shared freely and widely among the communities. Both Samburu and Turkana communities named and described up to 60 livestock 'diseases'. However, when translated to scientific equivalents, some of these so-called diseases were in fact conditions.

Out of these the Samburu selected 10 disease conditions while the Turkana selected 15 disease conditions that they treat confidently. Most of the treatments were found to be plant-based. Both the Samburu and Turkana listed up to 43 plant-based treatments. Unlike other communities, it was found that the Samburu and Turkana communities use preparations made from single plant species. There was a lot of consistency in the way these remedies are prepared and administered.

During botanical identification, a total of 49 specimens was collected, representing 45 distinct plant species. Of the 45 species collected, the most common and easily accessible belonged to the Euphorbiaceae, Caparaceae and Mimosaceae families. The field information was easily accessed and healers were confident in their identification of the plants. However, it was noted that in some cases, one local name was assigned two or more scientific names belonging to different species. It should be noted that spellings of local names differ among local collectors. This shows that indigenous taxonomy is sometimes not specific.

Literature search Two literature searches were conducted. The first one focused more on plant morphological description, propagation and ethnobotanical uses. The second search focused on documented ethnoveterinary and ethnomedical aspects as well as phytochemical and pharmacological properties of the plants. The results obtained from the search showed that 32 (74.4 per cent) of the 43 plants had documented uses as medicinal in both ethnoveterinary and ethnomedicine literature. No information was obtained regarding medicinal uses of the remaining 11 (25.6 per cent). Of the 32 plants, 26 (81.25 per cent) were used for treating various animal diseases while 30 (93.75 per cent) were used for treating human diseases. Information regarding toxicity of the plants showed that 10 out of 43 (23.2 per cent) plants had toxic characteristic. Only a few plants, e.g. *Withenia seminifera* and *Salvadora persica*, have been intensively studied and documented. It was interesting to find in the literature that in some species of plants, e.g. *Caparis tementosa*, fruits were reported to be edible in Nigeria while a report from Ethiopia said it is poisonous to camels and horned stock. One of the areas found lacking in documentation is on propagation, conservation, harvesting and storage of medicinal plants (Kaburia, 1998; Khayota, 1998).

Expert workshops During an intensive participatory workshop for production of information materials on ethnoveterinary knowledge, selected ethnoveterinary practices in Kenya were presented, reviewed and recorded by a team of veterinary scientists and traditional animal healthcare practitioners. Up to 180 medicinal plants used to treat various livestock diseases in Kenya were identified and described. The validity of this information was based on a scoring system which determined whether treatment was part of standard veterinary practice or close equivalent, whether this was common traditional practice supported by scientific knowledge or whether this was common traditional practice which animal health healers generally acknowledge. Based on this information, some researchers have attempted to carry out scientific validation of some of the remedies (Githiori, 2004). The selection of remedies to be validated drew on this information.

Cross-cultural workshops and exhibitions between the pastoralists and marginal farmers of Samburu, Turkana, Marsabit, Tharaka and Makueni districts facilitated the cross-referencing of the traditional veterinary knowledge between these communities. In the process a database has been developed that provides information on more than 100 plant-based remedies. In addition, healers' confidence and capacity to practice has been strengthened.

Field trials Formal field trials were conducted on three plant-based best remedies namely, *Myrsine africana*, *Albizia anthelmintica* and *Hilderbrantia sepalosa* used among pastoralists of Samburu. The results showed that, compared with an untreated control group of local sheep, the efficacy of these three remedies against internal nematodes in sheep was 77 per cent, 89 per cent and 90 per cent respectively (Gathuma et al., 2004). These parasites are present in most small ruminants in the project area and have a serious negative effect on their productivity. During the preparation and application of the remedies by the healers, it was noted that some the methods used were inappropriate as they were prone to wastage of the remedies and inaccuracy of dosage measurement.

Data from informal trials have yet to be analysed. However, initial reports indicate that a number of healers are 'discovering new remedies' in their trials.

14.3 Achieving wider impact

The project worked with an average of 30 healers, each one of them representing 100 households. It is therefore estimated that about 3000 households have benefited directly from the project (source: ITDG website), and many others indirectly. This project has made a substantial impact through the following activities.

Collaborative partnerships This ITDG East Africa project has been undertaken from the outset in partnership with pastoralists, local healers, local veterinary officers and formal research organizations. This broad coalition has helped to widen the project's reach.

Local healers contributed their knowledge to the researchers, and participated in the trials. The project organized several 'healers' workshops', which enabled healers, pastoralists and scientists to share their knowledge. Some of the healers were also involved in informal trials, which involved monitoring of their work.

The scientific partner organizations are the University of Nairobi, Kenya Agricultural Research Institute (KARI) and the International Livestock Research Institute. Their involvement has contributed to at least one of them (KARI) initiating related research elsewhere in the country. KARI has prioritized EVK as one of the research themes in its programme, and has commissioned scientists in a number of its regional offices to undertake the research.

Development partner agencies participated in stakeholder workshops in the initial stages of the project during which the project achievements were discussed and future plans developed. These workshops provided opportunity for influencing these organizations to adapt the EVK research and deployment approach. However, there is need for more collaborative work with development partners to facilitate this.

Capacity building has taken place in each of the main stakeholder groups (healers, vets, scientists). The traditional *healers* have been trained as community-based animal health workers. They have also been facilitated to form and register healers' associations in five districts, not only ensuring sustainability of the EVK activities but also building their confidence and facilitating formation of an institutional framework to lobby for and advocate recognition of their practice. *Veterinary practitioners* have been trained in EVK, which has helped to change their attitudes to it. However, one lesson learned is that it would have been better to involve more local vets and livestock extension workers in the research, to encourage better adoption of the results and approach.

Supply of raw materials A study was undertaken of the status of the plants involved in the validated remedies. EVK drug stores have been established in Samburu, as have community-based herbal gardens and shops.

Extension materials Information about effective EVK practices, particularly for the control of internal parasites, has been widely disseminated, both through training and publications. The project published a *Community-based Animal Healthcare Training Manual,* which incorporated the project's baseline information. It also published a two-volume book on socio-economic aspects of the practices used, including who holds the knowledge and how it is shared. It has also produced extension leaflets through local schools.

Policy The project facilitated the formation of the Kenya Working Group on Medicinal and Aromatic Plant Species. Through this group, a national strategy on research and development of these plants has been developed. The project has also been promoting appropriate IPR regimes that recognize practitioners' IPRs.

Lessons and issues

The project is tackling one of the main problems affecting pastoralists' livelihoods, namely livestock disease. The importance of the issue has raised their expectations a lot, and the project must ensure that these expectations are fulfilled, otherwise there could be a negative impact.

The project's experience suggests that the issue of IPRs should be raised and discussed at the beginning of the research, after the awareness-raising, rather than midway through the project.

Identification and validation of medicinal plants

Pastoralists have a wealth of knowledge on medicinal plants used in treatment of livestock diseases. This knowledge, which is detailed in nature, is widely and freely shared. To validate this knowledge a participatory approach is very useful. This approach should include collection of baseline information on the plants as well as the practice in general; conduction of a literature search to establish documented use and previous laboratory trials on the these plants, and subjecting the remedies to formal and informal field trials.

Participatory approach

Participatory research ensures that the healers, who are the custodians of traditional knowledge on which the validation is based and who stand to benefit from it, take control of the process throughout the research period. This also enables researchers to change their attitudes towards the roles of the local community in research and technology development.

The research has been an impetus for change, by relating knowledge to action. First the community members are now equal partners in all aspects of the research. Second it has been a bi-directional education process, in which researchers and healers have learned from one another and shared expertise and knowledge. Lastly, through participation of the healers, it is hoped that the benefit from this research will be accrued to the healers and the community at large. One lesson learned is that participation of the communities would have been strengthened further if there had been more participatory monitoring and more healers' workshops.

The challenges in participatory validation are the lack of clarity on mode of acknowledging all the players in the process. Participatory validation takes a very long time to carry out. Although the actual trial took only a few weeks to accomplish, the preparation of all the stakeholders to fully take part in the research took over two years. This preparatory phase could be made shorter by ensuring the availability of sufficient resources at the start of the project, and by avoiding selecting research sites in insecure areas with poor infrastructure.

Acknowledgements

The author wishes to thank the Turkana and Samburu healers who participated in the project, whose knowledge formed the basis for this participatory research. I thank the two institutions, i.e. the Intermediate Technology Development Group and the University of Nairobi, for providing logistical and institutional support. I specifically wish to thank: Prof. J.M. Gathuma, Dr J.M. Mbaria and Mr H.F.A. Kaburia, all from the University of Nairobi, and Dr L. Mpoke who collaborated with me during the scientific field trial stage of this project. Last but not least I wish to thank the funders – Department For International Development (DFID), CordAid, Drought Preparedness Intervention and Recovery Programme (DPIRP) and African Research Fund of the Kenya Agricultural Research Fund – who provided funds at different stages of this project.

15 Case study D: Improving the efficacy of concentrate usage by smallholder dairy farmers in Kenya

D. Romney, M. Wambugu, R. Kaitho, J. Biwott, L. Chege, A. Omore, S. Staal, P. Wanjohi, D. Njub and W. Thorpe

SOME INTERESTING ASPECTS OF THIS CASE STUDY

This case study describes a researcher-designed trial. Based on the results of an on-station trial, the researchers hypothesized that by temporally re-allocating the total amount of concentrates typically fed to a dairy cow by smallholders, without increasing the total, cumulative milk production would be significantly increased. The on-station trial had shown that if all concentrates were fed during the first 3 months, instead of being spread out at a fairly constant daily rate over many months, milk production increased.

The trial was unusual for a supplementation trial (and application of the technology was potentially more sustainable), in that the researchers did not provide any free inputs to the farmers. They did, however, arrange with the collaborating dairy co-operative that, during the first 3 months after calving, its members would be able to obtain larger quantities of concentrates than usual on credit.

The trial was also noteworthy (and participatory) in that smallholders were given discretion as to the extent to which they followed the recommended 'treatment'. In this respect the trial represented an interesting departure from the conventional approach of testing well defined biological treatments under conditions where (a) underlying variation is either minimized or taken account of, and (b) changes in application of the 'treatments' by farmers are often strongly discouraged and results discounted when they occur. The researchers were interested in knowing how farmers modified the recommended treatment. Rather than control for underlying variability, the study attempted instead to record the variability and use this to explain results, because data gathered in this way are more likely to be translatable into information useful to farmers since it allows farmer circumstances to be taken into account. There were no treatment and control groups as such.

15.1 Background

This case study describes work carried out by a consortium of partners from national extension and national and international research institutes under the Smallholder Dairy Project (SDP) in Kiambu District in the Central Highlands of Kenya. SDP is an integrated research and development initiative to support the sustainable development of Kenya's dairy sub-sector. The project is supported by bilateral funds from the UK's Department for International Development (DFID) and is led by the Ministry of Agriculture and Livestock Development (MoALD), which implements the project jointly with the Kenya Agricultural Research Institute (KARI) and the International Livestock Research Institute (ILRI). The project addresses a range of issues relevant to the dairy sub-sector in Kenya. Following identification of key constraints and on-station experiments to develop strategies, field studies to adapt and evaluate options are tested in the field.

15.2 Constraint identification

It has been estimated that in Kiambu District alone there are more than 80 000 smallholder households (of Kenya's estimated 600 000 smallholder dairy farms) involved in dairy production to supply the ready market within Nairobi and its environs. Milk yields reported by smallholders were low (Staal et al., 1998a), and the smallholders stated that inadequate feed supplies were the major cause.

A survey, using participatory rural appraisal (PRA) methods, found that use of feeds was generally opportunistic, with farmers using small quantities of whatever was available or could be purchased from outside the farm. Commonly used concentrates included dairy meal, maize germ, wheat pollard and maize bran, ranked in that order of preference by the farmers. Farmers said that they compensated for fodder shortages in the dry season by increasing quantities of concentrates, principally brans. A study by SDP observed an increase in the amount of concentrate from 0.9 in wet months to 1.58 kg DM TLU^{-1} in dry months. In contrast, farmers do not alter amounts fed according to stage of lactation, preferring a low, flat rate of concentrate, typical quantities being 2 kg/day (Romney et al., 1998; Staal et al., 1998a; Wambugu, 2000). The general practice of low flat rate concentrate feeding exists despite existing extension recommendations to increase the amount of dairy meal by 0.5–1 kg per day until no further response in milk yield is observed (NDDP extension booklet). One reason given by smallholder respondents for the low levels of concentrate offered was the high cost of concentrate feeds. Farmers favoured maize germ rather than the more expensive dairy meal, even though the latter is considered to have higher nutritive value, because the dairy meal's quality was known to be variable. Generally, farmers with access to a co-operative said they preferred to purchase concentrates at the co-operative, despite lower prices in local shops, in order to take advantage of the credit facilities offered.

15.3 On-station development of intervention

The project decided to explore how to improve the productivity and profitability of concentrate use, and one option tested by SDP was to exploit the increased efficiency of concentrate conversion into milk during the early stages of lactation. An on-station trial carried out by the project showed that milk production was significantly higher for dairy cows offered 8 kg/day for the first 12 weeks after calving, compared with animals offered 2 kg/day over 48 weeks, despite the fact that over the 48 weeks all animals received the same amount of concentrate. Milk yields were calculated in four periods (1–75, 76–150, 151–225 and 226–305 days) and yields were 45, 24, 6 and 8 per cent lower for animals receiving the flat rate in the four periods, respectively (Kaitho et al., 2001).

This led to initiation of a field study to determine if the re-allocation of concentrates was feasible under on-farm conditions, and to observe how farmers implemented and modified the strategy. Livestock researchers and government extension staff carried out the trial jointly in collaboration with Limuru dairy co-operative in Kiambu and members of the co-operative delivering to the Ngecha milk collection centre, the largest of the 16 Limuru collection centres.

15.4 Methodology to adapt and evaluate intervention in the field

Selection of farmers
A meeting was held with 450 of the 520 active members. The intervention was presented to them and volunteers were requested to test it on their farms. Of 90 volunteers with cows due to calve between April and July 1999, 60 were selected at random. Thirty non-volunteer farmers who originally said they did not wish to alter their feeding practices also agreed to be monitored during the experimental period. However, treating the farmers as discrete groups of treatment and control turned out to be invalid since some volunteers fed lower amounts than planned and some control farmers opted

to feed higher levels of concentrate after observing positive results on other farms.

Provision of concentrates

The project provided no inputs to any of the farmers. However, an agreement was reached with the co-operative that each volunteer farmer would be allowed to take four bags (280 kg in total)/cow of concentrate at calving, and three bags per month/cow for the subsequent two months. The payments would be spread through the whole lactation if a farmer was unable to clear the debt within the three months. This contrasted with the official credit rules by which farmers were only allowed to take concentrate to the value of the milk delivered to the co-operative in the previous month. This practice meant that during the critical first month of lactation farmers often found it most difficult to obtain concentrate because of lack of credit at the co-op. In the Ngecha area, the most common farmer practice was to feed purchased maize germ, rather than dairy meal, due to the latter's unreliable quality and the perceived high cost of the dairy meal. However, during the initial meetings the research team undertook to monitor the quality of the feed and most farmers chose to use dairy meal for the study.

Monitoring

The concentrate feeding management recommended to the farmers was based on the experimental findings described above, i.e. to reallocate the concentrate bought to the first three months of lactation, by feeding 8 kg/day rather than the standard 2 kg. However, there was no attempt to insist that the farmers follow any instructions from the researchers, since the primary objective was to monitor the farmers' modifications and to understand why they were made. Quantitative data were collected using formal questionnaires as well as qualitative feedback through informal interviews.

In a baseline questionnaire, information was collected to characterize the farm (including area of land farmed, herd size and household composition), as well as the animals themselves (including milk production and date since calving), and current feeding practices. Cows calving between March and October 1999 were monitored over a period of at least 200 days post-partum, with monitoring ending in May 2000. Quantities of concentrates and forage offered and milk yield were recorded, using a formal questionnaire. Frequency of monitoring varied, but was generally weekly to the 12th week of lactation and fortnightly thereafter. Monitoring was carried out by field extension staff, supervised by MoALD, KARI and ILRI staff attached to SDP. Qualitative information was collected during the survey and recorded by the extension officer leading the trials.

Information on credit used between July 1998 (approximately eight months before the farmers were introduced to the research team) and July

2000 was extracted directly from the co-operative records. Records were initially collected for 60 of the study farmers, and later, an additional group of 30 'control' farmers was selected at random. These controls delivered to the same collection centre but did not participate in the study. Expenditure at the co-op was recorded and categorized as dairy feeds (including dairy meal, maize germ and bran) and other items which included dairy items (such as udder salve and veterinary products or services) and non-dairy items (fertilizer, human food, etc.). Milk delivery records were also extracted.

Throughout the study regular visits by enumerators and their supervisors allowed collation of farmers' views, observations and comments. At the end of the survey farmers were invited to a feedback meeting where preliminary results were presented and their observations were recorded. A follow-up survey based on farmer recall, and using a formal questionnaire, was carried out 12 months after the end of the monitoring. Its purpose was: to allow comparison of feeding practices before, during and after the study; to collect information on calving intervals following the study; and to collect information on sources of purchased feed during and after the study.

Data analysis
The data were used to draw conclusions on the potential for the intervention to be implemented in the field by farmers and to improve milk production. They were analysed as follows.

- Information from the baseline survey was used to determine whether farmers in the study were representative of farmers in the study area.
- Lactation curves (Wood, 1979) were fitted to the data collected – (a) in the baseline survey, (b) during frequent monitoring of animals in the actual trial and (c) in the follow-up survey – to determine if there had been changes in milk production as a result of the study.
- Lactation curves were also fitted to production data from individual animals, and yields over 1–30 weeks were estimated. Mean milk yield for each animal was regressed against mean quantity of concentrate offered.
- Calving interval was estimated from calving dates recorded in the baseline survey, during the study and in the feedback survey. Pre and post intervals were compared using a t-test.
- Mean milk revenue, dairying-related expenditure and expenditure/revenue in the two periods before (July 1998–March 1999) and during the study (April 1999–May 2000) were compared for study farmers and the 'control' group, using simple t-tests. Trends in expenditure at the co-operative were plotted against month to show underlying trends.
- In the follow-up survey farmers were asked to recall concentrate offer rates before, during and after the study period. Average rates in

the first three months after lactation, as well as the relative change, were estimated. These data were regressed against household and farm characteristics in order to identify important factors likely to influence the likelihood of farmers changing their practices and of feeding higher amounts of concentrate.

15.5 Results

Farmer characteristics

Study farmers were self-selected. The mean area of land farmed (c. 3 acres), number of dairy cattle owned (about two) and income category were quite similar to average values for the district as whole, but the areas of land allocated to Napier grass and maize (which acts as both a food and forage crop) were at least twice as high (Staal et al., 1998a). This was interpreted as an indication of high relative importance of dairy to the study farmers.

Implementation of intervention

None of the farmers fed concentrates according to initial recommendations. Although some decreased quantities after 8–12 weeks, none withdrew concentrates completely, many stating that they did not wish to make such changes while milk yields remained higher than observed in previous lactations. Nevertheless, data from the follow-up survey indicated large differences between concentrate feeding before and after the study. Before the study, on average a flat rate of approximately 3 kg of concentrate was offered per day, decreasing the amount by about 15 per cent over a 10-month period. During the study, farmers offered approximately twice as much in the first months after calving decreasing by more than 30 per cent over a 10-month period. In the period following the trial farmers offered slightly less than during the study period but maintained high levels (Figure 15.1). Mean values for the observed data during the monitoring exercise show the close correlation with farmer recall values.

Observed values are actual mean values recorded during the study monitoring period included for cross-referencing with the farmer recall information.

Determinants of feeding patterns and changes in the feeding pattern

One of the main reasons given in the pre-trial PRA for using low levels of concentrate was their high cost and a lack of cash. Nevertheless, before the study neither greater wealth nor the presence of off-farm income appeared to contribute to higher offer rates, whereas years of education and farming experience had a positive effect, suggesting a knowledge-based decision (Table 15.1). In contrast, level of education had no effect on the degree to which farmers were likely to increase concentrate use following the study. It appeared that once farmers had received relevant information, and had

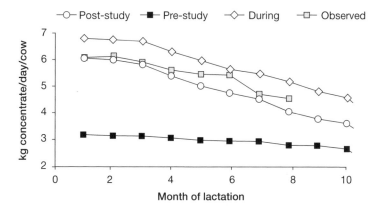

Figure 15.1 Farmer recall of mean concentrate offered (kg/day) 1–10 months post calving pre, post and during the study

observed the effects of higher rates of concentrate use, the main factor influencing uptake became the presence of off-farm income, which was taken as a proxy for the availability of ready cash. Those with more cows, considered as an indicator of greater market orientation, were also more likely to increase offer rates by greater amounts. The negative effect of age of the farmer may have reflected an unwillingness to change in older people.

Milk yield

Farmers reported higher milk yields during the study, which was supported by the observed data (Figure 15.2).

Figure 15.3 presents the relationship between concentrate intake and milk yield showing that the level of concentrate explained 55 per cent of the

Table 15.1 Effect of household characteristics on concentrate use and changes in feeding practices

Characteristic	Increase following the study	Amount (kg/day/cow) before the study	Amount (kg/day/cow) after the study
Age of household head (years)	–	NS	–
Number of dairy cows	+	NS	+
Years of education	NS	+ + +	NS
Years of farming experience	+	+	+
Off-farm income (yes/no)	+	NS	+
Concentrate offered before study (kg/day/cow)	– – –	Not tested	Not tested

+ = positive effect; – = negative effect; NS = no effect.

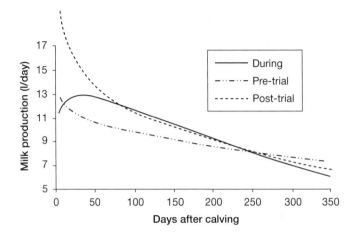

Figure 15.2 Milk curves fitted to all the data collected in the baseline survey (pre-trial), during the actual trial (during) and in the follow-up survey (post-trial)

variability in milk yield. The results indicate a 2.2 l/day increase in milk yield for every extra kilo of concentrate offered. During the period for which credit data were collected co-operative prices for concentrates varied from 8 to 15 KSh/kg and for milk from 14.5 to 18 KSh/l. Hence, over the range of concentrate rates observed, even at the highest prices for concentrates and lowest milk prices, farmers can expect to make a profit. Some of the variability will have resulted from individual animal variation, cow parity, cow genotype and other environmental factors, including month of calving and of sampling.

Calving interval
Calving intervals following the trial were significantly shorter than pre-trial values (445 cf. 542 days), which supports farmers' observations in the feedback exercises that body condition was maintained and that the animals came into heat faster.

Concentrate purchase and credit
In a study in Tanzania, where feed options to increase milk production were presented to farmers, the most important criteria stated for adoption were: money required for implementation, compatibility with the existing farming system and the knowledge required for implementation (Ashley et al., 2000). The Tanzanian farmers also observed that some options that seemed economically viable on paper were not appropriate because the farmers did not have the cash available for initial investment.

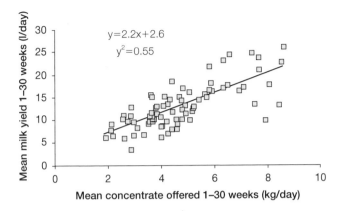

$y = 2.2x + 2.6$

$y^2 = 0.55$

Figure 15.3 Effect of increasing concentrate offered on milk yield

In the present study the likely influence of other factors on farmer behaviour, such as availability of credit, was expected from the outset and the study was carried out in collaboration with the managers of the dairy co-operative, who agreed to increase the credit facilities available to the farmers involved in the study. Despite agreement with the co-op, during the course of the trial a number of problems with the system were observed. Farmers reported refusal of credit in early lactation and refusal to spread the credit over subsequent months. In contrast the co-op complained that farmers continued to purchase high levels of concentrate so that there was no period in which to recover the money owed.

Examination of the co-operative credit data suggested that credit patterns were not altered greatly during the trial. Nevertheless, the percentage of concentrates represented by dairy meal changed from 20 per cent to over 60 per cent during the study period. Data from the feedback survey indicated that following the study purchase of feed from private sources became more important, rising from 46 per cent to 76 per cent of total expenditure on concentrates, and suggesting that in fact spending practices were altered during the study.

15.6 Conclusions

Technical implications

It appeared that the increased performance resulting from increases in concentrate feeding was financially viable under the observed price ratios. For many smallholder dairy farmers one of the key constraints to making technological changes expected to improve production is the lack of cash or credit to allow them to make investments. The results from the study showed that, although farmers did not implement the intervention according to initial recommendations, increases in concentrate offer rate were sustained following the study period. The pre-study observation that the level of concentrate feeding did not appear to be related to the income category or the presence of off-farm income, but to level of education and years of experience, suggested that knowledge rather than economic factors was a constraint. Once farmers had received information and support from extension staff and scientists, presence of off-farm income became an important factor influencing extent of adoption. Results related to the provision of credit were not conclusive, but the fact that farmers purchased less concentrate from the co-operative following the study while maintaining high offer rate, and the minimal changes in spending patterns during the study, suggest that credit was not the primary constraint. Promotion of increased concentrate feeding in areas where markets are reliable appears to be justified from this study.

Methodological critique

On-farm experimental studies generally conform to the conventional approach of testing well defined biological treatments under conditions where underlying variation are either minimized or taken account of, for example in blocking procedures. Changes in application of the 'treatments' by farmers are often strongly discouraged and results are discounted when they occur. The present study differed from that approach in a number of ways. First, there was only a single 'treatment' which was not only biological, but also attempted to address the working capital constraint faced by smallholders by making credit available for the timely application of the biological intervention, the feeding of concentrate in early lactation. Second, farmers were not forced to adhere strictly to a treatment and their modifications to the recommended practices were recorded. The analytical tools used allowed us to interpret the information collected despite there being no formal control group. Third, rather than control for underlying variability, the study attempted instead to record the variability and use this to explain results. Data gathered in this way are more likely to be translatable into information useful to farmers since it allows farmer circumstances to be taken into account. Data were collected in a variety of ways and the analytical methods used varied depending on the form of the data. The co-operative itself was considered part of the implementation team and although feedback was collected, a more systematic collection of feedback from staff may have provided additional insights to the work. Problems arose from the complexity of the situation. It was realized during the course of the study that additional information was required in order to understand the recorded information. The heavy data handling requirements resulted in long intervals between feeding back results to farmers, making it more difficult to have productive interactions between them and the extension and research staff.

Participation

The majority of the data was not collected in a participatory manner. The research scientists defined parameters and formal questionnaires were used to collect the information. Long delays in data handling meant that it was difficult to feed back information rapidly to farmers and the co-operative and to gather their opinions on it. Some data were collected in retrospect (e.g. credit information from the non-study farmers). Nevertheless, qualitative information was collected using informal methods and was invaluable in terms of interpretation of the data. The success of this component of the data collection was largely because of one dynamic member of the team who took the time to record observations made by farmers. A more structured method to collect informal feedback from members of the team may have been valuable. Farmers, based on the information provided to them, determined implementation of the technology. One can speculate that facilitation and support of farmers to test an intervention in the way they saw fit gave them enough confidence in the intervention to maintain the altered patterns of feeding, suggesting that farmers were convinced by the benefits of change. Collection of data from the co-operative records was valuable in that it allowed quantitative evaluation of assumptions made by the research team and feedback from farmers and the co-op.

Acknowledgements

This research was carried out through the Smallholder Dairy (R&D) Project (SDP) of the Kenya Ministry of Agriculture and Rural Development, the Kenya Agricultural Research Institute and the International Livestock Research Institute. SDP is funded by the UK Department for International Development (DFID). The views expressed are those of the authors and not necessarily those of DFID or SDP.

16 Case study E: Tree pods as a supplement to improve the productivity of female goats in India

C. Conroy, A.L. Joshi, M. Sharma, Shyam Singh Lakhawat and M.H. Wadher

SOME INTERESTING ASPECTS OF THIS CASE STUDY

In Bhilwara District, Rajasthan, poor reproductive performance (low conception rates) of does during the dry season (when naturally occurring feed is scarce) was identified as a serious constraint. To address this constraint, researchers suggested collection and storage of *Prosopis juliflora* pods for selective supplementation (in combination with barley grain) in the late dry season, when feed scarcity is most acute. On-farm trials were carried out in four successive years, with the barley component dropped in the last two years to reduce the cost of the treatment. In all trials kidding rate increased significantly, by 30–40 per cent. This technology was also applied effectively in another state, Karnataka, to address the constraint of high kid mortality in the rainy season.

An interesting aspect of this case study is that the supplement is one that is widely available in many parts of semi-arid India, and can be used even by poor and landless goat-keepers. There are no restrictions on collecting the pods of *P. juliflora* trees, as they are mainly found on common lands, unlike certain other fodder trees. The fact that *P. juliflora* pods can be collected rather than purchased can be a significant advantage for cash-constrained goat-keepers, provided that the collection period coincides with a time when the demand for labour for on-farm work is slack. The case study shows that optimizing the use of locally available feeds to address key constraints can generate significant improvements in animal productivity.

This case study describes one component of a goat research project that worked in various districts of semi-arid India. In Bhilwara District of Rajasthan, India, there is evidence that feed scarcity in the dry season is a constraint on the reproductive performance, particularly conception rates, of female goats belonging to poor people. On-farm trials in 1998 and 1999 fed breeding does a mixture of 250 g/day of *Prosopis juliflora* pods and barley in equal proportions for 10 weeks. The treatment was given during the later part of the dry season when fodder scarcity is most acute. The mean number of kids per doe in the treatment groups was significantly higher than that in the control groups, providing clear evidence that the treatment results in does producing more kids than they would otherwise have done. The benefits of the treatment exceeded the costs, but not by a large margin. To reduce the cost, the treatment was changed to 250 g/day of *P. juliflora* pods in subsequent trials in 2000 and 2001. This treatment proved to be as effective as the first one. *P. juliflora* pods were also used as a supplement for female goats in Karnataka, where they proved to be effective in addressing a different constraint, namely high kid mortality. This could prove to be a valuable technology for many goat-keepers in India, since trees of this species are widely distributed on common lands in dryland regions throughout India. The project has been promoting the technology in the two project states and elsewhere in India.

16.1 Background

Between October 1997 and March 2002 the Natural Resources Institute (NRI) and BAIF Development Research Foundation (BAIF) collaborated on a research project entitled 'Easing seasonal fodder scarcity for goats in semi-arid India, through a process of participatory research'. BAIF is one of India's largest rural development NGOs, operating in six different states, and has a strong track record in livestock development. The main researcher from NRI was a socio-economist with experience in participatory research. The project chose to focus on goats because they are an important type of livestock for poor people. It worked in five districts of four states altogether. The project, in collaboration with goat-keepers, tested a number of different interventions, including: the effect of supplementing particular feeds on feed-related production problems or opportunities; de-worming does around kidding time as a means of reducing kid mortality; and measures to alleviate water scarcity in the dry season.

In Rajasthan's Bhilwara District, the project conducted a programme of on-farm trials with goat-keepers, in four successive years (1998–2001), in which tree pods were used as a supplement. This district has a mean annual rainfall of about 700 mm, and every 3–4 years there is a drought year when rainfall is much lower than this. Most of the rural people here are involved in mixed farming that is dependent on rainfall, and the project worked with farmers who only had small or marginal landholdings. The project also tested the use of tree pods in Dharwad District, Karnataka. This district is also semi-arid, and here the project worked with landless people as well as poor farmers.

16.2 Participatory situation analysis

Systems description and characterization
The BAIF/NRI project team began by doing surveys in three or four villages in each of the project districts. The surveys, which lasted about three days per village, involved rapid rural appraisals with groups of goat-keepers, using semi-structured interviews and mapping and diagramming. The surveys generated descriptions of the goat production and feeding systems, and information about the principal constraints, as perceived by the goat-keepers.

Characterization of goat production systems Matrix ranking was used to determine the relative importance of different contributions that goats and other livestock make to people's livelihoods. Seasonal production calendars provided a valuable overview of the timing of conception, kidding, sales and disease.

Description of goat feeding systems The principal tools used were seasonal calendars, to show temporal aspects; and participatory mapping of forage resources to show spatial ones. Different types of seasonal calendars were used to explore different aspects of feeding systems – some calendars focused on fodder species, while others looked at sources (e.g. common grazing lands, private grazing lands, owners' fields, others' fields).

Identification of constraints and research issues
Preliminary identification of constraints and needs The project focused on people's perceived priority needs. Simple ranking was used to identify major problems and their relative importance, and the results of the ranking were generally cross-checked with other survey findings. In all of the villages in Bhilwara goat-keepers identified feed scarcity in the dry season as a significant problem.

In Bhilwara District the project also benefited from the fact that BAIF had been undertaking a goat development programme there for several years. It had already gathered evidence that the reproductive performance of does belonging to poor goat-keepers was unsatisfactory: for example, in one village about 25 per cent of poor goat-keepers' breeding does were not conceiving during the main breeding season. Thus, the project staff proposed to poor goat-keepers that they collaborate in a trial to test the effect of feed supplementation on the reproductive performance of their does.

The main breeding season is May/June. It is preferred by the goat-keepers, as it means that the kids will be borne in October/November, after the rainy season, when there is plenty of fodder available and there is comparatively little disease. However, the breeding season coincides with the late dry season when feed is scarce. It was hypothesized that inadequate feed was responsible for the poor reproductive performance, and that selective supplementation of does at this time would reduce the problem.

In the first two trials the project team suggested that the treatment, to be given daily, be composed of *Prosopis juliflora* pods and barley, and the goat-keepers agreed to this. *P. juliflora* is a tree species that was introduced into India from central America in the second half of the nineteenth century, and which has since spread rapidly across large parts of the country. It is now abundant along roadsides and on common lands in dryland regions, including parts of Bhilwara, where its production of pods is bimodal, concentrated around April/May and October/November. *P. juliflora* pods are a good source of protein and energy, and are easily digestible (Pasiecznik et al., 2001). In parts of the adjacent state of Gujarat, *P. juliflora* pods are widely collected and marketed for use as a high quality livestock feed. There is no commercial market for them in Bhilwara, although the forest department purchases them from villagers.

In Dharwad District, Karnataka, goat-keepers identified high kid mortality in the rainy season as the main problem they faced. *P. juliflora* pods were also tested here as a means of addressing this constraint.

16.3 Methods and materials

Treatments

In the Bhilwara trials, pods were collected during April/May, and stored for use over a 10-week period from mid-May to the end of July. The pods and the barley were fed in equal proportions (a combined total of 250 g/day). In the two later trials, in 2000 and 2001, the treatment was only *P. juliflora* pods, at 250 g/day. The barley was replaced by pods to reduce the cost of the treatment. The project staff suggested that half of the treatment be fed to the does in the morning and half in the evening, but most goat-keepers preferred to give it in the morning.

The average weight of the does, most of which were of the Sirohi breed, was 25 kg. The daily quantity to be fed was based on discussions between BAIF staff and the goat-keepers. It was thought that it would amount to 30–35 per cent of a doe's daily dry-matter intake, and would result in minimal substitution effects.

In Dharwad District, Karnataka, a trial was conducted in the rainy season of 2001, using *P. juliflora* pods as a supplement for pre-partum and early lactation does. The objective was to test its effect on kid mortality, and also on birth weights and growth rates of kids. The treatment was again 250 g/day.

The pods are not normally collected and stored, so this was a new practice for the goat-keepers. The pods were collected when they appeared on the trees in April and early May and stored (usually in gunny bags) for use later. Goat-keepers were advised to dry the pods thoroughly before storing them, otherwise there would be a risk of infestation by pod-borer. In the Dharwad trial, in which the pods were being stored during the rainy season, they were preserved in neem (*Azadirachta indica*) leaves, and there was weekly fumigation of the store with green leaves of neem.

Prior to the trials the goat-keepers were concerned that the pods might cause diarrhoea in their animals, but they were nevertheless persuaded to apply the treatment.

The goats in the treatment and control groups were also de-wormed. This was done partly because it gave goat-keepers in the control group an incentive to participate in the trials, and partly because BAIF wanted to be of assistance to the goat-keepers. A potential disadvantage of de-worming the animals is that this could mask any anthelminthic effect that the treatment might have. On the other hand, it can reduce variability between animals caused by differences in worm burdens.

The seeds of the pods are highly nutritious, and it was thought that most of them were not being digested by the goats. If this were the case, it could have been worthwhile to grind the pods, so that the seeds were broken open, thereby facilitating their digestion. Before testing this option, however, the project decided to obtain some objective information. Thus, in 2001 another trial was carried out at BAIF's Central Research Station, in which *P. julifora* pods were fed to goats, to measure what percentage of the seeds in the pods was digested and what percentage was excreted intact in the faeces. This trial was carried out on-station, because it would have been impractical to collect all the faeces under field conditions, where the goats are out grazing most of the day.

Selection of participants and goats

In each trial there was a treatment group and a control group. In Bhilwara the goats in the treatment group belonged to different herds to those in the control group. This design was adopted in order to avoid the possibility of control group goats getting access to the treatment. If breeding does belonging to both groups had been in the same herd, this could easily have happened by accident if they were feeding from the same bowl. It could also have happened intentionally if the goat-keeper had observed the benefits experienced by does in the treatment group, and decided part-way through the trial to make sure that all her/his does benefited from the treatment. By contrast, in the Dharwad trial goats were selected for treatment and control groups from the same herd. Despite the above reservations about this kind of design, the potential problem was avoided.

In the 1998 and 1999 trials, the participants were goat-keeping households in the villages who belonged to the poorest groups, namely scheduled castes (SCs) or tribes (STs). In the 2000 trial, the SCs in the selected village were not prepared to risk feeding their goats with the *P. juliflora* pods, so participants were selected from a slightly better-off caste, called Kumawats. (The attitude of SCs changed dramatically after the trial.) In the 2001 trial, it was decided to include a larger number of goat-keepers (40) from one village, in order to ensure that enough goats were included, and this necessitated including goat-keepers from different castes: 15 SC/ST, 16 Kumawats, 11 Gujars, and 8 others. Participants were divided between the treatment and control groups in such a way that there would be roughly equal numbers of trial does in each group.

Some experimental goats left the herds (i.e. died or were sold or slaughtered) during the course of the trials, particularly during drought years, and these were not monitored subsequently. It was important, therefore, to include larger numbers of goats initially to allow for this.

Monitoring and evaluation system

For each trial a local person was trained to undertake the monitoring of the trial animals. The monitors visited the participating households every 15 days during the supplementation period and the kidding season. In Bhilwara, they made records of: breeding activity (including heat, number of services and conception); the health and condition of the does; the number of kids born; and, in a few cases, their birth weight.

Most of the goat-keepers were illiterate, particularly the women. In order to give them the option of keeping their own records, the project team in Bhilwara designed a monitoring form that was based entirely on symbols, and could be understood and used by illiterate people. However, the goat-keepers declined to use it, saying that their visual observations were an adequate form of monitoring.

In addition, every month or so the BAIF field researcher met with participants to discuss with them how the trial was progressing. At the end of each trial the field researcher convened an evaluation meeting with participants from both the treatment and control groups.

16.4 Results

Conception

The conception data are summarized in Table 16.1. The treatments had the anticipated effect in all four trials, with does in the treatment groups having higher conception rates than those in the control groups.

Twinning

The incidence of twinning was also higher in the treatment groups (see Table 16.2), but the difference was not statistically significant.

Table 16.1 Conception data for mature does in each of the four trials

Group	1998		1999		2000		2001	
	P	E	P	E	P	E	P	E
Treatment	24	0	39	11	35	3	72	0
Control	18	5	34	22	28	7	50	7

P = pregnant; E = empty.

Table 16.2 Twinning rates in the four trials for does that kidded[a]

Group	1998		1999		2000		2001	
	Twins	One	Twins	One	Twins	One	Twins	One
Treatment	4	19	11	28	8	19	20	40
Control	1	16	6	26	3	14	3	26

[a] Does that aborted are excluded.

Kidding rates

Kidding rates were calculated by dividing the total number of kids produced by the number of serviced does completing the trial (i.e. that remained in the herd at the end of the kidding season). The combination of higher conception rates and higher twinning rates results in higher kidding rates in the treatment groups, as can be seen from Table 16.3.

Table 16.3 Kidding rates in the four trials (%)

Group	1998	1999	2000	2001
Treatment	116.6	100.0	116.6	138.7
Control	78.3	69.1	70.4	110.3

Results of the other trials

In the Karnataka trial the pods improved the health of pregnant does and increased their milk production. As a result, their kids were healthier and grew faster than those in the control group (statistically significant).

The results of the 'on-station' trial were surprising. They showed that the vast majority of seeds were digested by the goats, with only 5–6 per cent being excreted undigested. Consequently, the idea of grinding the pods and seeds was abandoned, as the extra nutritional benefit from doing so would have been very small.

16.5 Discussion

The goat-keepers' apprehension that feeding *P. juliflora* pods would induce diarrhoea proved to be unjustified. Some goat-keepers reported diarrhoea during the first few days of the trial, but otherwise there was no problem in this regard.

Profitability and benefits

In the two trials for which the treatment was a combination of *P. juliflora* pods and barley, the benefits of the treatment exceeded the costs, but not by a large margin. Based on the 1999 kidding rate data, a goat-keeper with ten breeding does would get three extra kids, on average, as a result of applying the treatment. The market value for a newly born kid was estimated by the project's field staff to be about Rs 300, giving a total benefit of Rs 900.

If one assumes that all of the supplement (both pods and barley) is purchased, the net benefit per ten does would be Rs 244, and the benefit:cost ratio would be 1.37:1. The effect of replacing barley with *P. juliflora* pods can be seen from the results of the 2001 trial, for which the reduced treatment cost raises the benefit:cost ratio to 1.71:1. In the 1999 and 2001 trials the number of extra kids per 10 does was about 3, but in the year 2000 trial it was 4.5. As a result, the benefit:cost ratio improves to 2.57:1. In other words, the return to the owner is more than 2.5 times the cost.

The fact that *P. juliflora* pods can be collected rather than purchased may be a significant advantage for cash-constrained goat-keepers. If the pods are collected then the opportunity cost of labour has to be taken into account. In Bhilwara, the collection period coincided with a time when the demand for labour for on-farm work was slack, coming after the winter season (*rabi*) crops had been harvested and before land preparation was required for the following rainy season (*kharif*). Thus, the opportunity cost of labour is low.

The trial results and the profitability analysis suggest that the collection and storage of *P. juliflora* pods for use as dry season supplement could prove to be a valuable technology for many goat-keepers in India. An extra two or three kids each year can be a valuable source of extra income for a resource-poor family. They are usually sold when they are about 5–6 months old, for about Rs 750–1000 each.

In August 2000, three women in Bhilwara who had applied the *P. juliflora* treatment in a pilot trial in 1999 were interviewed individually and asked how they had used the additional income from the sale of kids. Each said that they had spent the money on purchasing food grains. This probably made a vital contribution to the well-being of their families, since 1999/2000 was a drought year, with crop yields having been well below average, due to the monsoon rains.

In Bhilwara, goat-keepers tend to prefer having single kids, rather than twins; whereas in Dharwad they generally prefer to have twins. International experience has shown that mortality rates are often higher in twins, but among the Bhilwara participants' animals the rate (35 per cent) was only 10 per cent higher for twins than for single kids (25 per cent).

Accessibility of tree pods

A key characteristic of this technology is that there are no restrictions on collecting the *P. juliflora* pods, as the trees are mainly found on common lands. If the pods were not collected they would either be eaten by animals that grazed on the common lands, or would be left to decompose. They could be eaten by any kind of domestic ruminant, so by collecting the pods the goat-keepers are to some extent depriving other livestock-keepers of the benefit of them. Despite this, nobody objected to the goat-keepers collecting them.

The pods of other tree species in India, such as *Acacia nilotica*, may also provide similar benefits, but *P. juliflora* is the only species that is widely accessible to the poor, including the landless. The benefits of *A. nilotica* pods are only available to those with these trees growing on their farms, or who can afford to purchase lopping rights to them.

Environmental considerations

There was some concern that by encouraging the feeding of *P. juliflora* pods the project could accelerate the spread of this invasive tree species. However, the on-station trial showed that the vast majority of seeds are digested by the goats, which suggests that, if anything, increased consumption of the pods may hinder its spread.

Some people have expressed concern that increasing goat populations may have a negative effect on the environment. However, higher kidding rates do not necessarily lead to marked increases in goat populations. In Bhilwara, almost all male goats are sold by the time they are 6 months old, and additional female goats may replace older less productive ones. Surveys in the Dharwad project villages showed that there was little difference in the size of the goat populations before and after the research was conducted.

16.6 Dissemination

The project has been promoting the use of *P. juliflora* pods, primarily in the two states where the research was done, but also in other dryland regions of India where BAIF works. Posters have been produced in both Hindi (spoken in Rajasthan and other parts of northern India) and Kannada (spoken in Karnataka) that show pictorially, as well as in words, the technology and its uses. These materials have been distributed to BAIF staff in all six states where it works; and to a large number of other Indian NGOs and government agencies involved in livestock development. In addition, a more detailed technical bulletin has been produced in English.

Workshops were organized in both Rajasthan and Karnataka – each of which was attended by 50–60 people from NGOs, government extension services and livestock research organizations – at which the project's findings regarding this technology and others were presented. In Karnataka, a field-level workshop/demonstration day was also organized in the project area in Dharwad, in which livestock professionals from various parts of the state were shown the project's work. Presentations about the *P. juliflora* technology have also been given at national and international conferences and workshops concerned with goats and/or animal nutrition, and articles have been published.

16.7 Key points arising from project experiences

The testing and development of the *P. juliflora* technology was one of the most effective components of the project, and some other components were less effective. The points presented below draw on the project's overall experience.

The shift towards a collaborative relationship with farmers is not automatic. It is important to be aware of, and to address, factors that may hinder the adoption of a participatory approach. Some lessons learned are as follows:

- It is important that researchers have experience and/or training/orientation in participatory research from an early stage.
- It is also important to do a thorough needs assessment, which can be jeopardized by the pressure to move quickly from the diagnosis and needs assessment phase to the establishment of trials (due to the short lifetime of some projects).
- It is preferable to have a field researcher who works full-time on the project, otherwise competing demands may result in: them having insufficient staff time to encourage full farmer involvement; and/or in late scheduling of project activities.
- Staff turnover can create problems, particularly when staff who are experienced in PTD are replaced by inexperienced ones, so staff transfers should be minimized and a critical mass of expertise developed so that heavy dependency on one individual is avoided.
- Technologies tested must be low cost and profitable.

Acknowledgements

The work on which this paper is based was funded by the Livestock Production Programme of the UK's Department for International Development, whose support we gratefully acknowledge. However, the views expressed are not necessarily those of DFID. We would like to thank the goat-keepers who participated in the trials. We would also like to thank Mr David Jeffries for providing biometric advice.

17 Case study F: Women, livestock and innovation: campesino experimentation in Mexico

Julieta Moguel Pliego, Bernadette Keane, Susanne Clark and Simon Anderson

SOME INTERESTING ASPECTS OF THIS CASE STUDY

The project collaborated with campesinos in the PTD process, initially focusing on alternative feed sources. Better ways of partitioning maize and other food/feed resources between family and livestock needs were explored. A notable feature of the project, however, was its emphasis on demand-led research and its flexibility, which resulted in it also researching certain animal health issues. The research was primarily related to pigs and poultry, as these were the main types of livestock kept by the campesinos. It is unusual for a research project to cover more than one livestock type, and participatory research relating to pigs is rare.

Another interesting dimension of the project was the emphasis it gave to working with campesino experimentation (CE) groups: it facilitated their formation in its early stages, and each of them identified themes for experimentation. CE groups from the different project villages were also involved in exchange visits to view and discuss each other's work. Farmer research groups can help to strengthen participatory research by farmers, and to make the process more sustainable, but most of the other cases did not work with groups.

This case study is also unusual in that it includes an ex-post evaluation (or impact assessment) of the CE experience.

17.1 Background

Campesino[35] households in south-east Mexico, as elsewhere in Latin America, face situations of declining food security due to the disintegration of traditional agriculture, or poor natural resources management in colonized areas often at the forest/agriculture interface. The main livelihood activities of these households include crop and livestock production (mainly poultry and pigs) for subsistence and sale. Such marginalized agriculture depends largely upon endogenous processes of innovation. The project described here sought to overcome both technological and social constraints by identifying and validating improved livestock feeding systems through facilitating and strengthening local capacity in campesino experimentation and campesino to campesino extension. Campesino groups, NGOs and researchers were all involved in this process.

17.2 Who, where, when and what

The project involved campesino households of four villages – Mahas, Xohuayan, X'culoc and Sahcabchen – in the states of Yucatan and Campeche, south-east Mexico. The researchers came from an action-research group based at the Veterinary Medicine and Animal Science Faculty of the Autonomous University of Yucatan. Funding was provided by DFID's Livestock Production Programme. The project commenced in 1997 and finished in 2001.

The objective of the project was to optimize campesino livestock rearing so that household livelihood and food security were improved. Processes of campesino experimentation were facilitated through a version of participatory technology development. Animal science research supported campesino innovations. The results of these linked activities were disseminated using campesino to campesino methods.

17.3 How

The project explored ways to utilize the biomass produced in innovatory small-scale crop systems, by feeding to livestock, so that both the production of food and the utilization of feed and forage[36] could be optimized. The intended impacts of this were improvements in family livelihoods and food security, and the consolidation and uptake of agro-ecological innovations in

---

[35] The term *campesino* is used here to refer to those people in Latin America who are involved in agriculture for both subsistence and commercial reasons. Crop and livestock husbandry is central to the campesino culture and well-being.

[36] Food here is used to refer to products consumed by families, while feed and forage is that fed to livestock.

campesino agriculture. Further information on these innovations is available in Anderson et al. (2001).

Following the inception phase, during which contacts were established with local NGOs and through them with campesino groups, the project was operated simultaneously along three overlapping activity axes as shown in Figure 17.1. These were:

a)   Action-research:

   ■ participatory appraisals;
   ■ facilitating processes of campesino experimentation (CE).

b)   On-station research:

   ■ generating relevant scientific information;
   ■ trials to identify the feeding values of crops;
   ■ experimenting with crop/livestock interactions.

c)   Building uptake pathways and disseminating methods and findings:

   ■ promoting campesino to campesino interchanges;
   ■ promoting the use of participatory methods of appraisal and technology development by local NGOs and campesino organizations;
   ■ providing technical assistance to community development projects;
   ■ sharing results with other local research/educational institutes and local government.

This case study shows how the processes of CE were facilitated and evaluated. Details and discussion of the other two activities axes – on-station research and building uptake pathways and disseminating methods and findings – can be found in Anderson et al. (2003).

Action-research activities

The action-research activities followed an iterative sequence designed to establish and consolidate dynamic campesino/researcher linkages. The sequence consists of:

Appraisal

   ■ dynamic characterization of livelihood maintenance strategies and agricultural production.

Convergence

   ■ identify families interested in the theme of crop/livestock integration and willing to provide case study material
   ■ identify themes for the CE
   ■ establish CE groups
   ■ initiate case studies and socio-economic research methods.

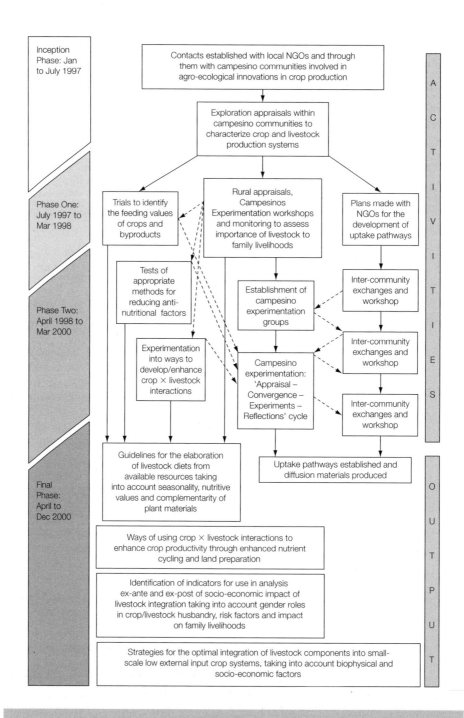

Figure 17.1 An outline of the project's methodology

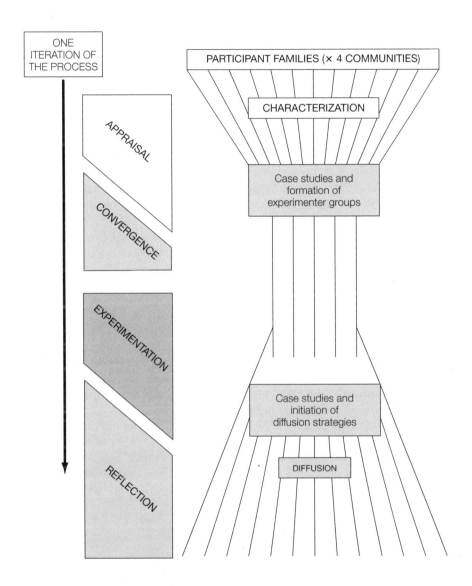

ONE ITERATION OF THE PROCESS

APPRAISAL

CONVERGENCE

EXPERIMENTATION

REFLECTION

PARTICIPANT FAMILIES (× 4 COMMUNITIES)

CHARACTERIZATION

Case studies and formation of experimenter groups

Case studies and initiation of diffusion strategies

DIFFUSION

Figure 17.2 The phases and the sequence of activities within each project community

Experimentation

- facilitate and monitor the CE
- continue case studies and socio-economic research.

Reflection

- consider the results and amend if necessary, and implications of CE
- discuss the possible future of the CE group
- diffuse the results and the process of the experimentation among more families
- diffuse new knowledge among families and communities.

Figure 17.2 shows the activities of the project's action-research axis within each of the participant communities. Here emphasis was upon facilitating the process of CE, collection of information to guide the on-station research, and establishment of the core CE groups that provided the basis for intra-community diffusion of the project outputs.

Table 17.1 shows the different tools used in the phases of the action research.

Appraisal

During the appraisal phase, contact was made with a cross-section of families in each community through existing campesino groups working with local NGOs and/or grassroots organizations. Participatory appraisal methods were used to gather the information needed to form a characterization of household livelihood strategies and of crop and livestock husbandry. Information gathered was also used to delineate priority issues from the campesinos' perspective. Several campesino families were already familiar with the participatory research methods, which not only facilitated application but also validated or qualified the method's usefulness. Secondary information was also collected where available about the communities and the zones.

Table 17.1 Tools used in the phases of the action research

Phase	Tools
Appraisal	Semi-structured interviews; mapping (villages and resource flows); institutional diagrams; well-being calendars; profiling for activities, production and responsibilities; gender disaggregated activity calendars
Convergence	Group meetings; dialogue; brainstorming; key question identification; well-being ranking; animal inventories
Campesino experimentation	Maize scarcity assessment; participatory budgeting; livelihood budgets
Reflection	Consultative evaluation; timelines; campesino experimentation books; campesino to campesino exchanges; participatory evaluation of on station research

Convergence

The process of action research should lead to a convergence of ideas and aims between researchers and campesinos. In this project, convergence did result from what proved to be a difficult but fruitful phase. Households interested in the theme of crop/livestock integration and willing to provide case study material were identified and CE groups were formed. Each group then identified themes for experimentation. In this phase, researchers attempted a more in-depth approach to understanding the socio-economic context, and the case studies of campesino households were initiated.

In each village, the campesinos who had participated in the appraisal stage were invited to a meeting where researchers determined their interest in forming a CE group that would specifically try out innovative animal husbandry techniques. The research team presented this idea to them. Brainstorming was used to focus in on why they would want to form their own group and how it would operate.

In all four villages, animal health was a priority issue for the campesinos. While health issues did not fall explicitly within the research team's remit, for collaboration it was felt that an attempt could be made to respond to their questions about poultry health. The opportunity could then be used to link the issues of animal health to problems with diet. If this were to work, then the collaboration would have a longer-term future given the research's goal of investigating crop–livestock interactions. Hence, responding to the demands expressed in the meetings, the researchers held animal health workshops in each village, open to all villagers – a process analogous to the farmer field school approach.

Animal inventory

The animal inventory technique was developed as a result of the researchers' interest in studying the portfolio of animals kept by each household and the quantity of maize dedicated to animal feed and human consumption. Pictures of the different animals hand-drawn by the children in the villages were used on a matrix-type table. The inventory was conducted every month, and the differences between one month and another (consumption, deaths, purchases) were listed and identified. This took about 10–15 minutes for a group of 8–10 people.

The purpose of the technique was to provide more detailed information on maize feeding to livestock and the source of the maize (grown by the family or purchased). This was used in discussions with campesinos, to facilitate the identification of feed shortage periods, and how trade-offs are made between allocating maize to the family or 'investing' it as animal feed. The initial analysis was carried out by the researchers who then developed easy to understand tables, which were then presented to the groups at six monthly intervals. Livestock population levels and animal feed quantities were graphed for each household, and explained. Questions were then asked as to what was understood from the graph, what had been learnt, and what this implied for the management of livestock. Campesinos saw the analyses a second time when they were presented at the village level (rather than the results of individual households). They also saw them at the end of the CE process, when results were relayed to the CE groups.

Experimentation

Once CE groups were formed the next question was how to facilitate and monitor the experiments and maintain momentum when experiments 'failed' or became 'uninteresting'. This proved a methodological challenge. A reflexive and iterative interaction between campesinos and researchers was essential for the researchers unused to 'uncontrolled' experiments and for the campesinos unaccustomed to words such as experiments and monitoring to describe something they are always doing.

A flexible use of participatory methodology is very important in facilitating the development of CE groups and enabling participatory monitoring and evaluation.

Invitation to form groups: getting to know each other's objectives In dialogues between the researchers and the campesinos a list of the campesinos' priority issues was drawn up. In each village, this led to the preparation of a list of objectives. In Box 17.1, the participants' objectives, and experimentation options based on those objectives, are presented for one of the villages.

BOX 17.1   Defining experiments: the example of X'culoc village

X'culoc

- Learn how to rear healthy and pretty animals

- Learn how to improve feed for poultry

- Have pigs that grow

- Learn what to do with ill animals

- Learn about cystercicosis

- Health problems to monitor and analyse in group: cystercicosis, parasites, clean water, dirt, colds, diarrhoea, sudden death (for pigs and poultry)

- De-worming poultry and pigs with local methods

- Feed with local forages, maize, maize drink, squash, mucuna (pigs and poultry)

- Compare differences in pigs and poultry according to origin and husbandry

Using participatory monitoring and evaluation (PM&E) methods objectives were defined for the experimentation process. These provided the basis upon which the CE groups monitored their experiments. In all the villages, the campesinos' aims and experiments were firmly based on animal health and feeding issues. The campesinos' emphasis on health issues initially caused the researchers to re-think their research strategy in the villages as it was not a priority area for the project. Calendars identifying seasonal differences in feeding strategies were also used in conjunction with brainstorming sessions, to identify and stimulate ideas for possible experiments.

As the group in Xohuayan had defined one specific experiment (construction of hen houses), the themes based on problems and benefits of the experiment (see Table 17.2) were developed before embarking upon the construction of hen houses. The other CE groups discussed potential problems and benefits during the process of selecting things to try.

Monitoring experiments An example of the monitoring process followed can be observed in the case of the CE group in Xohuayan. The benefits (as seen in Table 17.2) anticipated were represented in drawn images and presented in a matrix format by the researchers at the monthly meetings, following the construction of the hen houses, and were analysed with the campesinos. Two months after the construction of the houses, the women were very concerned about the absence of egg production and many blamed the enclosure of their birds. This type of straightforward monitoring process gave the campesinos early opportunities to discuss problems in-group, and to seek out possible solutions with other campesinos and the research team. However, it proved difficult to revise the benefits on a monthly basis due to the quantity of topics to be dealt with at the monthly meetings and eventually they were checked every three to four months.

Monitoring experiments via discussions Using lists written in bright primary colours proved to be an important technique. But, given the potential

Table 17.2 Working through the experiment before testing: hen houses in Xohuayan

Benefits	Potential problems	How can they overcome these problems?
■ Poultry will not eat chilli seedlings. ■ Poultry will not get wet ■ Poultry will not die ■ Poultry will not enter their homes ■ Excrement can be collected ■ Poultry will not be eaten or attacked by other animals ■ More eggs will be collected	■ More work as they have to be fed more frequently ■ The poultry may get ill ■ The poultry may not be fed enough	■ Ask their families for help ■ Mix chicks with turkey chicks who have initial eating problems so they teach them how to eat? ■ Women get up earlier ■ Attend poultry health workshop ■ Give the poultry lemon with water and other remedies ■ Plant more mucuna ■ Collect forage ■ Plant forage

problems surrounding testing new husbandry techniques, the researchers also spent large parts of each monthly meeting discussing problems related to experiments, and this led to new actions being taken.

These activities were discussed, debated and some were tested out during the eight months. The vaccination option was discarded after a lengthy debate between the CE group and researchers about the risks of applying the vaccination to weak/ill poultry. However, the women pursued the other activities.

Visiting sites of experiments In all four villages this simple process of visiting the experiments of other campesinos in their own village and others was key to CE group meetings. For example in Mahas a woman commented that she had fed her chicks whole maize grains since the age of three days old and they were growing fine. This diet had saved her time and money that would have been spent milling maize. However, other women said feeding whole maize grains to chicks had not worked for them and their chicks had died. A rich and enthusiastic discussion ensued among the women about variations in diets.

Several exchange visits to experiments in other villages were organized by the researchers and NGOs. This was considered important for the researchers as one village in particular, Xohuayan, had been cultivating mucuna for several years and had a successful pig-rearing experience based on alternative feeding strategies.

These types of visits facilitated reflection upon the constraints and opportunities available to campesinos in the different villages. Market access, soil types, local vegetation for forages and seed varieties were key themes discussed and compared by the campesinos. However, these topics were sometimes considered negative as many campesinos reflected upon the lack of resources in their village when compared to others. Nevertheless, they did serve to stimulate experiments in their own villages as the campesinos expressed desire to carry out innovations in animal husbandry techniques.

Village maps and illness calendars In all villages, the workshops on poultry and pig health utilized participatory methods to assist in the shared learning experience. One small example of this can be observed in the following case. In one workshop session, the causes, effects and treatments of fowl-pox were discussed using visual aids. To consolidate the learning process the women (24 in total) were divided into two groups. One group constructed a seasonal illness calendar, while the other drew a map of the village on which households with ill poultry were identified, as were locations where dead and infected animals were thrown. Each group then presented their findings to the whole group and discussions followed as to why seasons influence their poultry's health. The map allowed the researchers to re-emphasize how diseases are transmitted by other animals, a novel concept for these women. Furthermore, the application of these methods gave the research team valuable information on seasonal variations in Mahas and a detailed map of the village, which continues to serve as a reference point in meetings between researchers and the women's group. In addition, these resources proved useful to PM&E.

Drawing illness In the animal health workshops with the campesinos from Sahcabchen and X'culoc, the farmers drew pigs and identified where cysticercosis could be found. This was part of an important discussion on the causes of this illness and led to important local beliefs being expressed to the researchers. Several campesinos believed that cysticercosis was caused by eating a local plant and/or fruit. This type of belief could prove to be a severe limitation in testing out alternative locally available forages and plants. Hence, the health workshops also helped establish a common ground, based on trust and sharing knowledge that would enable testing of alternative animal husbandry strategies.

Problem–opportunity tree analysis Problem trees enabled collaborative identification of problems, their causes and effects. They were carried out within group meetings to enable reflection about cause and effect, and opportunities available to campesinos to resolve animal health problems. A tree is drawn on a large sheet of paper, or sticks are used to create a tree. The trunk is the problem (e.g. high poultry mortality), the roots are the causes and the branches are the effects of the problem. The opportunity tree turns the situation around and the trunk becomes the desired situation (e.g. healthy chickens). The participants then think about ways in which this can be achieved by converting the causes of the problem into means to avoid illness. From this technique, experiments were also defined.

Seasonal feed calendars The animal health workshops were also used to reflect upon seasonal influences on poultry and pig diets and the preparation of mucuna and its use as a feed supplement. This was done via calendars, depicting monthly variations in feed availability.

Thus, the animal health workshops facilitated the identification of links between health and crop/livestock interactions. Furthermore, a wider context was presented within which experiments could be considered and evaluated.

Analysis and evaluation
Regional workshops The results for the four villages are extensive. The results from one village, X'culoc, will be used as a specific example of the process and the results generated in the workshops, but generalized conclusions for all four villages will also be presented.

The objective of the first 1-day regional workshop (June 1999) was to enable a participatory analysis of the initial analysis, developed from well-being rankings and animal inventory. The all-women groups were invited to participate in this workshop in order to scrutinize and criticize the analysis of the techniques undertaken by researchers. To facilitate this, the researchers divided the workshop participants into their CE groups and first discussed the technique of ranking and its objectives.

The results of well-being rankings in their villages were depicted with a hand-drawn pie-chart, showing percentiles and numbers of families belonging to each well-being stratum, with symbols of the assets that characterize each stratum. The pie-chart was entitled: 'How we live'. The responses ranged from a despondent: 'yes, we really are that poor', to: 'no, there is one person who's poorer than all the rest', and in one village, the diagram was rearranged. Each group then presented their ranking results, with their own comments and changes back to the entire group. Their insights and changes were incorporated into the ranking results for two of the villages.

Later that same day the analysis of the animal inventories was presented to each CE group by facilitators, using a fictional character and discussing her animal husbandry according to season. The villagers then discussed whether this was a true case from their village, the nature of her difficulties and how she could improve her animal husbandry.

The purpose of this workshop to the CE process was crucial for researchers. The joint analysis facilitated a reflection on the results and hence changes could be incorporated before the conclusions were drawn and presented to all CE groups nine months later in March 2000. The June workshop was particularly important for the animal inventory results as many of the limitations of the technique were nullified, in particular the confusion over animal age-types.

The objective of the final 1-day workshop in March 2000 was to facilitate a sharing of the experiences of each of the CE groups. It was also used to provide a forum whereby the campesino groups could think about how they wished to continue in the future. Approximately 70 campesinos attended and several local NGOs participated so that the future could be considered with potential NGO involvement. Each experimenter group informed the participants of the types of experiments they had tried, methods used and the benefits and problems experienced. They used mostly large sheets of paper with key words and images to explain their stories, told in Spanish and Maya. In addition, each group shared their books with the other groups. In Table 17.3, a summary is presented of the CE X'culoc group's evaluation.

17.4 Results

Ex-post evaluations of the process and outcomes of the campesino experimentation were carried out at the end of the process and almost two years after the researchers had withdrawn from the villages. The results presented below summarize the findings.

Accessibility of experiments

The results of the animal inventory when analysed according to family well-being strata demonstrated that the experiments were not 'exclusive' to any particular socio-economic group. They were equally accessible to the poorest and the poor.

Table 17.3 CE X'culoc: final evaluation of experiments and look to the future

Problems starting CE	Achievements
<ul><li>Sick animals</li><li>Lack of knowledge about de-worming</li><li>Excessive use of maize</li><li>Lack of knowledge about alternative and important feeds for animal rearing</li><li>Lack of awareness about traditional maize production</li></ul>	<ul><li>Pigs are now healthier</li><li>Learnt and apply biological and conventional de-worming techniques</li><li>Animals fatten quicker and sold</li><li>Learnt about mucuna as a forage and grain for pigs</li><li>Learnt about other alternative feeds for animals</li><li>Diminished amount of maize used for feeding animals</li><li>Learnt a great deal about animal husbandry</li><li>With what have learnt and are doing have a better opportunity to improve living standard</li><li>Awareness about traditional maize production</li><li>Mucuna planted in traditional maize plot</li><li>Increased maize harvest</li><li>Proved that where mucuna is planted maize harvest improved</li><li>Disseminated in village and in other villages what have learnt in CE</li></ul>
Current problems	**Future actions**
<ul><li>Unable to learn more about experiments due to lack of technical advice</li></ul>	<ul><li>Keep trying out what have learnt with animals</li><li>Spread what have learnt in our village and in other villages</li></ul>

Collection of forage, poultry pens and cold remedies appeared to be the most accessible innovations, showing the highest experimentation rates. It is interesting to note that both forage and cold remedies were suggested by the campesinos rather than the researchers. There was an 80–100 per cent experimentation rate for these two experiments, and 30–40 per cent for the other experiments (experimentation rate refers to the numbers of households that tried out the innovation). Poultry pens, which were initiated within the villages, should be treated separately given that an NGO donated the fencing.

The innovations that involved mucuna were problematic, given the scarcity of the seeds and the high prices which campesinos could sell them for in 1999. This meant that many households sold them rather than feeding them to their pigs. In addition, there was little time to be able to produce enough.

Other analyses were conducted which revealed that there was no significant difference between other characteristics of the innovations in terms of accessibility and experimentation levels. Thus, it appears that the main characteristic, which affected the level of experimentation, was whether the experiment was locally suggested and 'demand-led'.

Utility of experiments

For the poorest households, the **reduced use of maize** was considered an important benefit of feeding forage and mucuna to livestock. It was recognized that the reduction of maize used for livestock increased maize availability for family consumption. This was particularly true of the poorest households who experience severe maize shortages.

The **rate** at which animals fatten was an important benefit raised for all feed alternatives. The **income** generated from sales was highlighted as being beneficial to the family for different purposes.

The increase in the **number of animals** was highlighted as an important benefit. In the case of the poultry pens, numbers of poultry reared increased. Both poultry pens and vermiculture appeared to increase the number of eggs laid.

Changes in the **aesthetics** of the animal were also important. 'Pretty animals' was the term used to describe healthy animals. This was mentioned for all the alternative feed innovations, for both pigs and poultry. The extra animal husbandry **workload** did not seem to be a constraint to experimentation for the majority of experiments.

The speed of the impact of the benefits is important to the experimentation level. Those innovations for which tangible benefits were seen quickly such as cold remedies were experimented with widely – results were discussed within workshops and, participants, hearing positive results from other group members, attempted the experiments. The visual, quick, tangible benefits thus tend to be adopted and diffused more quickly. Those experiments for which benefits were delayed or over a long period (mucuna experiments) had a lower experimentation level.

In conclusion, it has been seen that the experiments were accessible to all of the participants, and were appropriate to the different resource endowments of households.

Results of an ex-post evaluation

Almost two years after completion of the research project an opportunity arose to carry out an ex-post evaluation of the CE experience. The objective of this ex-post evaluation was to collect sufficient information to objectively assess the impact of the action-research.

The ex-post evaluation assessed:

- continuing adoption of the experiments related to crop–livestock husbandry tried during the project's lifespan;
- achievement by the campesinos of their objectives as identified and modified during the project;
- continuation of CE groups;
- the impact of the experiment according to the campesinos of CE groups;
- variations in adoption according to well-being strata (categories defined during well-being rankings carried out by the project).

The continued adoption of the innovations developed during the project and the percentage change in numbers of households using the innovation are shown below.

Experiment/technique and percentage **increase** in adoption:

- Lemon with water for colds   67%
- Hen house management changes   50%
- Minimum tillage   44%
- Mucuna forage feeding   37%
- Mucuna seed feeding   33%
- New hen house   29%
- Other types of forage   22%

Experiment/technique and percentage **decrease** in use:

- De-worm with epazote and garlic   62%
- Mucuna planted in back-yard   57%
- Vermicompost   50%
- Chicken excrement   50%
- Pigpen   13%

In Table 17.4 an analysis is shown of the benefits of the experiments and their limitations, as identified by ex-members of the CE groups during the ex-post evaluation.

In Table 17.5 the negative and positive impact of the experiments, with adaptation and reduction in adoption are presented.

17.5 Recommendations for livestock PTD processes

From the experience gained in the project and the evaluation of the campesino experimentation process the following recommendations can be made:

1. The agenda of the facilitators must be sufficiently flexible with regard to the constraints and problems addressed to be able to find a fit with the priorities of the participants.
2. The form of the experimentation (use of controls, numbers of animals, repetitions, etc.) need not be prescriptive. Indeed, it is better to maintain as loose a set of experimentation protocols as possible as this will enable greater participation and inclusiveness. The way findings are sought and agreed requires the participation of all and the researchers should not dominate the process.
3. Issues that require answering under controlled conditions are best addressed through on-station research. This can also be 'participatory', where the livestock keepers define the research questions, agree the types of treatments applied and evaluate the results and outcomes.

Table 17.4 Impact of experiments with increased adoption

Experiment/technique	Positive impact of techniques	Negative impact and/or limitations of technique
Mucuna forage	Stimulates pig rearing as it reduces dependency on maize Pigs can eat a lot of forage	The leaf is used as a fertilizer in the milpa Cutting leaf reduces the size of seed harvest
New hen house	Other animals cannot eat the hen's food Hens kept out of house It is cheap to copy Families have improved access to eggs	Unsuccessful for egg laying and hatching Pigs break fence Men do not repair hen house Need to have more than 15 birds to use it
Lemon with water for colds	Reduce deaths from colds	They do die if cold too far gone
Mucuna seed	Saves maize for family consumption Fattens good and quick with no need for purchased commercial feed	Husband will not harvest it as sees no utility No market for it Not all pigs will eat it, even when cooked with maize No seed More work to plant Have to harvest at right time Pigs consume more if it is cooked A lot of work to prepare it as feed Not all pigs thrive on it Pigs cannot eat too much of it It is the woman's responsibility to cook it When there is sufficient maize they do not give it
Minimum tillage	Feeds the soil Gives shade and keeps out weeds Protects maize from birds	Migration of husbands to USA
Other types of forage	Helps to use less maize	Not used to using it Distance from home to carry it
Hen house management	Hens protected from predators Reduces chance of infection from contagious diseases	Lack of habit (forget to clean it, etc.) Other tasks have higher priority

Table 17.5 Impact of experiments with reduction in use

Experiment	Positive impact	Negative impact and/or limitations of experiment
De-worm with epazote and garlic	Less illnesses Eat well The hens get pretty	The hens eat all the epazote in the backyard
Mucuna planted in back-yard	It is close by	Hens eat it
Vermicompost	The hens eat them very well	The hens eat them all Fear of worms Dislike of worms Could not get used to feeding them Grandparents taught them not to touch worms
Collect chicken excrement	Produces very good vegetables	No utility??? Lack of time to dedicate to vegetables
Pigpen	Pigs have a high economic benefit Pig rearing not damaging to others Makes birthing much easier	Not all pigs grow well in pen It is expensive to copy The pigs can get ill

4. Support innovations and experiments that are cheap, easy to apply and based on local traditions (e.g. lemon with water); in the case reported here these have spread widely and persist despite there being no technical assistance.

5. The researchers have to be committed to continually adapt their role in the multi-dimensional situations that arise in PTD.

6. A lengthy period (five years minimum) is required for considerable adoption and adaptation of techniques/experiments that require significant labour input, and a new and alien management (e.g. mucuna as a crop and feed).

7. Poverty definition and distribution in villages must be identified as this influences the ability and willingness of people to try out major innovations (e.g. new crops that can substitute maize) which are crucial to well-being.

8. Consideration of gender aspects needs to be included. In the Yucatan women, in general, do not make crucial decisions for crop husbandry; e.g. in Mahas the women were interested in cultivating mucuna but their husbands were not incorporated within the CE group; mucuna was not planted. In this situation the project needs to work wih both sexes, separately.

9. Work with NGOs that can follow up the work after the project finishes. This increases adoption and spread of techniques.

10. Ensure the speedy diffusion and promotion of PTD results to a wide variety of governmental institutions.

Acknowledgements

The authors have the pleasure of thanking all the different members of the campesino experimentation groups in Xohuayan, X'culoc, Sahcabchen and Mahas for letting us work with them and for teaching us so much.

18 Case study G: Adoption and scaling out – experiences of the Forages for Smallholders Project in South-east Asia

Ralph Roothaert and Peter Kerridge

SOME INTERESTING ASPECTS OF THIS CASE STUDY

This case study describes a project that has been operating for eight years, currently in six countries. Perhaps because it covers such an unusually large geographical area, it has identified important ways of enrolling in-country partners, both organizational and individual, into supporting and promoting the project. At the organizational level, it has learned that building partnerships at local, provincial and national level is crucial to obtain broad support for the initiative. Therefore, the project makes a serious effort to invite key agricultural or political officials at district or provincial levels for various training workshops and courses.

At the individual level, the project seeks to identify enthusiastic farmers and extensionists. In every new community exposed to cross-visits from participating farmers, champion farmers emerge, whose enthusiasm and experience is harnessed by the project. They in turn will become key farmers able to receive other farmers from new areas, to show them their experience in forage evaluation and utilization.

Promising field staff are often identified during training courses: apart from skills, attitudes are also an important selection criterion for staff. In very remote areas, where extension workers can be scarce, another option that has worked well is the use of experienced farmers as extension workers.

Another reason for the project's success has been its recognition that no two smallholder farms are the same, and that farmers need to experiment with and develop their own forage systems. Thus, the project aims to provide 'building blocks' and not 'finished products'. In other words, the project shows the farmers the species and forage systems that have worked in other places, while at the same time allowing the new farmers to evaluate a range of optional species and develop their forage systems within their overall farming system.

18.1 Introduction

The Forages for Smallholders Project (FSP), convened by the International Centre for Tropical Agriculture (CIAT), started in 1995 to move research on tropical forages from the experimental stations to farmers' fields, which created scope for evaluating the potential of improved forages in smallholder farming systems in Asia. The target farming systems were those in upland areas. The FSP now operates in six countries in South-east Asia through national partners, namely: China, Indonesia, Lao PDR, the Philippines, Thailand and Vietnam.

The strategy has been to concentrate farmer participatory research activities in one or two sites in each country, which subsequently have been used as focus sites for dissemination of forage systems developed at these sites. This case study describes the methods that the project developed and how they evolved, the meaning of adoption of forage technologies, how adoption was achieved, and how dissemination took place in new areas, and includes an example of impact on farmers' livelihoods at these focus sites in Indonesia.

The term 'forages' is used here for crops that are specifically cultivated to provide feed for animals. This is different from the broader definition often used for forages as 'any plants or parts of plants used for animal feed, including agro-industrial by-products'.

18.2 Developing technologies with farmers, and adoption

The project aims to work with resource-poor upland farmers. However, it can be argued that livestock-keepers are not the poorest farmers, because keeping livestock means having some wealth. On the other hand, upland livestock-keepers in South-east Asia do not have large herds, and it is uncommon to find smallholder livestock-keepers with large pasture or fodder banks. This is likely to remain so even if numbers of livestock per household or production levels increase. A common scenario is to find forage crops planted within a complex pattern of other food and cash crops, utilizing farm space and labour in a multiple and optimal way. After many years of working with these farming communities, we now see the integration of a range of some 25 introduced grass and legume species: in lines along contours on farm land; as cover or green manure crops in fruit trees, coffee and tea; as live fences for demarcation of external and internal boundaries; and as pastures and fodder banks in backyards or under young oil palm or coconut plantations.

The main difficulty with forage research is that it is complex. Unlike food crops, forage crops need to pass through an animal for an end benefit to be obtained. Inevitably, forages are often of secondary importance to poor farmers, as food security is their main concern. The interest of farmers in participating in evaluation of forages is influenced by these and other factors. The decision whether to work with new communities and farmers in forage technology development is guided by five questions:

1. **Is there a genuine problem?** Very often, when we meet farmers for the first time and we are strangers to them, they will say, 'Yes, we have a problem' because they would like to work with us. Sometimes forages are just an entry point for them as they expect to receive free fertilizers or animals.
2. **Are there committed local individuals who can work with farmers to solve this problem?** There are few staff employed by the FSP project and we do not have fieldworkers. At the field level, we depend on availability of staff from the district agricultural services. We look for persons who are motivated and will not go into an area where such people are not available to help us.
3. **Do farmers think that this problem is important enough?** During the dry season, farmers' cattle often do not have enough feed. At the same time, their children might not have enough food to eat or they are malnourished. Farmers may have a higher priority than providing for animal feed needs, e.g. engaging in on-farm or off-farm activities that will bring in immediate cash to buy food.
4. **Are there many other farmers with the same problem in a region?** In order to ensure efficient use of resources we only work in locations where there is a minimum number of farmers interested in collaborating with us.
5. **Do we have potential solutions for substantial benefits?** There might be a problem of shortage of feeds but in certain circumstances we do not have options to offer. If for instance, the system is irrigated rice, every square metre is cultivated and there is very little land to plant forages for the buffaloes that plough the fields.

Role of participatory research

A major contributor to farmer adoption of forage technologies has been the process of farmer participatory research; that is where farmers are involved in planning and carrying out the evaluation of new species and in adapting the management of them to their farming system.

In practice, when scientists first begin to work with farmers in new projects, the degree of participation may be small. For example, it may be necessary to plant a demonstration in a village to enable farmers to become aware of various options. As farmers gain interest and confidence, so they naturally show more initiative and take on more responsibility.

FSP's research and development strategy

A research and development strategy using participatory approaches has been developed following many years of experience of working with farmers (Figure 18.1). The normal sequence of events is from 1 to 10 but there is no fixed formula. The first step is to gather secondary information and to carry out a rapid rural appraisal. Secondary information, from reports and key local informants, gives us an indication of the nature of the farming systems, livestock densities and farm problems. From this information, we can assess whether there is a need and opportunity for working in the area. If there is a need, we train extension workers from several districts in forage agronomy, participatory research and gender analysis. The training lasts for two weeks and may involve 20 participants. During this training, the more active and motivated extension workers, who can effectively lead work in the project, are identified.

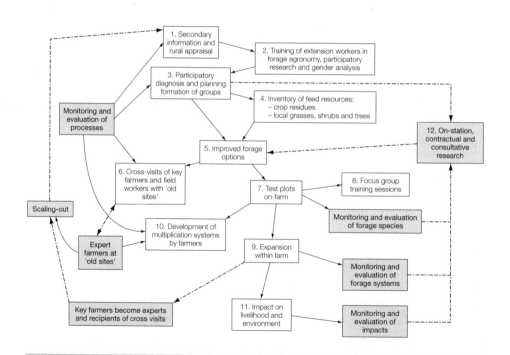

Figure 18.1   Participatory research and development processes

After we have selected motivated extension workers, we conduct participatory diagnoses and planning in selected villages where the initial appraisal has shown that there is a need and opportunity. This process normally takes 1–2.5 days. Problems are identified by the village community using participatory tools, such as mapping, calendars and flow diagramming. The problem diagnosis is followed by planning research and development activities to evaluate solutions to specific problems that might be solved using the farmers' own resources supplemented by seed and technical inputs from the project. Farmer groups may already exist. If not, we work with those farmers who have identified themselves during the diagnosis as being willing to invest their time and resources in testing new technologies. Regular farmer meetings are facilitated by fieldworkers, and often stable groups develop from these meetings.

Research issues identified at step 3 often lead to the evaluation of improved forage species, for biomass production, drought resistance and quality, under farm conditions. Researchers and experienced fieldworkers are able to provide forage species, and suggest forage systems that have been screened, modified and developed by other farmers in the region that will meet the specific needs of the new group of farmers. The project initially evaluated some 500 species and accessions of forage grasses and legumes. Out of those, 25–40 were well adapted to climate, soils and diseases, and are now widely adopted. They are the species options recommended for evaluation by new farmers.

The choice of introduced forage varieties to offer to farmers depends on the seasonal availability of existing feed resources. Sometimes the quality and availability of existing feed resources cannot be easily assessed during the participatory diagnosis phase. If local trees and shrubs form an important part of animals' diet, their quantity, availability and nutritive quality are often unknown. A high availability of good quality local tree fodder would reduce the need for research on exotic fodder trees. The inventory of feed resources, step 4, can be made a researchable issue if little is known about this. Nutritive value of local vegetation can be determined through participatory studies with key informants, and through laboratory analysis (Roothaert and Phengsavanh, 2001).

Where feasible, new farmers are taken on cross-visits to other farmers who have been working with the project for several years (step 6). Farmers with extensive forage experience are the best advocates to show how forages can make an impact on livelihoods, the livestock and the environment. Farmers learn a lot from other farmers. During these cross-visits, new farmers receive planting materials from the old farmers, and take them home to plant on their own farms. New farmers are encouraged to try more species than only the ones that grow well on the farms that they have visited. The new farmers plant test plots or strips, which are evaluated regularly by both farmers and field staff (step 7). In every new community, new champion farmers emerge, whose enthusiasm and experience is harnessed by the project. They in turn will become key farmers able to receive other farmers from new areas, to show them their experience in forage evaluation and utilization.

Some key farmers receive training on certain topics that interest them and that complement their on-farm research (step 8). Such topics have included training in animal nutrition, nursery techniques for forage trees and seed production. Farmers that have evaluated new forage germ plasm in small plots or strips expand the area planted with those species or accessions that show good growth (step 9). There are also other factors that determine whether or not a farmer expands, such as palatability of the forage, ease of harvest, ease of propagation, and low weediness potential. Later on, we find that farmers take other factors into consideration, e.g. whether the introduced forages can play a role in improving soil fertility, whether they compete with crops, and usefulness in soil and water conservation. Concurrently with the expansion activities, an interest in multiplication systems is developed (step 10). Often, the original test plots become multiplication plots to produce vegetative planting materials. Seed production is often low, especially in humid climates. If there is a strong market demand for seeds, such as improved accessions of *Leucaena leucocephala* or *Centrosema pubescens*, some individual farmers may choose to develop seed production systems.

Availability of planting material or seed can be a bottleneck for developing and expanding forage systems if it is not addressed systematically, and is essential for sustainability of forage development. Seeds of improved forages are rarely found in markets in rural areas. In the areas where FSP has been operating for five years, there is now a lively trade in vegetative planting materials and some legume seeds among farmers. Sale of planting materials also contributes to farmers' incomes.

Monitoring and evaluation are used to provide feedback to farmers and project implementers. It is relatively easy to monitor and evaluate forage technologies in terms of test plots on-farm, expansion within farm, and impacts on people, livestock and the environment. What is more difficult to monitor and evaluate is the effectiveness of the processes, such as collecting secondary information, conducting rural appraisal, participatory diagnosis, and cross-visits. How do we quantify the success of these elements? These processes are probably more appropriately evaluated by qualitative case studies than quantitative assessments.

Farmers' experience with growing improved forages often generates the need for new research. The results of such research are fed back as new options for farmers to evaluate.

The adoption process

Farmers' evaluation is a prerequisite for adoption. When a farmer has experimented with a species or a forage technology, and subsequently expands his cultivated area with the technology using his own resources, then we can talk of meaningful adoption or an adoptable forage system.

Farmer evaluation does not always result in adoption. About 25 per cent have dropped out of evaluating or using improved forages after between one and three years for various reasons, although this is highly variable between sites. Some farmers never reach the stage of expanding from test plots to larger areas due to labour constraints. Sometimes the forage plots cannot be properly protected, resulting in grazing by stray animals. Some had planted improved forages with the aim of qualifying for receiving animals from government loan schemes but, when the animals were not dispersed, they abandoned the plots.

What is a typical adoption process? First, the farmer tests grass and legume varieties and accessions in small plots and observes such things as yield and whether the grass stays green in the dry season or not. The second step is to evaluate the species by incorporating and/or adapting it in a forage system (Figure 18.2). The forage system includes the forage variety or species, the way it fits in with other crops, the cutting management, the contribution to soil fertility or degradation, the type of animals it can be fed to and the effect on the animals.

Some unique systems have been developed, such as feeding cut fodder to carp (*Ctenopharyngodon idella*) instead of cattle, because farmers discovered that this was more profitable. When such forage systems are tested and developed on-farm, and they are appreciated, more land is allocated to grow forages and expansion within the farm occurs. Expansion usually happens after every planting season, and can take place over many years.

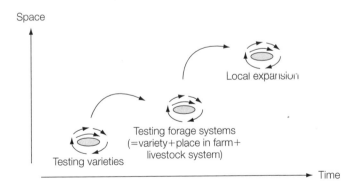

Figure 18.2   Adoption: from on-farm test plots to on-farm expansion

18.3 Some FSP research highlights

Developing forage technologies with smallholder farmers (Horne and Stür, 1999) was the outcome of screening of some 500 accessions of forage germ plasm on experimental stations in Indonesia and the Philippines, ending with about 40 varieties that are now widely adopted by farmers in more than six countries. The booklet is meant for fieldworkers and gives practical information about the most popular forage species and varieties. The way the forages can be grown and utilized, their adaptation to climates and soils, and their comparative advantages are all explained. The publication is also available in Chinese, Indonesian, Lao, Thai and Vietnamese.

The relationship between natural feed resources, improved forages and adoption of forage technologies is shown in Figure 18.3. Traditionally, farmers in South-east Asia have used natural grasses and crop residues to feed their cattle, goats and sheep. 'Adoption' of this system is 100 per cent, but ruminant productivity is only 25–35 per cent of its potential. In terms of animal nutrition, the limiting factor for productivity is energy intake and year-round feed supply. The first forage innovation that farmers usually adopt is the cultivation of new grass species. The new grasses establish easily and show impressive growth and biomass production. Most grasses are readily accepted by cattle. Adoption rates for improved grass accessions are high; about half of the farmers with livestock within the community that we work with start growing them within a year of introduction. Livestock productivity improves because of higher dry matter intake, more available energy and good quality feed in the dry season. Maximum ruminant productivity, however, is still not obtained, due to limitations of available rumen nitrogen and shortage of by-pass protein. It is only in the very intensive systems, such as

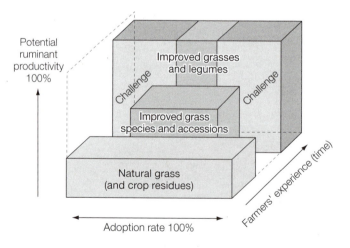

Figure 18.3 Relation between adoption rate of forage technologies, potential ruminant productivity, and time

the dairy cattle and dairy buffalo systems in Mindanao, Philippines, that farmers realize the protein limitation. In those systems, there is a demand for herbaceous and tree legume species that, when fed, cause a remarkable and immediate increase in milk production or milk fat content. Young stock fed on a mixture of grass and legumes get all the nutrients they need and can attain potential growth rates. The challenge of the project is to have more farmers experimenting with the optimal feed regimes, and to overcome constraints of initial slow establishment of legumes, seed availability and misconceptions of cattle and buffaloes not being able to eat herbaceous or tree legumes.

18.4 Scaling up

If all stakeholders, that is the farmers and government staff, are happy with the results of the forage evaluation and adoption, the next challenge is to allow more farmers to benefit. Replicating a forage system on new farmers' fields would seem ideal, but experience has taught us that this does not work. No two smallholder farms are the same, and farmers need to experiment with and develop their own forage systems. In addition, farmers need to learn to manage new systems. Identifying new areas where there is a need is another challenge. The FSP therefore uses the same strategy as described in Figure 18.1 when it comes to scaling up, proceeding through all ten steps. However, the process can be speeded up by using farmer to farmer visits and ensuring that there is ample planting material or seed.

Skilled and motivated local staff are essential for scaling up. New staff need training about forage accessions, agronomy, systems and participatory approaches. They must be equipped with good listening and facilitating skills, and they need to be able to analyse data and write reports. During the training courses, field staff with potential can be selected. Apart from skills, attitudes are also an important selection criterion for staff. Only those staff that are willing to accept change and learn new principles can learn about participatory approaches. Even then, it often requires a big mental change to be prepared to learn from farmers, listen to them and respect them.

In very remote areas, extension workers can be scarce. Another option that has worked well in the FSP is the use of experienced farmers as extension workers. In East Kalimantan, Indonesia, this is now a common practice. These farmers have detailed agronomic knowledge about the forage accessions and can provide useful tips that they have learned by experience. Cross-visits being facilitated by these leading farmers are lively and very convincing to new farmers. In every village key farmers can be found and used for extension purposes, if a modest remuneration for their service is provided.

Other lessons we have learnt are that it is important that focus sites where the technology is first developed are readily accessible and that it is impor-tant to have 'buy-in' at the provincial or other level that is responsible for decisions on extension, as well as involving district officers in the process. A serious effort is made to invite key agricultural or political officials at district or provincial levels to various training workshops and courses. Even though some rarely stay for the whole duration of the workshop, if they are given the opportunity to give opening speeches or keynote addresses, a bond is automatically created. Courtesy calls to some politicians or administrators at municipal or provincial levels during some stage of the project have done wonders for creating acceptance of methodologies, gaining logistic or financial support, or straightening out misunderstandings.

Capacity has been created among national partners to conduct training events autonomously. These events and other cross-visits are also vehicles for inviting and networking with NGOs and other government administrative units that the project is not directly involved with, but who can promote a further scaling out. It is very likely that more farmers benefit from the forage methods and technologies than the project actually records. At several sites where FSP has been operating for more than five years, and where local multiplication systems have been established, the testing, evaluating, utilization and scaling out of improved forages have become a sustainable process.

FSP scaling up

Table 18.1 shows how the FSP scaled up its activities, with many more farmers beginning to evaluate forages and forage systems. Some 5400 farmers participated in 297 participatory diagnosis sessions conducted in the six participating countries. Not all these farmers are necessarily adopters. Field staff note which farmers show enthusiasm and these are offered a trip to visit more experienced farmers who are evaluating and adopting forages. Although only 3163 farmers participated in the cross-visits, 4155 farmers planted forages. The higher number can be attributed to the 'ripple' effect of these visits; many farmers are organized in groups and share new experiences in group meetings.

Multiplication systems are essential for scaling up; without planting material scaling up cannot happen. In East Kalimantan farmers have organized themselves in groups for the purpose of producing planting materials. In several

Table 18.1 Scaling up of FSP and number of new farmers involved

Year	No. of participatory diagnoses conducted	No. of farmers participated in PD	No. of new groups	No. of cross-visits organized	No. of farmers participating in cross-visits	No. of new farmers planting forages
2000	45	1087	52	NA	NA	748
2001	151	2173	179	187	1330	1537
2002	101	2148	52	141	1833	1870
Total	297	5408			3163	4155

NA, not applicable.

cases a piece of land is made available by a farmer who has spare land. Every Friday, farmers come together to work on this multiplication area. They weed the field, uproot plants of improved species, divide them into splits, bag them and sell the material to other farmers. A few splits are returned to the land to produce more splits. If the forage becomes rank, the owner of the land is entitled to harvest fodder for his animals, a reward for making his land available. The whole group benefits from the income of the sales of planting material. Members of the group can obtain materials free of charge.

Production of seeds is more difficult and is usually done by individual farmers. Regulations on seed importation are still a problem in some countries. Seed-producing countries such as China, Thailand and Vietnam face difficulty in trading with other countries because of the lack of knowledge on individual countries' export–import regulations.

After the initial germ plasm screening at regional level, investments were made at each site in terms of rural appraisal, creating partnerships, participatory diagnosis and planning, and capacity building. This resulted in modest numbers of farmers adopting forages in the first few years. However, when local research and development systems were well established, the project gained momentum and the number of farmers adopting the new forage systems increased exponentially.

18.5 Benefits

Socio-economic studies were conducted in East Kalimantan, Indonesia; northern Vietnam; and Mindanao, Philippines, with farmers who had been with the FSP project for two years or more (Bosma et al., 2001, 2003). The aim of the study was to measure impact. Benefits that were mentioned across sites were: increased forage availability; better growth rates, health, fertility and body condition of animals; and reduced labour requirements to feed animals. The drastic reduction in labour requirements was because the farmers had to spend less time collecting the natural forages which are traditionally stall-fed at night. In the Philippines and Vietnam, women and children benefited more than men from reduced workload. In the Philippines and Vietnam, work capacity of draught animals increased. In Indonesia, the value of manure applied to food and cash crops often contributed to 40 per cent of the income generated by livestock, and manure production has become a lifeline in crop agriculture.

The benefits mentioned resulted in better financial performance of the livestock enterprises at household level. In Indonesia, the income from livestock increased from US$311 to US$392 per household per year, for systems with beef cattle and sometimes goats. In Vietnam the income increased from US$99 to US$199 for mixed systems with cattle, buffaloes and ponded fish. In the Philippines, the income increased from US$54 to US$157 for beef cattle systems, and from US$68 to US$503 for dairy cattle or dairy buffalo systems. When saved labour was valued in money, the additional increases in income were US$87, 52, and 36, respectively, for Indonesia, Vietnam and Philippines, respectively. Poorer farmers in Vietnam benefited most from improved forage technologies.

18.6 Conclusions

Several lessons were learned that have helped to develop the current research and development strategy used in the FSP.

- We need to provide 'building blocks' and not 'finished products'. In other words, the project should show the farmers the species and forage systems that have worked in other places and at the same time allow the new farmers to evaluate a range of optional species and develop their forage systems within their overall farming system.
- Adoption is a continuous process, taking into account that farmers modify the technology options that we provide and expand the areas cultivated with forages only if benefits are experienced.
- Impacts of forage technologies are on individuals within families and on particular groups within communities (e.g. wealth, gender and ethnic groups). If women, for example, spend most of the time cutting feed, then labour savings from introduced forages would benefit them. If the poorer sections of the community do not own cattle, forage technologies directed towards cattle feeding would provide them with no benefits. It is essential to be aware of the effect of technologies on different groups within the community.
- Investment in training of attitudes and skills of field staff is more difficult than training in technical subjects, but not less important. Results of some of these training courses can only be observed in the field.
- There are no short cuts in scaling up, new farmers need time to experiment as did the old farmers. However, advantage should be taken of the 'momentum' that is generated by the enthusiasm of staff, and the rapid expansion of training, development and research activities in the initial years of the project.
- Participatory approaches are fragile. Even where the project is highly effective at the local level, if officials at higher levels do not appreciate the use of participatory approaches, the project field staff will receive little support for what they believe in.
- Building partnerships at local, provincial and national level was crucial to obtain broad support for the initiative.

19 Case study H: Development of herbaceous forage legume technologies in central Kenya

David Miano Mwangi

SOME INTERESTING ASPECTS OF THIS CASE STUDY

Several attempts have been made to introduce herbaceous legumes on smallholder farms in central Kenya, but a survey undertaken in 1994 suggested that less than 20 per cent of farmers had started growing them. The project described in this case study investigated the reasons for non-adoption of the technology, and then sought to overcome the constraints that had been identified. These included: availability, cost and ease of handling seeds; and poor persistency of the legumes when grown together with Napier grass, which is quite widely grown. The researchers addressed these problems directly, and tried disseminating planting material in the form of stem cuttings, instead of seeds, promoting farmer-managed nurseries to supply the cuttings.

Previously, researchers had emphasized intercropping legumes with Napier grass, but in this project farmers were allowed to plant the legumes wherever they liked. This resulted in them identifying new niches, such as under avocado trees, where little else would grow. The on-farm research also revealed (to researchers) that the main species promoted, once established, was effective at suppressing weeds. Where the legume was intercropped with Napier grass, this characteristic proved to be a major benefit, as pure stands of Napier grass require a lot of weeding.

When evaluating legumes, researchers have traditionally focused on dry matter yield as their main criterion. However, this research shows that the main factor considered should be the ability of the legume to fit into the cropping and farming system; and that this can only be determined with confidence by actually testing the legumes in participatory on-farm research.

To promote the technology the researchers decided to work with 20 existing farmers' groups, and gave them responsibility for managing the nurseries, which proved to be very successful. The project was unusual in that it used GIS tools to determine areas in the country where the legume would grow well and would stand a good chance of adoption, based on milk market access, etc.

19.1 Introduction

The benefits of integrating forage legumes into fodder systems have been demonstrated adequately. A review by Saka et al. (1994) looks at the benefits of integrating forage legumes into different farming systems in sub-Saharan Africa. Recent work in Kenya has provided more information on the benefits in terms of dry matter yield (Mwangi et al., in press) and livestock performance (Kariuki et al., 1998a, 1998b). Despite all this the adoption of forage legumes by smallholder farmers has been very poor.

Several attempts have been made to introduce herbaceous legumes on smallholder farms in central Kenya. *Desmodium intortum* and *D. uncinatum* were introduced to smallholder farms in central Kenya by the national dairy development project (NDDP) a decade ago. The project recommendation was that the legumes should be grown together with Napier grass (*Pennisetum purpureum*) and harvested together with an aim of improving the nitrogen supply to the dairy cattle. More recently, the Kenya Agricultural Research Institute (KARI) introduced both herbaceous and shrubby legumes into the same area. The legumes were to be intercropped with food crops and planted grasses (Wandera, 1995). The Legume Research Network Project (LRNP) also introduced herbaceous legumes mainly as a green manure crop in areas of Embu in central Kenya.

In 1994, NDDP reported that out of 222 farms with a total of 536 ha surveyed in eastern Kenya, only 42 farms were growing herbaceous legumes on approximately 7.2 ha of land. The report did not indicate the proportion of the legume in the dry matter and therefore the importance of the legume in the system could not be determined.

Through the livestock feeds project funded by the UK's Department for International Development (DFID), which was part of the KARI's National Agricultural Research Project II (NARP II), an attempt was made to re-introduce forage legumes into the Napier grass (*P. purpureum*)-based fodder system in central Kenya. In an effort to improve the chances of smallholder farmers adopting the forage legumes the project employed a participatory approach. The project went through constraint identification and combined on-station and on-farm activities.

19.2 Constraints

Constraint identification

A survey was conducted in central Kenya to identify the major constraint to dairy production in central Kenya. A total of 254 farmers were interviewed in a formal survey. The survey identified lack of year-round feed (quantity and quality) as the main constraint limiting dairy production in the area. It was established that maize stover, which is low in nitrogen content, con-tributed a large proportion of the feed – especially during the dry season. This was associated with low milk production. Possible solutions to the prob-lem were discussed during the feedback sessions with farmers. The follow-ing potential solutions were discussed.

1. Planting of nitrogen-rich forages (NRF), i.e. forage legumes.
2. Feeding of protein-rich supplements, i.e. cotton seedcake, meat and bone meal, etc.
3. Increasing the amount of balanced dairy meal fed during the dry season.

The feeding of protein-rich supplements and dairy meal were not favoured due to the high cost involved; therefore, the growing of NRFs was thought to be the potential solution.

As NRF had already been introduced in the area without much success a topical PRA was conducted to determine the constraints that curtailed the adoption of the forages. A total of 33 farmers and 13 key informants (farmers involved with the previous attempts to introduce NRF) were interviewed. The farmers identified the main constraints to adoption as:

■ availability and cost of *D. intortum* seeds;
■ slow growth during the seedling stage;
■ failure to demonstrate clearly the benefits of herbaceous legumes especially at the farm level;
■ poor persistency of the legumes when grown together with Napier grass.

Availability, cost and ease of handling of seeds

The main source of legume seeds so far in Kenya has been small quantities supplied by researchers conducting on-farm experiments. The introduction of forage legumes has not been matched by the supply of seeds by commer-cial seed companies as is the case with other crops like hybrid maize. When available, most of the seeds are imported and are expensive: *D. intortum* seed costs approximately US$25 (Ksh 2000)/kg. Farmers grow on average 0.2 ha of Napier grass (Staal et al., 1998b) and therefore to grow *D. intortum* together with Napier grass they would require 500 g of seed (at a seed rate of 2 kg/ha). This amount would cost US$12.50 (Ksh 1000). In an area where the monthly income is estimated at US$83.3 (Ksh 6664) (Staal et al., 1998b) the seed would take approximately 15 per cent of the total monthly farm income. This high cost of seed, and the fact that the seeds are not readily available, make this otherwise good technology unattractive to farmers.

The legume seeds are small. Consequently, sowing requires extra care and hence requires extra labour at a time (planting season) when the demand for labour for planting food crops is high. The tiny seedlings that emerge make weeding difficult. Many farmers indicated that this weeding problem would be a major issue if they had to adopt the legume. In several instances the farmers unintentionally uprooted the legumes together with the weeds. The incidences of uprooting the legume were higher where labour was hired.

The conclusions from the study were that if the issues of availability, cost and difficulty of handling the seed and the seedling were not addressed then the technology was unlikely to be adopted. An alternative method of establishing the legume through stem cuttings (vines) was envisaged. Experiments conducted on-station showed no difference in dry matter (DM) yield when D. intortum was established through seed or stem cuttings: the survival rate of the stems was over 90 per cent. The survival rate of the stems was not different whether the legumes were established as a pure stand or in an intercrop with Napier grass. The farmers could easily relate to the planting of stem cuttings as this was similar to planting sweet potato vines, which they do all the time.

When the farmers learnt that they could establish D. intortum from stem cuttings and that the number of stems that the research team could provide was limited they started small nurseries, mainly near shallow wells on the farm or under banana plants where water and shade were available. These nurseries have now become sources of planting material, thus ending the dependency on the research team. Farmers used the materials from the nurseries to experiment with the legume. When the experiments started the only niche for the legume that was discussed with the farmers was the Napier grass stands. Farmers later planted the legume under coffee, banana and avocado trees, and on soil conservation structures. This planting and experimentation by farmers would not have been possible if the legume had to be established from seed. Planting stem cuttings made weeding the stand easier. Therefore, solving the propagation issue and putting the solution into farmers' hands increased the potential of adoption of the D. intortum technology. It must be emphasized that difficulties with propagation are a critical constraint to fodder adoption. The widespread adoption of Napier grass is mainly attributed to the ease with which it can be propagated (Mwangi et al., 1995).

The rest of this case study will focus on recent (1996–2002) activities to introduce D. intortum cv. Greenleaf through the National Agricultural

Research Project phase II (NARP II) and under the Smallholder Dairy (R&D) Project (SDP). Factors that affect the adoption of the legumes, and methods used in an attempt to overcome constraints, are discussed.

19.3 Legume characteristics and the production system

As indicated earlier, Napier grass is the main planted forage in central Kenya. Therefore, all attempts to integrate *D. intortum* into the farming system have focused on its role as a companion crop to Napier grass. In this work a participatory approach was used. A survey was conducted in Kandara division of Maragua District, one of the areas where the NDDP introduced *D. intortum* in central Kenya with the objective of identifying constraints to adoption and documenting farmers' experiences with the legume. A total of 33 farmers and 13 key informants (farmers involved with NDDP work) were interviewed. After the survey on-farm studies involving 15 smallholder farmers in the area were established. The on-farm studies were looking at the effect of growing Napier grass with or without legumes on DM yield. During the duration of these studies (approximately 1½ years) dialogue with the farmers was maintained and the experiences shared below were mainly from this period of constant interaction with the farmers.

Initial slow growth

As stated before, the main constraint to dairy animal performance in central Kenya is the inadequate year-round supply of good quality forage. As most forage legumes have a slow initial growth, farmers decided that the potential was low, and that the legumes were a waste of time and resources. Therefore, to have a good chance of adoption, any forage introduced to the area must be fast growing and high yielding. Napier grass is easy to establish, high yielding, and the planting material is readily available: these characteristics explain the adoption of the grass by a majority of smallholder dairy farmers (Mwangi et al., 1995; Staal et al., 1998b).

Failure to demonstrate clearly the benefits of herbaceous legumes, especially at the farm level

If farmers have to adopt a technology they must be able to see the benefits clearly. Sometimes technologies are not adopted not because they are not beneficial but because the benefits cannot be clearly demonstrated or are long term. The main benefits of forage legumes have included higher DM yield (Keya et al., 1971; Keya and Kalangi, 1973; Reategui et al., 1995; Shehu and Akinola, 1995; Mwangi, 1999); biological nitrogen fixation (BNF) (Cadisch et al., 1989; Thomas and Sumberg, 1995; Mwangi, 1999); improved soil fertility; and better animal performance, due to the improved nitrogen supply in the diet (Kariuki et al., 1998a, 1998b, 1998c). Some of these benefits are difficult to demonstrate on-farm, while others (like soil fertility improvements) are long term.

Poor persistency of the legumes when grown together with Napier grass

Poor persistency of forage legumes when grown together with Napier grass was cited by farmers as a major constraint in this technology. One farm had a substantial amount of *D. intortum* growing in a pure stand; but, apart from this, there was no trace of the legume in the Napier grass plots. It was suspected that Napier grass, which is a very competitive grass, had edged out the legume through competition. This apparent lack of persistency could have been caused by one of several things.

- The management (i.e. spacing, harvesting frequency, manure application, etc.) of Napier grass was not adjusted to accommodate the legume in the intercrop.
- The legume was planted in the same row with Napier grass tending to maximize between-species competition.
- The legume seed was drilled into an established stand of Napier grass, giving the young seedlings little chance to survive.

19.4 Combining on-station and on-farm experiments in technology development

On-station experiments were designed to deal with some of the factors identified in the survey. This included: identifying 'best bet' forage legumes that would fit into the Napier grass production system; defining suitable agronomic practices; and determining benefits associated with the forages. *D. intortum* and *Macrotyloma axillare* were identified as the potential companion legumes for Napier grass in terms of persistency and production. The on-station experiments were used to define the biological relationships.

The farmers who were carrying out the on-farm trials visited the on-station experiments and during the visits they discussed their observations with the research team and any concern they had. The visits helped the farmers evaluate the forage legumes grown on-station. This also helped farmers assess the growth of the legumes on their farms and compare this with what was happening on-station.

On-farm experiments were set up on 15 smallholder farms in central Kenya. Two of the 'best bet' forage legumes, *D. intortum* and *M. axillare*, were used in the trials and were intercropped with Napier grass. Seeds were used to establish the legumes. Germination was poor, and accidental weeding out of the legumes also occurred as farmers were managing the experiments. These problems were discussed with the farmers. As more seeds were not available, the possibility of establishing the legumes from cuttings was proposed. Experiments were set up on-station to determine whether the 'best bet' legumes could be established from cuttings: the findings were positive for *D.*

intortum and *M. axillare.* Farmers then established small nurseries near water wells and under bananas. These nurseries provided planting material, which meant that the farmers did not have to depend on the research station for planting material. As adequate planting materials of *D. intortum* were available, farmers started experimenting with the legume by growing it in niches that had not been discussed before. These included under coffee, under fruit trees like avocados and on soil conservation structures. Currently farmers are using these niches and also intercropping the legume with Napier grass. Planting under avocado trees became very popular with the farmers, as they discovered that *D. intortum* was doing very well in this niche where little else could grow.

The benefits of the legume forages discussed with farmers included higher biomass yield, nitrogen fixation and improved supply of nitrogen to the dairy cows. The research team overlooked the fact that *D. intortum* suppressed weeds after establishment. It is recommended that Napier grass plots should be weeded after every harvest, which is every 6–8 weeks: therefore, with a minimum of four cuts per year, the plot has to be weeded four times. Farmers indicated that it takes eight man-days to weed 1 ha of Napier grass. At the current rate of Ksh 150 (US$1.9) per day, it would cost at least Ksh 4800 (US$60) per year to weed a hectare of Napier grass. This became one of the most important benefits cited by the farmers as they spend a lot of time weeding their Napier grass plots.

The balance of legumes and grass in the intercrop was discussed with the farmers and management practices that would help maintain a productive legume in the intercrop were developed. These included cutting height, harvesting frequency and, in some cases, manure application.

19.5 Scaling up and scaling out

After evaluating forage legumes and validating the results on-farm, the main challenge is scaling up and out of the technology. If a technology is to have impact in an area then many more farmers than those involved in the pilot/testing group must adopt it. In the past, introduction of both herbaceous and shrubby legumes has been through individual farmers. This approach has its limitations, especially where nurseries have to be established.

In the scaling up and scaling out stage the group approach was adopted. The group approach means that the farmers can share the cost in terms of labour or inputs required for the nursery establishment. The presence of many community-based organizations (CBOs) (self-help groups, farmer co-operatives, NGOs, etc.) provided an opportunity to link with these groups. The groups helped in mobilizing the farmers and provided a favourable environment for awareness creation, training and distribution of planting materials. The ministry of agricultural and rural development (MoARD) extension staff, the Dairy Goat Association of Kenya (DGAK), Systemwide

Livestock Programme (SLP), LRNP and 20 farmer groups were involved in the scaling up activity. Participatory approaches were used in training and working with farmers and partners from the public extension service, CBO and NGOs. This aimed at developing and enhancing strategic partnerships between farmers, researchers and extension agents (both public and private).

GIS (geographical information system) tools were used to determine areas in the country where the legume would grow based on biophysical conditions. This was then taken further to determine areas where adoption of the technology was most likely, based on milk market access, production systems and levels of intensification. The three areas chosen were: Maragua District, representing an area with good access to milk market; and Embu and Kirinyaga Districts, representing medium and low access respectively. Four farmer groups were selected in Maragua District, eight each in Embu and Kirinyaga Districts. The groups were then supplied with a small number of *D. intortum* cuttings to establish nurseries, and with information on how to grow and utilize the legume. Some of the groups decided to start group nurseries while others shared out the materials and started individual farmer nurseries. The group nurseries were a big success and within the first season it was estimated that close to 25 000 cuttings had been produced and distributed to group members for planting. There are indications at the moment that groups that decided to share out the planting materials to start individual nurseries have not produced as many cuttings as those that decided to start groups. Anecdotal information suggests that farmers not involved in the study have received planting material from farmers with nurseries and in turn started their own nurseries.

19.6 Implications and lessons learned

One of the lessons learnt from this work is that germ plasm availability and cost can curtail the adoption of an otherwise excellent technology. As in the case of herbaceous legumes presented here, information available from the SLP on the introduction of shrubby legumes like *Calliandra calothrysus* indicates that availability of planting material and the ease of propagation are critical issues that must be addressed if the legume technologies are to be adopted by farmers. Giving farmers free seedlings or seeds from international research centres, research projects or NGOs, reduces their ability and willingness to use resources available at farm level to produce their own planting material, as they will be expecting more free material to be provided. On the other hand, it will be futile to introduce the technology without ensuring that some planting material is available. Therefore, the aim should be to move the farmers from the point where they are dependent on research institutions and NGOs to a point where they can handle the technology with little or no intervention from outside their systems. Therefore, it would be wise to address the problems of germ plasm availability and propagation early in the phase of forage technology development, otherwise adoption will be poor. The survival rate of the stems was over 90 per cent on-farm for *D. intortum*.

Adoption of any technology is enhanced when farmers can easily see the benefits. Therefore, short-term benefits should be emphasized, although the long-term ones should also be mentioned. Visits to research centres or to other farmers will help farmers visualize the potential of the technology. In situations where mother–baby trials can be set up, they should be encouraged as the mother trials help the farmer see the potential of the technology in their own environment, unlike in research centres where the situation might be very different. Visits to research stations by farmers could also enhance their understanding of the technology, but where possible the experiments should be carried out on-farm. Controlled experiments could be carried out in institutions such as public schools, co-operative society farms and farmer training centres close to the farmers. These would enable the farmers to visit the experiments often and reduce the cost of moving farmers long distances to research stations.

Working with farmer groups enables the research and extension agents to reach more farmers using the resources available. The approach enhances adoption of technologies as the farmers share experiences, labour and other inputs required for the technology to succeed. In this particular case group nurseries succeeded as farmers took turns in watering the nurseries. Therefore the time taken in watering the nurseries per farmer was significantly reduced. It may also enhance wider adoption as each farmer can potentially pass the technology to a few other farmers. There is a risk, however, that the most proactive farmers may be upset, because they feel they are making effort for the weaker farmers who gain benefits they feel should remain with them. It is necessary to tell the farmers the minimum they would have to do to see any effects/benefits of the technology.

Germ plasm evaluation should be done in the system where the forage will be grown. Currently forage legumes are evaluated in small plots and in pure stands while maybe the aim is to grow them together with companion grass. In the current method of evaluation DM yield is the main factor considered while the ability to fit into a system, i.e. intercropping, might be the issue to consider.

Farmers should be encouraged to assess every technology in their own environment and to use their own criteria, as this will bring up technology benefits that are important to farmers but possibly not considered important by the researchers.

The participatory approach is expensive and time-consuming, but the benefits in terms of potential adoption are likely to be far greater and hence outweigh the cost.

20 Case study I: Development of the Kebkabiya donkey plough in Western Sudan

Mohamed Siddig Suliman

SOME INTERESTING ASPECTS OF THIS CASE STUDY

The Kebkabiya Smallholder Project (KSP) was initiated by Oxfam after the 1984–85 drought. KSP aimed to empower the communities, strengthen the position of the poor and increase food security. Animal traction was seen as an important means of increasing food security, but it was largely absent from the area, and the only widely owned animal capable of ploughing was the donkey. A careful needs assessment was undertaken, which proved to be a prerequisite for success. It was decided to develop a donkey-drawn plough suitable for the local conditions that could address farmers' main constraints on crop production, which were weeding and excessive run-off. A participatory process was adopted, involving blacksmiths as producers, and farmers as users. After several years of experimentation an effective plough was developed that reduced labour requirements, and increased crop yields, planted area and food security.

However, there was another major challenge to overcome, namely ensuring that the poorest farmers could use the plough. They faced two constraints: lack of cash to purchase ploughs and lack of donkeys – about one-third of the poorer households had no donkeys. A pay-by-instalment system was developed to address the first constraint. The second was addressed by facilitating the sharing of a donkey and plough between two households, one owning the donkey and the other the plough. Now more than 3000 ploughs have been distributed.

Capacity building of blacksmiths and farmers, through training and group formation, has been an essential part of the project, as has provision of credit. These activities were made possible because the PTD process was part of a larger development project. Furthermore, the development of the plough took about 10 years, which is longer than most research projects last.

20.1 Introduction

The greater Darfur region is divided into three states: west, south and north Darfur. North Darfur state, which lies on the southern edges of the Sahara Desert, has been identified as one of the poorest states in Sudan. The population was estimated to be 1 364 294 (1993 census). The area has intermittent variable rainfall, suffering consecutive drought years. This results in poor harvest and loss of animals; and collapse of the rural economy, which is based on rain-fed agriculture.

Kebkabiya province is situated in the south-west of North Darfur state, at the bottom of Jabal Marra, a famous mountain. The area is characterized by remoteness, lack of infrastructure and low rainfall (less than 400 mm). The main soil type is sandy loam with a hard surface crust (locally called *qoz* soil), which leads to excessive run-off. Water courses, locally known as wadis, drain from the mountains.

Ploughs were not known to the majority of North Darfur's farmers until 40 years ago. Some ploughs were hired during the 1980s from plough owners who travelled with their camels from the southern parts of greater Darfur to the northern parts, providing plough services to richer farmers on irrigated farms with wadi (clay) soil. Due to various factors, including an upsurge in camel theft, the use of camels has been declining.

Farming system

Rain-fed subsistence farming, complemented by transhumance with small ruminants, is the basic means of livelihood in the area. The farm unit is based on a nuclear family. Land for cultivation is the basic resource: every household has access to land in qoz (sandy) or wadi.

Millet is the main staple crop, covering 70 per cent of the total cultivated area, and is mixed with sesame and sorghum. It is mainly planted in qoz soil. On wadi land okra and tomato have been traditionally cultivated for household consumption, but recently this land has been used intensively for cash crop production. In spite of drought, wealthy farmers still practice small-scale irrigation on wadi land where the water table is still high, producing cash crops such as onion, broad beans, chickpeas and carrots.

20.2 History of plough development

Oxfam Darfur started work in the area in 1984, providing relief support during the famous drought. Kebkabiya Smallholder Project (KSP) was initiated by Oxfam after the 1984–85 drought. The ultimate goals were: (i) empowering of the KSP communities; and (ii) strengthening the position of the poorer men and women. The three intermediate objectives were: increasing food security, increasing control over available resources and empowering the most disadvantaged groups. Animal traction was seen as an important means of increasing food security, and as relevant to the other objectives too.

Initial Oxfam trials on animal traction: replication of Jabel Marra Rural Development (JMRDP) and Western Savanna Development Corporation (WSDC) project implements

JMRDP, which was implemented from 1971 to 1994, developed the traditional mouldboard camel plough to suit the soil conditions of the area and the donkey as the source of draught power. WSDC developed a donkey-drawn seeder/weeder, after unsuccessfully promoting tractorization. The early work in Kebkabiya conducted by Oxfam tested the seeder/weeder developed by WSDC. This implement had shown very good performance on the sandy qoz soil of Southern Darfur State, but proved unsuitable for use on the hard surface sandy loam soil of Kebkabiya. It facilitated quick sowing, which was the main constraint in the WSDC area, but it was less effective in

---

BOX 20.1 History of ITDG in the area

ITDG started working in Darfur in 1988. A primary survey study was conducted to identify suitable areas for ITDG intervention according to the organization's mandate, and it was decided to provide technical support to Oxfam. The work has passed through several phases.

- **Investigatory phase 1988–89**: conducting survey for primary study

- **Provided technical support to Oxfam Kebkabiya smallholder project (KSP) 1989–94**

- **Consolidating phase 1994–96**: working with Kebkabiya smallholder's charity society project (KSCS). Oxfam handed over the project to the community

- **LINK project (linking indigenous knowledge) 1996–98**: as part of this project, the animal traction experience gained by ITDG was spread and replicated in a new and larger Oxfam operational project targeting 100 000 households

- **Scale up of LINK to DARLIVE project 1998–2001**: the core was the package developed in the LINK project, complemented with new technical areas (agro-processing and rural transport)

- **Food security programme 2002– to date**: food security is the main focus. The programme is replicating the experience gained, using the ITDG development package, which remains the key element in this project

weeding, which was the main constraint in Kebkabiya. It was also light and not stable during operation.

UK prototype mould board plough: 1987–88

In 1987 Oxfam sent an agricultural engineer to the UK for training in animal traction technology. The engineer brought a mouldboard donkey plough from the UK, whose frame was made of steel pipes and which had a front wheel. Testing showed that it was small in size, light in weight, and that adjusting the cutting depth through the wheel was time-consuming. Oxfam decided to support further plough modification and development, and to train local blacksmiths from a marginalized ethnic group, the Zaghana. They are very skilled, and it was envisaged that they would play an important role in donkey plough modification, although they had never made ploughs before. To do this they needed to be equipped with the basic tools and knowledge for designing and manufacturing.

At the other side of greater Darfur, in Nyala, there was a blacksmith called Halato. He had considerable experience in plough design and manufacture, gained through his large workshop, which had benefited from the high demand for donkey ploughs from JMRDP and WSDC. The projects used him as a pioneer designer. Halato is a cunning entrepreneur. He has trained many blacksmiths, but in such a way that each of them can produce only one plough part, and none of them can produce a whole plough, assembling all the parts himself in his workshop.

Oxfam contracted Halato to train seven Zaghawa blacksmiths from Kebkabiya. Seven donkey ploughs produced by them were tested in community demonstration farms, in four villages in Kebkabiya area, adjacent to the main roads passing to Kebkabiya. Farmers observed the ploughing operation. At first they laughed at the idea of using a donkey, but a few farmers showed interest and borrowed the donkey plough and used it in their plots.

The testing showed that the plough was too heavy for the donkey, and it did not speed up agricultural operations significantly. Nevertheless, the farmers and village extension agents who had used the plough recommended continuing with plough modification. ITDG was contracted to provide technical support in identifying, testing and developing an appropriate donkey implement to solve farmers' constraints (i.e. weeding and excessive run-off), and to develop a suitable training package.

ITDG involvement in plough development

Oxfam Darfur requested technical support from ITDG for the animal traction component in 1988. To provide background information for identifying an appropriate animal-drawn implement, two surveys were undertaken at the beginning of ITDG involvement.

1) A technical survey of the status of animal traction in the area and the technologies available.
2) A socio-economic survey, which obtained information about food security, agricultural problems, possible solutions, social wealth strata among the community, animals owned, and affordability of project inputs to poor farmers.

The major findings of the surveys were as follows.

1) There was considerable interest in using animal traction in the area, some farmers already being familiar with camel ploughs.
2) A large proportion (32 per cent) of poorer households had no donkey.
3) The percentage of women-headed households was particularly high: they represent 30 per cent of the community, and women in general had not seen ploughs or heard about testing the donkey plough.

Based on the technical and social survey findings, it was decided that the plough developed should be:

- affordable for the majority of farmers (particularly women);
- suitable for cultivating the specific soil types and farming system in the area;
- easy to operate and maintain;
- suitable for operations that farmers found most arduous;
- suitable for the draft animal available to the majority in the project area;
- suitable for manufacturing locally.

Halato's plough design was not good enough to be promoted in the area. However, animal traction is not only confined to mouldboard ploughs. According to the climate and soil type a chisel plough would be most appropriate. In addition, it would not require a large amount of steel. The project thought about the Ard, which is an old type of chisel plough, with only the blade made of steel. To give farmers choices, ITDG decided that the mouldboard plough and Ard would be developed and tested in parallel.

Modification of Ard plough: KSP

A prototype Ard was brought from the UK, which was the product of work done by a consultant, together with the University of East Anglia's Rural Technology Unit. Blacksmiths at one of the KSP centres copied the blade with two wings, and produced the wooden frame from live wood. The Ard was tested by the blacksmiths. The results showed various problems. Further modifications to the Ard were made to address them. The blacksmiths developed their own solutions and produced modified Ards that were then tested in the four KSP centres in demonstration farms and by individual farmers.

At the same time, modifications to the mouldboard design were being made by another blacksmith group. The Ard and the mouldboard plough were tested in the same demonstration farms. The results of the Ard trials were not encouraging: difficulty in adjusting it was the main problem. Farmers also complained that it had not formed ridges or controlled weeds effectively. Another disadvantage was that it was environmentally unsound, in that the main beam was made from live wood. The modified Halato mouldboard plough showed significant acceptance by farmers, despite having its own disadvantages, i.e. needing larger quantities of steel and having a higher draught requirement.

Development of donkey mouldboard plough process (Kebkabiya plough)

Trained blacksmiths (Halato trainees) produced seven mouldboard ploughs. All of these were tested in 1990 in four demonstration farms, and 16 village extension agents (VEAs) were trained in plough use. Farmers' interest was raised by the work on the demonstration farms, and a few farmers borrowed a plough from VEAs and used it in small plots about one-quarter Fedan in size (1 acre = 2.5 Fedan), for comparison, and to assess the benefit. The results were encouraging, so it was decided to continue with the Halato version. The project ordered 100 more ploughs from Halato, to be sold to richer farmers who could afford to take on the risk. These farmers tested the plough, which gave a good opportunity to measure the plough benefit and to assess the farmers' acceptance and demand. Encouraging results provided the impetus to plan strategically on several fronts. Development of the plough was taken forward in a participatory way in a process involving blacksmiths as producers, and farmers as users, with a little technical advice from the project engineer. The issues addressed were:

- tackling technical problems of the Halato plough design;
- Halato's monopoly on production;
- affordability (high price);
- steel problems;
- technical know-how, software and hardware.

The plough had several technical problems, including the following ones. It was very heavy (weight = 32 lb); it twisted during ploughing and was difficult to control; and steel used in the frog part (locally called the chair) was light, making it bend easily. The mouldboard was very large, which increased soil resistance and required strong draught animal power (not suitable for donkey power). The land side was very short and made of steel angle, which made the plough unstable and difficult to control and keep in a straight line. Some parts welded during assembly posed difficulties for repair and maintenance, as welding was not available at the village level.

Work continued for three years to tackle the technical faults until the final and accepted donkey plough (called the Kebkabiya plough) was successfully developed in 1994. Each year farmers observed some technical problems, and fed back their views in a participatory process through exchange visits, either farmers to farmers or blacksmiths to farmers or vice versa. Then modifications were made before the next rainy season.

In 1990 training began of two of the seven blacksmiths who had been trained by Halato. Plough problems were discussed, they showed interest in collaborating and they accepted further on-the-job training in plough design and manufacture. The project provided steel and their food. The blacksmiths' training took more than six months. These blacksmiths subsequently trained others. They produced another 17 ploughs. The changes made over the three years resulted in:

- a decrease in the plough's weight, from 32 to 22 lb;
- a 40 per cent decrease in the size of the mouldboard;
- use of stronger steel in the frog part of the plough; and
- use of bolts and nuts to assemble the plough parts, instead of welding.

20.3 Distribution of ploughs

Getting them to the poorest

The socio-economic survey conducted in 1989–90 showed that the majority of households were not able to afford the plough. Ploughs had been sold to better-off pioneer farmers, counter to the project's overall philosophy of targeting the poorer farmers. The project decided to find a more equitable approach or system. An instalment system was introduced, based on how much poor women could afford to pay. Plough uptake by women at the beginning was less than expected, considering that women carry out 80 per cent of agricultural activities: this was partly due to their belief that ploughs are only for men and not for women. At the beginning women were given 50 per cent of the total number distributed to each centre, but women used to purchase a plough on behalf of their husbands. Nevertheless, demand from women grew over the years, from 3 per cent of the total number distributed in 1993 to 60 per cent after 1995.

In 1993 ploughs were distributed with payments in two instalments: 50 per cent of plough price, when the farmer received the plough, and 50 per cent after the harvest. Later this was increased to four instalments. The price of the plough was one barrier, and another was lack of access to a donkey. This problem was solved by sharing one donkey between two families: one owned the plough and the other owned the donkey. A donkey can also be borrowed from relatives, although it is not easy to obtain one for heavy work like cultivation.

Number of ploughs produced

The number of ploughs produced and purchased has increased over the years, and dissemination continues without the involvement of the project. More than 3000 ploughs have been manufactured and distributed since 1990, and now they can be seen everywhere. In Kebkabiya, 1364 were distributed by the projects between 1990 and 2000; and in the locations covered by the LINK project 872 were distributed between 1997 and 2000. In Kebkabiya, the numbers distributed annually by the projects declined during the 1990s, as blacksmiths increasingly manufactured and sold ploughs independently.

20.4 Capacity building

Human capacity building

Large numbers of blacksmiths and farmers have been trained in plough manufacture and use respectively. About 100 blacksmiths have been trained altogether. Since 1990, training has been provided to farmers using the ploughs in the following:

- practical used of ploughs using a video film show;
- how to train a donkey to pull the plough and donkey feeding regime;
- technical extension package (plough pattern, ploughing timing, use of donkey, intercropping, cash crops, crop spacing);
- design and selection of local material for harnessing.

Institutional capacity building

ITDG has supported the formation of charitable societies for blacksmiths in different locations, whose main aim is to supply their members with steel and assist them in marketing. ITDG provided them with working capital and training in book-keeping and management, and in some cases supported the construction of premises. These societies are now functioning effectively, which should help to ensure the sustainability of plough-making in the state. Innovation is continuing, with the development of larger ploughs that can be used by camels or horses.

ITDG has worked in 186 villages through their village development committees (VDCs), whose formation it has supported. The VDCs co-ordinate development activities, and facilitate access by members to seeds and tools, including ploughs, through purchasing, renting or borrowing.

20.5 Benefits of the mouldboard donkey plough

Impact on farmers

Promotion and adoption of the donkey plough in North Darfur State has had a huge impact on the lives of farming households. The area ploughed each year is about 7500 hectares. The major change in traditional cultivation activities is the first cultivation, in which three activities are now combined – ploughing, weeding and planting. This has resulted in improved tillage and seedbed preparation, increased water infiltration and retention, and less time (> 50 per cent reduction) spent on land preparation, weeding and planting. The benefits for farmers are reduced drudgery, diversification of crop production, and increased yields and food security. Yields have increased by

50–114 per cent, and the cultivated area by 86–200 per cent. In addition, most of the farmers started diversifying their crops, mainly introducing cash crops.

There have also been improvements in children's health and education that may be indirectly attributable to the widespread adoption of the mouldboard plough.

Impact on blacksmiths

Blacksmiths' weekly income has doubled, enabling them to double their expenditure on household needs. They are now food secure; and they have built up their assets through restocking animals, purchasing fertile irrigation farms, etc. Social barriers facing this previously marginalized group have gradually dissolved. Blacksmith's children are now accepted and enrolled in the neighbouring villages schools for the first time. Plough production has given them high recognition and some of them are members of village committees.

20.6 Conclusions and lessons learned

The project faced a number of weaknesses and challenges during the first few years that were gradually overcome and from which lessons can be learned. These were:

- development of the technology took longer because of a lack of animal traction experience among farmers, blacksmiths and the project staff;
- there was insufficient training in plough use at the village level, training being confined to KSP centres;
- exclusion of the poorer households when plough distribution was through direct sale and no credit facilities were available;
- Scarcity of steel in the state resulted in high plough prices, again reducing its accessibility to the poor.

Several other lessons can be learned from more than 10 years involvement in plough development.

- Effective development and adoption of the plough was made possible by the fact that this was done as part of a development project, which meant that credit and training could be given to both blacksmiths and farmers.
- Involvement of producers and users early in the project enhanced the contributions of each in the technology development process, enabling them to contribute their knowledge and giving them enthusiasm and a feeling of ownership of the innovations.
- A careful needs assessment is an essential element for the success of any project, particularly those focusing on technology development,

in this case indicating the type of tool required and the donkey as the source of power.

- The farmers' and blacksmiths' CBOs have proved to be essential in institutionalizing plough production and utilization.
- CBOs formed as a result of natural growth from an informal body are more successful than those started formally, and the pace of group formation and development should not be forced.
- The development of the plough was a long-term process, taking about 10 years, and would have been impossible without financial support over that period.
- The technology development process facilitated producers (blacksmiths) and customers (farmers) to interact closely, so that the design continuously improved until it eventually satisfied the customers' requirements.
- Special steps are required to ensure that the poorest households are able to acquire the technology.

21 Case study J: Tzotzil shepherdesses and Chiapas wool sheep, Mexico

Raul Perezgrovas

SOME INTERESTING ASPECTS OF THIS CASE STUDY

Participatory technology development (PTD) is usually carried out by farmers and researchers on-farm: this is the only case study in this book that describes PTD that has been conducted on-station. This distinguishing feature arises from the nature of the research – research aimed at genetic improvement would be difficult to implement on numerous small farms.

Previous initiatives to improve the local sheep in this part of Mexico, which are kept for wool production, had involved the introduction of exotic breeds for cross-breeding purposes, but they had failed for two reasons. First, the exotic breeds were poorly adapted to the local environment, and second, their wool was not amenable to the traditional spinning and weaving techniques of the Tzotzil women. This project was the first to seek genetic improvement through selective breeding of the local sheep themselves. Largely unsuccessful cross-breeding programmes have been the norm in research on genetic improvement in various types of livestock, and improvement of local breeds the exception, which gives this case study a relevance beyond sheep.

A small flock of the local Chiapas sheep was built up at the University's Sheep Centre in the Highlands region. The Tzotzil shepherdesses visited the centre to see the sheep that they had sold to the University, and they became partners in the selection process. The initial emphasis was on increasing the quantity of wool, but later improving quality became the main focus. A fleece quality grade was designed jointly by the women and the sheep scientists, and the assessment of fleece quality was done using the women's own measurement system, based on finger distances. Fleece quantity in the University flock has roughly doubled, and quality has improved by about 25 per cent, but disseminating the benefits among the villagers is proving to be a major challenge.

21.1 Introduction

Very little is known about either Tzotzil shepherdesses or Chiapas sheep, and yet both have significant roles for the livelihoods of thousands of Tzotzil families living in the mountains of Chiapas State, in Southern Mexico. Nine ethnic groups are settled in Chiapas, each one of them speaking their own language, and having unique culture and traditions. The Tzotzils live under extremely marginal conditions, and they are characterized by their typical woollen clothes and by the special form in which they carry out the husbandry of sheep.

Facts of Tzotzil life

The Tzotzils live in small hamlets spread all over the mountains, and they live very simple lives. Men are in charge of crops, for which they have to travel and rent land in the valleys situated in the lower parts of the State. They stay out of the hamlets most of the time, preparing the land for the cultivation of maize and beans. It is very common to see them walking up and down the paths on the mountains, wearing their heavy black coats or their white sleeveless jackets, both of them made out of wool by the women, who transform the fleeces of their sheep by means of ancient textile techniques.

A quick view of the Tzotzil household shows a single-room house, a small annexe for cooking purposes, a wooden shelter for the sheep, small patches of crops of different vegetables, and a few fruit trees. A number of chickens are kept free range, and occasionally a pig is observed nearby, tied with a rope. Women are in charge of the households while the men stay at the lowlands, and they care for the family, the animals, and the crops. You can see them very busy all the time, proudly wearing their black woollen skirts and shawls, and their brown woollen blouses richly embroidered with colourful motifs.

We all know that sheep were introduced into the New World early in the sixteenth century, but it is not so clear how these animals became such an important feature of the Tzotzil culture. The fact is that, nowadays, all the sheep in the mountains are in the hands of Tzotzil women, and sheep husbandry accounts for up to 36 per cent of the family income, through homemade clothing and the selling of fleeces, sheep, woollen handicrafts and manure. Besides, sheep are the only domestic animals which are considered sacred, and the Tzotzil religion prohibits the killing of these animals or the consumption of their meat. Tzotzil men do not participate in any of the sheep-related activities or in the transformation of wool into clothes; these are the exclusive responsibility of women.

The importance of sheep for the Tzotzil livelihood is evident, and several government programmes were developed over the past 30 years aiming to improve the local breed and the traditional husbandry practices. A number of exotic sheep breeds have been introduced, such as Rambouillet, Columbia and Romney Marsh, but they suffered the same fate: lack of adaptation, sickness, and death within a few weeks. Besides the survival problems, Tzotzil women were not able to transform the fleeces of these animals using their traditional spinning and weaving techniques: the wool was too short, too fine and too white. For the expert Tzotzil artisans, all those exotic sheep were considered 'foreign', and could not compare with their sacred *batsi chij*, their 'true sheep'.

21.2 A sustainable alternative approach

A different approach was necessary, and the initial characterization of the local wool sheep, undertaken by the University of Chiapas, led to the comprehensive study of the traditional sheep management system designed by many generations of Tzotzil shepherdesses. These two elements – a perfectly adapted breed of sheep, and an efficient husbandry system to keep them alive and productive – were considered as the basis of a new way to improve the livelihood of the Tzotzils. For the first time, the cross-breeding approach was avoided, and a genetic improvement programme was proposed in order to have sheep of the local breed selected to produce heavier fleeces of higher quality.

The genetic improvement programme got started in 1991, when a dismantled federal research and extension facility in the Highlands region – the Sheep Centre – was lent to the University of Chiapas, and a small flock of the local breed, now identified as 'Chiapas sheep', was formed. An open nucleus scheme was chosen as the selection strategy. Tzotzil women are not used to selling ewes, especially the lambs and the young ones, and the initial flock took some time to develop. Being used to selling the sick and the old sheep, it was difficult to convince the shepherdesses that the yearlings were not going to be slaughtered, but kept only for breeding purposes. A strategy that paid dividends was to invite those women selling sheep to come to the Sheep Centre at will, to visit their former flock members.

At the beginning, greasy fleece weight within a given phenotype was used as the only selection parameter. The objectives of the programme were easily established since meat production has no cultural or economic significance for the Tzotzil families, while heavier fleeces of different colours were very important to them. The three phenotypic varieties of the local sheep were used as reference within the selection programme. The white Chiapas sheep has white skin and fleece, with distinctive black markings on eyelids, lips, nostrils and ears. The black variety has black skin and fleece, with white markings on top of the head and tip of the tail. The brownish-greyish variety has yellow to brown skin and creamy white wool.

These three varieties produce fleeces of different colours, and all of them have a place within the Tzotzil culture. Ceremonial and daily-use clothes are made by the women using the fleeces of their sacred Chiapas sheep, spinning fibres into thread with a wooden spindle, and weaving thread into garments with a back-strap loom. The textile process is very complex and time-consuming, and requires great skill and physical strength. Even though a girl can be a capable shepherdess at a very young age, she will be a teenager by the time she masters the art of weaving. She is then ready to inherit her initial flock of two or three sheep and get married, starting the cycle once more.

Most ceremonial clothes are black, and there are also daily-use skirts and shawls of that colour, but white and brown woollen garments are part of the typical clothing too. The traditional clothes were the reason for the conservation of coloured sheep, and the requirements of the traditional textile process have directed the empirical selection of sheep carried out by the Tzotzil shepherdesses over a period of almost five centuries. The contribution of these women to the preservation of genetic biodiversity still awaits proper acknowledgement.

It took the University of Chiapas five years to form a sizable nucleus flock. At least 20 ewes were bought directly from Tzotzil shepherdesses each year, while visiting different hamlets, and they were introduced into the selection nucleus. Eventually, superior rams from the programme would be taken into village flocks to sire superior lambs. Parameters associated with the production of wool have high heritability and thus have a good chance of passing to the next generation.

The colour and weight of the fleece were important parameters and the basis of the selection programme during the first five years. In 1996, however, the high correlation between body weight and greasy fleece weight suggested the inevitable selection bias towards larger and heavier animals, which would have a terrible time trying to meet their nutritional demands with the scarce forage availability in the highlands of Chiapas. This situation triggered the quest for more adequate selection variables, including qualitative parameters; these should necessarily be indicated by the experts, the Tzotzil shepherdesses and weavers. The regular presence of women from the villages at the Sheep Centre – visiting the former members of their flocks – was the clue, and a participatory approach was used to establish the qualitative criteria used empirically by the women for the selection of Chiapas sheep.

Defining the local standards

A series of participatory exercises with women from different hamlets gave valuable insight information on their empirical basis for the selection of sheep. All Chiapas sheep have a double-coated fleece, with loose conical staples including both the short-fine and the long-coarse fibres. The existence of these two types of fibres had not been acknowledged until the Tzotzil women shared their expertise with the sheep scientists, and it was going to become one of the most important aspects of the selection programme. The importance of a third type of fibre – the unwanted kemp – was also recognized at the time.

Preference ranking matrices were used to identify the concepts and to establish the relative importance of the different selection parameters used empirically by the Tzotzil shepherdesses. Staple length was always at the top of the list, along with a high proportion of long-coarse fibres. A low amount of kemp, the colour of wool, and the softness and cleanliness of the fleece were also signalled. This was the 'theoretical' basis of empirical selection, and a series of 'practical' exercises followed when the women evaluated fleece quality in sheep of the nucleus flock.

As a result of the participatory approach, a 'fleece quality grade' was designed with input from both the Tzotzil women and the sheep scientists, and it was to be incorporated into the databases of the nucleus flock. Since then (1996), women from different Tzotzil villages have been responsible for the practical assessment of fleece quality, which is now a standardized procedure within the selection programme. As a novelty in Mexican agricultural research, Tzotzil women – mostly illiterate – were collaborating as research scientists in a joint academic programme, the genetic improvement of Chiapas sheep.

Interacting with the sheep scientists, women from the villages would assess the characteristics of the fleece in all the animals under two years of age within the nucleus flock. This grading of the fleeces would be carried out a few days before the shearing of the sheep, twice a year, in spring and autumn.

The combination of key words exchanged among the women while performing the assessment of fleece quality of an animal allowed the sheep scientists to assign a compounded quality grade going from 1 (poor) to 4 (excellent), integrating both staple length and textile aptitude. Grades would be included in the databases for statistical analyses.

At the time, the aim of the programme was no longer the production of greasy fleece weight but the 'efficiency' in wool production, which is fleece weight divided by body weight. With this objective in mind, a convenient technique to establish 'wool growth' (milligrams of fibre produced by squared centimetre in the unit of time) was then included as part of the selection variables.

The assessment process

The fleece grading exercises were carried out every six months with Tzotzil women from different villages, so in a couple of years it was possible to standardize and systematize them properly. This showed that women perform an initial assessment of 'fleece volume' by observing the sheep as they move around in the pen; the way in which the staples 'make waves' is an indication of their length and looseness. Once there is agreement among the Tzotzil graders, usually four of them, over which is the animal with the best fleece, a closer inspection is undertaken. Women press the fleece with their hands at different places, with firm but gentle grips, to confirm their initial assessment of volume. Handling of the fleece gives a preliminary appraisal of its potential use during the textile process: the 'textile aptitude'.

What follows is the assessment of the single most important criterion: staple length. Even though most of the Tzotzil women are illiterate, they have developed an efficient quantitative method of measuring the staples using a series of distances that can be established with the fingers of their hands They use from one to four horizontally stacked fingers for the shorter distances, and they calculate the larger ones measuring from the tip of their thumb to the tip of their index or their middle finger.

To validate the empirical method, this series of finger distances was measured with a ruler and plotted on a graph, and they were highly correlated, which means that each woman has an integrated ruler in her hands. This measuring system is also used by Tzotzil women in other household and agricultural activities; it is a convenient tool for them, very useful and efficient. Direct measuring of the different finger distances in different women at a given time, and in one of them over a period of eight consecutive shearing seasons (four years), showed that they are highly repeatable and thus a trustworthy selection tool under village conditions.

A second qualitative criterion considered by Tzotzil women is the 'textile aptitude' of the fleece. Through inspection and handling of the fleece and individual staples, women establish if the wool would be appropriate for the spinning of threads that will go either to the weft or the warp of the loom. Any wool can be spun into thread for the warp, but fleeces with a good amount of long-coarse fibres to spin the weft are not so common, and thus are highly regarded and valued by the weavers. Manual counting of individual fibres on wool staples of different fleece quality grade showed that an excellent fleece had around 24 per cent of long-coarse fibres, as compared with the amount found on poor quality fleeces (17 per cent).

In summary, the fleece quality grading in animals of the nucleus flock is based on the translation of the subjective assessment of staple length (measured 'by hand') and textile aptitude of the fleece. These two elements are co-dependent, and long staples are mostly related to a good textile aptitude for spinning the weft.

Tradition meets formal science

When these findings were presented in an academic forum, the 'subjective' nature of the fleece quality grade was pointed out, questioning its inclusion in a formal selection index for Chiapas sheep. However, subsequent statistical analyses showed that fleece quality grade correlated significantly with a number of very objective productive variables, such as staple length, greasy fleece weight, wool growth and the proportion of long-coarse fibres. Analyses of variance demonstrated that these objective parameters differ significantly across the range of fleece quality grades, and it was concluded that a selection index including them would in fact incorporate the empirical criteria of the Tzotzil women. This selection index is being tested at the present time in animals of the nucleus flock, and it is being adjusted for its use within given age ranges. Preliminary results showed that this selection index can properly discriminate animals according to the quality of their fleece. The aim of the programme is to identify rams of superior wool characteristics at a young age (24 months old), so that they can have a long life siring equally superior lambs within village flocks.

21.3 Benefits of the programme

Within the nucleus flock at the university sheep farm we have recorded an increase of 100 per cent in fleece quantity. Our selected rams are producing at least twice as much wool (800–1200 g per 6-monthly shearing) as the rams in the village flocks (400–600 g). Repeatability of this trait (an indicator of its heritability) has been calculated at around 39 per cent, which is quite high and within the range reported in the literature (10–60 per cent). Our estimates of fleece quality improvement within the nucleus flock in the last five years reach a figure of 25 per cent, using the subjective scale designed in collaboration with the Tzotzil women.

At this time, different extension and development agencies of the government are implementing programmes utilizing rams from the nucleus flock: at least 110 superior rams have been introduced directly into village flocks in the last two years. The results are promising, judging by the amount of women who are requesting a 'true sheep' of this quality, and who are willing to pay for it. In the near future, not only rams but also superior ewes will be available for such development strategies. There has not yet been any monitoring of the performance of these rams and their offspring.

Not much is known yet about the economic impact of the programme on the shepherdesses. However, they and their families could be experiencing benefits in the form of: (a) increased income, from sales of ram lambs sired by superior rams from the university, or sales of fleeces; and (b) better clothes. Greasy fleeces in highland Chiapas are normally sold for about 5 pounds sterling, and the fleeces from the programme's sheep reach up to 10 pounds sterling per kilogram.

21.4 Final reflections and thoughts

In retrospective, the use of participatory methodologies has proved to be a breakthrough in the design and application of appropriate selection strategies of Chiapas wool sheep. Tzotzil women taught the sheep scientists what should be the parameters of cultural and economic value to select for, and they have remained as active collaborators of the programme. To ensure that diverse opinions are always considered, 'newcomer' women from different Tzotzil villages are invited every six months to join the group of 'regular' graders. The interaction among them enriches the whole process. The women's involvement has made the improvement programme faster, more precise and more effective.

The participatory approach has been adopted and systematized within the programme. It is one of the basic elements of the improvement of Chiapas sheep. The researchers who work on a daily basis in this effort, and those who collaborate indirectly from other academic institutions, are happy with what is being done. However, our convictions are still questioned at most academic forums, and we think that not many researchers from other institutions would adopt these ideas.

The extension challenge

It has been difficult to take the experience learned at the Sheep Centre back to the Tzotzil villages. The ideal situation would be that every woman attending the Sheep Centre to assess fleece quality grade would have information or lessons to share with her neighbour shepherdesses. For example, she could inform them that the university sheep farm is producing excellent animals, and that it is actually using the local breed of sheep; and that these improved sheep do not require any major changes in the management system or extra expenditure.

Unfortunately, the sharing of information and lessons has been limited. This could be explained on cultural terms, since sheep husbandry is undertaken as a family activity and not as a collaborative action among a group of peer shepherdesses. Grazing areas in the Highlands of Chiapas are considered community land, but each woman only takes care of her small flock of about ten sheep. Sharing responsibilities would give the shepherdesses a good amount of free time to do different things, to go to the markets, to work on the fields, to visit relatives, etc. But this is not the case, and women prefer to leave the animals within the pens when they have to go to the market instead of requesting a neighbour to take care of the animals while they are away.

Furthermore, there is still a gap between jointly developed research and the appropriation of knowledge at the village level. It seems that not only research, but the area of extension also has to be revisited, and new alternatives have to be designed when there are large cultural differences and considerable language barriers. Participative methodologies can help to make this task a more successful experience.

PART IV Conclusions

22 Maximizing the contribution of participatory livestock research

This concluding chapter addresses a few key issues relating to the future of participatory approaches in livestock research and development. In particular it seeks answers to the following questions.

- What impact have participatory projects had to date? Have they made a difference?
- How much potential is there for increasing their impact?
- What are the barriers to maximizing impact, and how can they be overcome?

It concludes that there is a need for two revolutions – an institutional revolution and an information revolution.

22.1 Benefits of participatory approaches

The case studies and other examples of PSA and PTD in this book have shown that participatory approaches can be highly effective in improving understanding of constraints facing poor livestock-keepers, and in developing technologies to address them. Table 22.1 summarizes the benefits generated by the various case study projects/initiatives. The benefits from the technologies take various forms. Some relate directly to the animals (e.g higher livestock productivity, reduced mortality rates) and others relate to the owners (e.g. reduced or zero cash requirement, reduced labour requirements, increased income, higher consumption of livestock products). Animal productivity benefits will, of course, be converted into benefits to owners in the form of increased income, etc.

The penultimate column of the table shows the numbers of households that have benefited from the technologies.[37] In most cases these are households

---

[37] In addition, at least seven of the case study initiatives have developed improved methodologies that could and should be used more widely; and, if they were, this too could generate major benefits on a much larger scale – see Table 22.2.

Table 22.1 Benefits of PTD case studies

Project constraint/opportunity	Benefits	Number of households Benefited	Reached
Animal health			
(A) Control of Newcastle disease, Mozambique: *mortality in chickens*	More effective and lower cost ND control, leading to increases in: ■ chicken numbers ■ household purchasing power ■ home consumption of chicken products ■ decision-making power for women	>10 000 using I-2 vaccine in Mozambique, Tanzania and Ghana	
(B) Development of mange treatment technology, Kenya: *mortality in goats*	Effective, zero-cash expenditure mange control, resulting in: ↓ goat mortality, ↓ expenditure on veterinary drugs, ↑ incomes	16 in trials	3500 farmers at field days
(C) Ethnoveterinary Knowledge Project, Kenya: *parasites in sheep, etc.*	Effective, zero-cash expenditure, de-worming, resulting in: ↑ productivity, ↓ expenditure on veterinary drugs, ↑ incomes	3000	
Feed and/or nutrition research			
(D) More effective usage of concentrate with dairy cows, Kenya: *low milk yields due to feed constraints*	■ Increased milk production, leading to increased income ■ Shorter calving intervals	90 participants in research	Feedback sessions conveyed outcome to c. 400 co-op members
(E) Easing seasonal scarcity for goats, India: *insufficient quality feed → low conception rates in does*	Effective, zero-cash expenditure, feed supplement, resulting in: ↑ conception and twinning rates; ↑ kidding rates by 30–45%; income from extra sales	105 participants in trials in 4 villages	Other villages via posters, technical bulletins
(F) Improved integration of livestock into LEI crop systems, Mexico: *various constraints affecting pigs and poultry, e.g. feed scarcity and health*	■ Smallstock are now healthier and more productive due to de-worming and better feeding ■ More animals are available for sale as and when needed	About 50 participant families (in 4 villages) + spread to others	People in other villages, via NGOs, projects and booklets

Project constraint/opportunity	Benefits	Number of households	
		Benefited	Reached

Forage research

Project constraint/opportunity	Benefits	Benefited	Reached
(G) Forages for Smallholders Project – China and 5 SE Asian countries: *various feed-related constraints, mainly affecting ruminants; also labour constraints*	*Increased forage availability*, resulting in: $\uparrow$ growth rates, better health, $\uparrow$ reproductive performance, and better body condition of livestock; $\uparrow$ draught power *Financial benefits:* $\uparrow$ income (US\$ 81–435 p.a.) *Other benefits:* Income from sales of planting materials; $\downarrow$ labour requirements. Manure.	4155 new farmers planted forages in 2000–2002	Additional 1250 participated in diagnosis sessions
(H) Legume supply and cultivation adapted to facilitate adoption, Kenya: *lack of year-round feed for dairy goats and cows (quality and quantity)*	Improved availability of planting material, and greater ease of propagation led to large increase in adoption rates for forage crops. 25 000 cuttings distributed from group nurseries to members. In addition: ■ Higher biomass yield ■ Improved supply of nitrogen to cows ■ Suppression of weeds by forage crop led to reduced labour on weed control	600 definitely. Possibly c. 6000[a]	>3000 farmers have been reached through field days

Tools research

Project constraint/opportunity	Benefits	Benefited	Reached
(I) Development of a donkey traction technology, Sudan: *high labour requirements of crop production, especially weeding*	186 Village Development Committees established, ploughs distributed, 100 blacksmiths trained in making them, → 7500 ha ploughed annually *Changes in cultivation practices*, leading to: >50% $\downarrow$ in time spent on land preparation, weeding and planting; improved tillage and seedbed preparation; $\uparrow$ crop production *Other benefits are:* $\uparrow$ yields by 50–114%; $\uparrow$ cultivated area by 86–200%; $\uparrow$ incomes	3000 have received ploughs	Not known

Genetic improvement

Project constraint/opportunity	Benefits	Benefited	Reached
(J) Participatory breed improvement of the Chiapas sheep, Mexico: *potential to $\uparrow$ women's income from wool products*	■ Fleece quantity of rams on station is double that of rams in village flocks ■ Improvement in fleece quality estimated to be 25% in last 5 years ■ Superior rams distributed to villages	150 ♀ have received superior rams	>300 ♀ received lambs of superior rams

[a] An adoption study in the project area (population of over 20 000) is showing up to 30 per cent adoption rate

who have participated in the testing and development of the technology, because information is not usually available on numbers of adopters: for this reason the numbers should be seen as very conservative. However, in one case, an adoption study provided an estimate of the number of users in the project area; and in another case (the donkey plough) data were available on the numbers who had received the plough. In five of the projects the number of known beneficiaries in the project area is a few thousand, but in a few other projects they are 150 or less.

In the final column, livestock-keepers who have been reached refers to those who are known to have attended field days or meetings about the technologies, or to the number of copies of extension materials distributed to livestock-keepers. For example, in the mange control case it is known that about 3500 farmers attended field days at which the technology was demonstrated. Again, these figures are likely to be highly conservative, because any farmer to farmer extension that has taken place is not captured by them.

22.2 Potential for horizontal scaling up

The number of beneficiaries of the technologies developed in the case studies has been limited until now. Is this because the technologies are only appropriate for a limited number of livestock-keepers, or is it more to do with inadequate dissemination or promotion?

The potential for horizontal scaling up of case study outputs (i.e. the geographical spread and expansion to more people and communities within the same sector or stakeholder group) is summarized in Table 22.2. In most cases[38] there appears to be a large unrealized potential use of the technologies. (See also Tables 11.1–11.3 in Chapter 11 for estimates of potential numbers of adopters for certain technologies.) This suggests, therefore, that inadequate dissemination is the main constraint on adoption of the technologies. One factor contributing to this situation is that most of the technologies have only been developed during the last 5–10 years, and hence there has not yet been sufficient time for dissemination on a large scale. Other likely reasons will now be discussed.

22.3 Barriers to horizontal scaling up

The organizational barrier
One reason why the number of users is well below potential is the division that often exists between research and extension, which can take three forms.

---

[38] The technologies described in the final two case studies, i.e. the donkey plough and the improved Chiapas sheep, appear to be exceptions, i.e. their recommendation domains may be limited to their respective project areas, due to agro-ecological and/or socio-economic conditions.

Table 22.2 Potential for horizontal scaling up of case study technologies and approaches

Project	Relevant outside original project area?	
	Technology	*Novel methodology*
Animal health		
(H1) Control of Newcastle disease, Mozambique	Yes, similar laboratory and field trials already conducted in Ghana and Tanzania	Methodology relevant throughout LDCs
(H5) Dryland Applied Research and Extension Project, Kenya	Yes, semi-arid regions of SSA and India[a]	
(H6) Ethnoveterinary Knowledge Research and Development Project, Kenya	Yes, proven technologies may be relevant in other countries where the plant species are found	Similar approach can be taken in other countries.
Feed/nutrition research		
(N1) Re-allocation of concentrates during lactation, Kenya	Yes, potentially relevant in smallholder dairy sector in any country where good market access warrants use of concentrates	Potentially relevant in smallholder dairy sector in any country
(N3) Easing seasonal scarcity for goats, Rajasthan, India	Yes, related work done in Karnataka, India Potentially relevant[b] in Horn of Africa, parts of west Asia, Pakistan, Venezuela, Colombia, NE Brazil, etc.	
(N4) Enhancing the integration of livestock into LEI crop systems, Mexico	There has been some uptake of feeding of *Mucuna pruriens* to monogastrics elsewhere in Mexico. Other technologies may be location-specific	General methodology being applied in central Mexico and also Bolivia (Altiplano and sub-tropical valleys)
Forage research		
(F2) Forages for Smallholders Project: South-east Asia	Yes, forage species suitable within upland areas of SE Asia, but may not be suitable outside SE Asia, due to different climatic conditions	Methodology for testing and developing forage technologies, and promoting them, is of general relevance
(F3) Legume supply and cultivation adapted to facilitate adoption, Kenya	Yes, other dairy areas in the country would benefit from the technology. It is estimated that approx. 300 000 smallholder dairy farmers in Kenya could benefit from the technology. Farmers in parts of Tanzania and Uganda where smallholder dairying is developing could also benefit	Approach relevant elsewhere – i.e. identify constraints (e.g. cost, availability, ease of handling) to adoption of legumes and address them through PTD

Table 22.2 cont.

Project	Relevant outside original project area?	
	Technology	*Novel methodology*
Tools research		
(T3) Development of a donkey traction technology, Sudan	No, relevance of technology more or less limited to project area, due to specific soil type, etc.	Methodology for developing animal traction technologies is of widespread relevance
Genetic improvement		
(B2) Participatory breed improvement of the Chiapas sheep, Mexico	No, relevance of technology is probably limited to Chiapas region, as this breed has evolved to adapt to agro-climatic conditions here	Methodology for improving indigenous breeds is of general relevance

[a] See Table 11.2 for further details.
[b] See Table 11.3 for further details.

One form of division is organizational (see also Box 1.2), i.e. an organization's mandate may state that it is responsible either for research or for extension, but not for both. The other is the basis on which funds are provided: in many cases donors specify that funds are to be used specifically for research, and that promoting adoption of the technology should be done by other organizations and/or funded from other sources. Unless there are very strong linkages between research and dissemination organizations, which is rare, this stipulation tends to result in poor dissemination of project findings and technologies.

A third organizational barrier is that, even where organizational mandates cover both research and extension, organizations tend to have a stronger *capacity* for one area than the other. Government NARIs, for example, are far stronger on research than on extension. Organizational *incentives* may also skew the effort put into research versus extension, favouring one rather than the other.

It is interesting that, among the five projects with a few thousand direct beneficiaries to date, the lead organization was an NGO (ITDG-East Africa and ITDG-Sudan) in two of them. One of these was a multi-stakeholder project in which the linkages were strong and the research/extension divide was bridged effectively. One of the other three projects, the Forages for Smallholders Project, benefited from having the development of methods for scaling up as one of its main project objectives. The Mozambique Newcastle disease control project, another of the 'high beneficiary numbers' projects, was primarily a development project, but with some applied research included.

Common research barriers – funding and duration

In the case studies, the number of livestock-keepers or farmers benefiting from a technology tends to be correlated with: (a) the size of the project budget; and (b) the length of time over which the project received support. Research funding sources tend to support smaller and shorter projects than development funding sources, which can place severe limitations on the number of users reached. Developing an effective and appropriate technology tends to take at least two years or seasons, and may require several years, so shorter projects (three to four years) may not have a long enough dissemination phase built into them. Furthermore, the size of the dissemination effort, and hence the number of potential users reached, is inevitably constrained by the amount of funds budgeted for this purpose. It is often the case that once the funding for a specific project comes to an end the activities related to that project also terminate or tail off.

In an ideal world, when effective technologies have been developed under the auspices of research projects development or extension funds should be available to promote them. Unfortunately, the organizational divide between research and extension tends to stop this happening. This divide exists not only between different agencies and ministries in less developed countries (LDCs), but also within bilateral development agencies, such as those of the OECD countries. A notable exception is the Mozambique Newcastle disease (ND) control project (Chapter 12), funded by the Australian Agency for International Development, which follows on from and expands upon the ACIAR/National Veterinary Research Institute of Mozambique ND Control research project, which ran from 1996 to 2001.

The information barrier

Another barrier to widespread adoption is the poor flow of information – people and organizations that could use a particular technology to their benefit are often not aware that it exists. Where profits can be made from the sale of products related to a technology, private sector companies (producers and distributors) find it worthwhile to publicize their existence through numerous media and to produce extension materials on how to use them. Thus, there is a reasonable chance that farmers and development agencies will be aware of the existence of commercial fertilizers, pesticides, seeds, etc., and will be able to obtain technical guidance on their use.

However, many, if not most, technologies that are suitable for poor farmers or livestock-keepers are ones from which private sector agents may not be able to make a profit, because they are usually low-external-input technologies involving little or zero cash expenditure. In these cases publicity and information provision depends heavily on government organizations and civil society, i.e. NGOs and CBOs. Unfortunately, publicly funded livestock services have not been functioning effectively in most developing countries for many years; and NGOs have limited geographical coverage and are often technically weak. Nevertheless, even within existing funding limits, there is scope for huge improvements in the performance of livestock service providers, through institutional changes and improved information systems and access to information. Measures for achieving these improvements are described below.

22.4 The institutional revolution: increasing the use of participatory approaches

In this twenty-first century era of globalization, if small-scale livestock producers are to survive they must increase the efficiency of their operations and the productivity of their animals. This will require more effective support from livestock development agencies and service providers than has generally been available until now.

A whole raft of measures is required to boost the small-scale livestock producer sector in developing countries. In particular, there needs to be an *institutional revolution* on the scale of the 'livestock revolution' itself. Livestock service organizations must be made more accountable and responsive to poor livestock-keepers, by facilitating the articulation of the latter's priorities and demands. Fortunately, the institutional revolution is already under way in many countries, although often in a piecemeal fashion. This process needs to be accelerated and made more comprehensive, combining improvements to the enabling environment with capacity building of all major stakeholder groups.

Reforms to extension and other services have been promoting comprehensive changes for the agriculture sector as a whole (e.g. in Chile, Uganda, Venezuela). However, there is a risk that livestock may continue to be marginalized in some countries, and it is important that the particular issues and needs of the livestock sector are taken into account. Capacity building of both livestock-keepers and livestock service providers is required, at various levels.

Capacity building of livestock-keepers
Group formation The formation of groups of farmers or livestock-keepers can have a number of benefits, including:

- making livestock and other services more client-driven and efficient;
- strengthening livestock-keepers'/farmers' bargaining power with traders;
- reducing transaction costs for input suppliers and output buyers;
- economies of scale (e.g. from bulking up in the supply of milk);
- facilitating savings and access to credit;
- reducing public sector extension costs.

Group formation is often related to a particular species. For example, in Rajasthan, India, groups of sheep producers have been formed in some districts, focusing on the processing and marketing of wool; and groups of goat-keepers in other districts. In many parts of India milk producers' co-operatives have been formed, focusing primarily on buffaloes and cross-bred cows. This happened under the auspices of the government-supported dairy programme, commonly known as 'Operation Flood', that has helped to make India the world's largest milk producer.

It should be noted, however, that effective and sustainable group formation is not easy, and requires considerable skill on the part of the development organization concerned. The groups must be reasonably cohesive, hijacking of benefits by elites must be avoided, and members must perceive the benefits of being in the group as significantly higher than the costs (including time spent at meetings, etc.).

Training livestock specialists The creation of village para-professionals has been more widely used in relation to animal health than in any other sector.[39] A committed villager is selected (preferably by her or his community) to be trained as a specialist in a particular subject and to provide services to the community, such as de-worming, treatment of wounds and identification of diseases. It is generally assumed that they will charge for their services, to make the service sustainable, and that this will become a major livelihood activity for them.

There is now extensive experience with community animal health workers (CAHWs), or paravets as they are more popularly known, in many countries. They can help to fill the void in livestock services (from private, public and civil society), and can also help groups of livestock-keepers to interface more effectively with livestock service providers. They have had a positive impact in a variety of situations, ranging from pastoralist communities in lowland Kenya to settled farmers in highland Nepal (Catley and Leyland, 2002). However, there have also been concerns about their long-term viability, partly because in most countries they are not legally recognized.

In some countries professional veterinary organizations have launched anti-CAHW campaigns, questioning their technical competence, etc. Some of the anti-CAHW propaganda has been unfounded, and there is evidence that where valid technical concerns have been raised these can be addressed satisfactorily (IDL Group and McCorkle, 2002). In some countries, such as Kenya, processes are under way to harmonize CAHW training approaches and curricula at the national level.

In Indonesia, where there has been a process of institutional change and privatization of services, CAHWs have been accepted by government as an effective type of service provider (Leksmono and Young, 2002). In Bolivia,

---

[39] It is interesting that, as with professional extension workers, training of villagers has tended to focus exclusively on animal health. Notwithstanding the importance of animal health, there is a strong case for training village para-extensionists in animal husbandry in general.

an NGO-supported programme to support community-based animal health training and service delivery has been promoted in various parts of the country (Stewart, 2002). Excellent results continued to be generated, even after project funding was discontinued.

One way to improve the financial sustainability of CAHWs, but which has not yet been widely tested, is to link them to private suppliers of veterinary medicines. As these linkages develop, a key issue will be the extent to which community perceptions of an ideal CAHW compare with the qualities preferred by private pharmacy owners, veterinarians, etc. There is still plenty to learn about the compatibility of community participation and privatization, and options for combined approaches to primary animal health service delivery (Catley and Leyland, 2002).

Capacity-building of livestock service providers

Capacity-building of livestock service providers is needed at three different levels: the task network, the organizational level and the individual level.

Task network *Horizontal* partnerships and linkages between different types of service organizations need to be strengthened to improve information-sharing and co-ordination of service provision. Such organizations include: government extension agencies, research institutes, NGOs, credit providers and commercial input suppliers. Co-ordinating committees may be useful at more than one level – for example, national, state/regional and local. The ITDG East Africa project on EVK established 'collaborative partnerships' with a range of stakeholders (see Case study C).

Linkages between service providers and farmers also need to be strengthened at different levels. Uganda's National Agricultural Advisory Services project (which is currently in its pilot phase, but will eventually be implemented across the country) provides an interesting example of how this can be done (Nahdy, 2002). It involves the formation and/or strengthening of farmer groups, which are the building blocks of the system. Representatives of these groups are then elected onto farmers' fora at the sub-county and district levels, where they are given 'voting rights' on agricultural services co-ordinating committees. This system improves both *horizontal* and *vertical* linkages between farmers and service providers.

To be client-orientated service provision needs to become 'bottom-up' instead of 'top-down', so the *vertical* flow of information and needs must be effective upwards as well as downwards. Bolivia has the beginnings of a livestock diseases surveillance system that operates in this way, and hence has the potential to improve the priority-setting for animal disease control at local, regional and national levels. In Uganda and Venezuela this kind of vertical structure, combined with participatory needs assessments, is being used to influence the priorities of extension service providers, and a similar approach could be applied to influence research priorities.

Organizational capacity building is needed in participatory, client-orientated work. Ways of achieving this are discussed in Chapter 11, sections 4 and 5, and Box 11.3 describes the experiences of Kenya's government research institutes. Major issues that need to be addressed are organizational mandates, incentive systems and resources.

Human capacity building Research and extension staff have been receiving training and exposure in participatory methods and approaches for many years now. Nevertheless, the process has a long way to go in some countries. International donors have encouraged and funded the shift in some countries (e.g. Kenya), but some other countries that have been less exposed have made less progress on this front (e.g. India, Nigeria).

Extension There is a need to move from a one-way to a two-way flow of information and knowledge, and from a prescriptive approach to a facilitatory one. Several of the case studies describe how ITK has contributed to technology development and improvement, and indigenous technologies can be as effective as commercially available ones developed by formal science. Livestock extension and development workers need to have respect for livestock-keepers' indigenous technical knowledge, and be receptive to utilizing it. They also need to recognize the value of para-extensionists, and to see them as complementary agents rather than as a threat to their own positions.

Livestock extension services have been dominated by veterinarians and have tended to focus on animal health issues. A large proportion of extension workers may benefit, therefore, from further training in systems-based approaches so that they have a holistic view of the contribution of livestock to livelihoods and the relationships between animal and crop production. Conversely, agricultural extension workers who are also responsible for livestock may need training in livestock production. All extension workers need to be aware of the fact that livestock often have multiple roles (see Chapter 1), of which production of products for human consumption is only one.

Research Livestock-keepers, and farmers in general, should have stronger inputs into research priority-setting. Structures for facilitating that were outlined above. In addition, the voices and negotiating power of poor livestock-keepers and farmers can be strengthened by allocating funds to them for use in commissioning research on what they regard as priority topics. The allocation of funds in this way has been tried in Kenya (Gustafson, 2002).

Equally important are changes in the way in which much research is carried out. The application of PTD in livestock research and development projects and programmes should be increased. Livestock research needs to move from the backwaters of PTD to the forefront and needs to be mainstreamed. Livestock NARIs and universities should become much more field-oriented in their research. This may require the strengthening of intermediate agents (e.g. local extension staff trained in PTD) between researchers and livestock-keepers.

Donors can support the *institutional revolution* by:

- funding major capacity building initiatives, including the development of new courses and curricula;
- pressing for improvements in the enabling environment, including institutional reforms that will enable the voices of the poor to be heard; and
- prioritizing funding for research that is clearly pro-poor and demand-led.

22.5 The information revolution

In many LDCs extension workers, and to a lesser extent researchers, tend to have limited access to relevant printed materials, such as books, extension materials, journals and newsletters. More effective use of modern information and communication technologies (ICTs) can help to overcome the information barrier. They are dramatically reducing the cost of processing and exchanging information, require less fixed infrastructure, and some are more interactive. While most are not currently directly accessible to poor farmers, they are increasingly available to service providers. Potentially important ICTs include: the internet, CDs, the use of geographical information systems, mobile phones, television and radio. Electronic products can be circulated on CDs or via the internet. Electronic publishing avoids the costs of printing, binding and heavy postage (although it does transfer printing costs to the end user if hard copies are required), and has a potentially larger reach than printed materials.

Radio is already an important source of information for many farmers in LDCs, and is becoming increasingly used as FM radio stations spring up in many countries. Furthermore, it may be widely used by poor farmers and women. For example, a survey in Uganda found that 90 per cent and 88 per cent of male and female farmers, respectively, had listened to radio broadcasts during the previous month (Garforth et al., 2003).

CDs Distribution of livestock-related information through CDs is starting to take off. Organizers of some livestock conferences have distributed papers to participants in this way, and some livestock research donors have begun to distribute research findings on CD too. For example, DFID's LPP has produced six CDs, and is developing another one with DANIDA that will focus on smallstock.

Internet Livestock service-providers can be reached better through appropriate websites and by email, including the distribution of electronic newsletters. Various internet-based initiatives to improve information flow and access have been launched in recent years, ranging from electronic journals to websites containing information about ethnoveterinary knowledge and practices. Some internet-based sources of livestock-related information are given in the Appendix. They include electronic peer-reviewed journals, and websites on specific subject areas or species.

22.6 Final comments

If the institutional and information revolutions outlined above take off rapidly, then the livestock revolution can become an opportunity for resource-poor livestock-keepers in LDCs rather than a threat. Their ability to take advantage of the burgeoning demand for livestock and livestock products can make a significant contribution to poverty eradication and broader social and economic development.

Appendix

Internet-based livestock and development information sources

Electronic journals There are at least two peer-reviewed electronic journals that focus primarily on livestock. One is *Livestock Research for Rural Development*, which has been published since 1989, and is available in English and Spanish (*www.cipav.org.co/lrrd*)

Another is FAO's *AGRIPPA* (Agri-Publishing for People in Agriculture), a journal that carries both research papers and extension materials. Although not exclusively concerned with livestock, it has so far focused on animal nutrition, feed resources and livestock production in general (*www.fao.org/agrippa*)

Livestock and environment The Virtual Centre for Research and Development in Livestock Environment Interaction has been established by a consortium of donors, to improve communication and enhance the relevance of research and development issues regarding livestock–environment interactions. The Virtual Centre, which is hosted by FAO, promotes multidisciplinary research and development activities and increases awareness among key stakeholders of the complex interactions of human needs, animal production and the sustainability of global natural resources. See: *http://www.virtualcentre.org/en/frame.htm*

In particular, the Virtual Centre hosts the Livestock–Environment Toolbox. This is a highly structured website intended to provide policy makers in developing countries with information on livestock–environment interactions and options for monitoring them. It also includes large numbers of pages summarizing policy/institutional options and technologies for mitigating environmental impacts. See: *http://lead.virtualcenter.org/en/dec/toolbox/homepage.htm*

Ethnoveterinary knowledge Information about ethnoveterinary medicine, including publications and projects, is available at *www.ethnovetweb.com*

Family poultry information sources There are three important internet-based information sources on family poultry. One is the 'International Network on Family Poultry Development', an international voluntary organization funded by FAO whose website is: *www.fao.org/ag/againfo/subjects/en/infpd/home.html* Various publications can be downloaded from the website, and occasionally there are e-conferences. It also publishes an electronic newsletter twice a year. In addition, the Australian Council for

International Agriculture Research funds the *Rural Poultry* website (*www.vsap.uq.edu.au/ruralpoultry*). This site aims to provide a resource for farmers, researchers and development workers, to encourage collaboration between different groups and to provide a forum for information exchange about rural poultry. Both extension and research materials can be accessed. There is also an associated electronic newsletter on Rural Poultry. Finally, there is the Network for Smallholder Poultry Development, which is associated with Denmark's Royal Veterinary and Agricultural University, and whose email address is: *www.poultry.kvl.dk* This contains information primarily about DANIDA-funded poultry projects.

List of contributors

Robyn Alders is associated with the Rural Poultry Centre and is the Team Leader of the Southern Africa Newcastle Disease Control Project based in Maputo, Mozambique.

Simon Anderson is a Principal Research Fellow in the Department of Agricultural Sciences, Imperial College, University of London, UK.

Filomena dos Anjos is a lecturer at the Veterinary Faculty, Maputo, Mozambique.

Brigitte Bagnol is an anthropologist working as an independent consultant and is a Research Associate with the Institute for Women and Gender of the University of Pretoria, South Africa.

J. Biwott was a Livestock Extension Officer for Kenya's Ministry of Livestock and Fisheries Development in Bomet District, and is now working for a consultancy firm, Tropical Harvest.

Andy Catley works in the Community-based Animal Health and Participatory Epidemiology (CAPE) Unit, Organization of African Unity/Interafrican Bureau for Animal Resources, Nairobi, Kenya.

L. Chege is an extension officer for the Ministry of Livestock and Fisheries Development, working as a District Dairy Officer in Kiambu District.

Susanne Clark was a research student at Imperial College, University of London, and is now a member of DFID's Sustainable Livelihoods Support Office in London.

Czech Conroy is Reader in Rural Livelihoods at the Natural Resources Institute, University of Greenwich, UK.

Raúl Fringe works for the National Veterinary Research Institute, Maputo, Mozambique.

A.L. Joshi is Executive Vice-President of BAIF Development Research Foundation, whose head office is in Pune, India.

R. Kaitho is a ruminant nutritionist who was working as part of the ILRI Market Oriented Smallholder Dairy team, and is now working for Texas A&M University.

John N. Kang'ara is a researcher in livestock production and nutrition with the Kenya Agricultural Research Institute, based at Embu Research Centre.

Bernadette Keane was a research worker at the Universidad Autonoma de Yucatan, Mexico, and is now an independent consultant working out of Uruguay.

Peter Kerridge is a researcher at Centro Internacional de Agricultura Tropical, PO Box 783, Vientiane, Lao PDR.

Shyam Singh Lakhawat works for BAIF Development Research Foundation, whose head office is in Pune, India.

Quintino Lobo works for the National Veterinary Research Institute, Maputo, Mozambique.

Belmira Mata works for the National Veterinary Research Institute, Maputo, Mozambique.

Dr David Miano Mwangi is a researcher in forage production and utilization with the Kenya Agricultural Research Institute, based at National Agricultural Research Centre, Muguga, PO Box 30148–00100 Nairobi, Kenya.

D. Njubi is a data management specialist at the International Livestock Research Institute, Nairobi.

A. Omore is an epidemiologist seconded from the Kenya Agricultural Research Institute's National Veterinary Research Centre to work at the International Livestock Research Institute, Nairobi.

Raul Perezgrovas works at the Instituto de Estudios Indigenas-UNACH, University of Chiapas, Mexico.

Julieta Moguel Pliego was a research worker at the Universidad Autonoma de Yucatan, Mexico, and now manages the university's social work programme.

D. Romney was a Feed Resources and Nutrient Cycling scientist in the International Livestock Research Institute (ILRI) Market Oriented Smallholder Dairy team, and is now contributing to ILRI's new innovations and markets themes.

Ralph Roothaert was a researcher with the Forages for Smallholders Project, Centro Internacional de Agricultura Tropical (CIAT), and is currently a researcher at the International Livestock Research Institute (ILRI/CIAT), PO Box 5689, Addis Ababa, Ethiopia.

M. Sharma works for BAIF Development Research Foundation, whose head office is in Pune, India.

S. Staal is a livestock economist who was working as part of the ILRI Market Oriented Smallholder Dairy team, and is now Deputy Director of the new livestock markets theme.

Mohamed Siddig Suliman is Food Security Programme Manager in North Darfur State with ITDG Sudan.

W. Thorpe was head of the ILRI Market Oriented Smallholder Dairy team and is now co-ordinating activities for ILRI in South Asia.

M.H. Vadher works for BAIF Development Research Foundation, whose head office is in Pune, India.

M. Wambugu was a Livestock Extension Officer for MOLFD working in Kiambu District, and is now working for the USAID Kenya Dairy Development Programme based at ILRI.

P. Wanjohi is a data management specialist at the International Livestock Research Institute, Nairobi.

Jacob Wanyama is Project Manager, Reducing Vulnerability Programme, Intermediate Technology Development Group – Eastern Africa, Nairobi, Kenya.

Mary Young is associated with the Rural Poultry Centre and is a Long Term Advisor with the Southern Africa Newcastle Disease Control Project based in Dar es Salaam, Tanzania.

References

Acharya, R.M. and Bhattacharyya, N.K. (1992) Status of small ruminant production, Paper presented at the Vth International Conference on Goats, New Delhi.

Amir, P. and Knipscheer, H. (1989) *Conducting On-Farm Animal Research: Procedures and economic analysis*, Winrock and IDRC.

Anderson, S., Gündel, S., Pound, B. and Triomphe, B. (2001) *Cover Crops in Low-input Agriculture: Lessons from Latin America*, Intermediate Technology Publications, London.

Anderson, S., Clark, S., Keane, B., Mogel Pliego, J. and Trejo Diaz, W. (2003) *Parcela-Solar: an experience in combining campesino and conventional experimentation*, Final Technical Report to the Livestock Production Programme, DFID, UK.

Ashley, S.D., Holden, S.J., Massawe, N.F., Owen, E., Mtenga, L. and Romney, D.L. (2000) *Compromise and Challenges: The process of participatory livestock research in Tanzania*, Research Report, Livestock in Development, Crewkerne, UK.

Bayer, W. and Waters-Bayer, A. (1998) *Forage Husbandry*, Macmillan Education, London and Basingstoke.

Biggs, S. (1989) *Resource-poor Farmer Participation in Research: a synthesis of experiences from nine agricultural research systems*, OFCOR Comparative Study Paper No. 3, ISNAR, The Hague.

Bosma, R.H., Roothaert, R.L. and Ibrahim (2001) Economic and social benefits of new forage technologies in East Kalimantan, Indonesia, CIAT Working Document No. 190, Centro Internacional de Agricultura Tropical, Los Baños, Philippines.

Bosma, R.H., Roothaert, R.L., Asis, P., Saguinhon, J., Binh, L.H. and Yen, V.H. (2003) Financial and social benefits of new forage technologies in Mindanao, Philippines and Tuyen Quang, Vietnam, CIAT Working Document No. 191, Centro Internacional de Agricultura Tropical, Los Baños, Philippines, pp.92.

Cadisch, G., Sylvester-Bradley, R. and Nosberger, J. (1989) ^{15}N-based estimation of nitrogen fixation by eight tropical forage-legumes at two levels of P:K supply, *Field Crops Research*, 22, 181–194.

Carney, D. (1998) *Sustainable Rural Livelihoods: What contribution can we make?*, DFID, London.

Casley, D. and Kumar, K. (1988) *The Collection, Analysis and Use of Monitoring and Evaluation Data*, Johns Hopkins University Press, published for the World Bank, Baltimore and London.

Catley, A. (1999) *Methods on the Move: A review of veterinary uses of participatory approaches and methods focusing on experiences in dryland Africa*, International Institute for Environment and Development, London.

Catley, A. and Leyland, T. (2002) 'Overview: community-based animal health workers, policies, and institutions', In: *Community-based Animal Healthcare, PLA Notes 45*, International Institute for Environment and Development, London.

Catley, A. and Mariner, J. (2002) *Where There is no Data: Participatory approaches to veterinary epidemiology in pastoral areas of the horn of Africa*, Drylands Programme Issue Paper 110, International Institute for Environment and Development, London.

Catley, A., Okoth, S., Osman, J., Fison, T., Njiru, Z., Mwangi, J., Jones, B.A. and Leyland, T.J. (2001) Participatory diagnosis of a chronic wasting disease in cattle in southern Sudan, *Preventive Veterinary Medicine*, 51/3–4, 161–181.

Catley, A., Osman, J., Mawien, C., Jones, B.A. and Leyland, T.J. (2002a) Participatory analysis of seasonal incidences of diseases of cattle, disease vectors and rainfall in southern Sudan, *Preventive Veterinary Medicine*, 53/4, 275–284.

Catley, A., Irungu, P., Simiyu, K., Dadye, J., Mwakio, W., Kiragu J. and Nyamwaro, S.O. (2002b) Participatory investigations of bovine trypanosomiasis in Tana River District, Kenya, *Medical and Veterinary Entomology*, 16, 1–12.

Chambers, R. (1997) *Whose Reality Counts? Putting the first last*, Intermediate Technology Publications, London.

Chambers, R., Pacey, A. and Thrupp, L.A. (1989) *Farmer First: Farmer innovation and agricultural research*, Intermediate Technology Publications, London.

Coe, R. (1997) *Aspects of On-farm Experimentation*, Statistical Services Centre, University of Reading, Reading, UK.

Conroy, C. (2002) *Participatory Technology Development with Livestock-Keepers: A Guide*, BAIF Development Research Foundation, Pune.

Conroy, C. (2003) *Easing Seasonal Feed Scarcity for Goats in Semi-Arid India*, Final Technical Report, Livestock Production Programme Project 2003, NRI, Chatham, UK.

Conroy, C. and Rangnekar, D.V. (2000) *Constraints Facing Goat-keepers and Ways of Addressing them through a Participatory Approach: Some experiences from semi-arid India*, BAIF/NRI Goat Research Project Report No. 2, NRI, Chatham, UK.

Conroy, C. and Rangnekar, D.V. (2003) 'Participatory research at the landscape level: Kumbhan water trough case study', In: Pound, B., Snapp, S.S., McDougall, C. and Braun, A. (eds), *Natural Resource Management for Sustainable Livelihoods: Uniting science and participation*, Earthscan, London and International Development Research Centre, Ottawa.

Conroy, C. and Y.A. Thakur (2002) 'Increasing the productivity of indigenous goat production systems through participatory research in ethno-veterinary medicine: a case study from India', In: *Proceedings of international conference on Responding to the Increasing Global Demand for Animal Products*, 12–15 November 2002, Merida, Mexico, pp.67–68.

Conroy, C., Sutherland, A. and Martin, A. (1999) 'Conducting farmer participatory research: what, when and how', In: Grant, I. and Sears, C. (eds), *Decision Tools for Sustainable Development*, NRI, Chatham, UK.

Conroy, C., Thakur, Y. and Vadher, M. (2002) The efficacy of participatory development of technologies: experiences with resource-poor goat-keepers in India, *Livestock Research for Rural Development*, 14 (3).

Conroy, C., Sparks, N., Chandrasekaran, D., Ghorpade, A., Acamovic, T., Pennycott, T., Natarajan, A., Anetha, K., Pathan, R.L. and Shindey D.N. (2003) *Key Findings of the Baseline Survey on Scavenging Poultry in Trichy and Udaipur Districts, India*, Scottish Agricultural College, Ayr, Scotland.

Conway, G (1999) Feeding the World: Ecology, biotechnology and farmers as experimenters, Second Annual Peter Doherty Distinguished Lecture, 24 September 1999, International Livestock Research Institute.

DAREP (1994a) Report of an informal diagnostic survey of farming systems in Tharaka North and Central divisions, Tharaka-Nithi District, Kenya. Eds A.J. Sutherland and J. Ouma.

DAREP (1994b) Report of an informal diagnostic survey of farming systems in lower Embu, Kenya. Eds A.J. Sutherland, J. Ouma and J. Ndubi.

Delgado, C., Rosegrant, M., Steinfeld, H., Ehui, S. and Courbois, C. (1999) *Livestock to 2020 – The next food revolution*, Food, Agriculture and the Environment Discussion Paper 28, IFPRI/FAO/ILRI.

Devendra, C. and Burns, M. (1983) *Goat Production in the Tropics*, Commonwealth Agricultural Bureau, Farnham Royal, UK.

Douthwaite, B. (2001) *Enabling Innovation: A practical guide to understanding and fostering technological change*, Zed Books, London and New York.

Farrington, J. (1998) 'Organisational Roles in Farmer Participatory Research and Extension: Lessons from the last decade', *Natural Resource Perspectives*, 27, January, ODI, London.

Garforth, C., Khatiwada, Y. and Campbell, D. (2003) Communication research to support knowledge interventions in agricultural development: case studies from Eritrea and Uganda, Paper presented at the Development Studies Association Annual Conference, Glasgow, 10–12 September 2003.

Gathuma, J.M., Mbaria, J.M., Wanyama, J., Kaburia, H.F.A., Mpoke, L., Mwangi, J.N., Samburu and Turkana healers (2004) 'Efficacy of *Myrsine africana*, *Albizia anthelmintic* and *Hilderbrantia sepalosa* herbal remedies against natural mixed sheep helminthosis in Samburu District, Kenya', *Journal of Ethnopharmacology* 91, 7–12.

Githori, J.B. (2004) *Evaluation of anthelmintica properties of ethnoveterinary plant preparations used as livestock dewormers by pastoralists and small holder farmers in Kenya*, Doctoral theseis, Swedish University of Agricultural Sciences, Uppsala.

Grandin, B. (1988) *Wealth Ranking in Smallholder Communities*, Intermediate Technology Publications, London.

Grandin, B. and Young, J. (1994) Ethnoveterinary question list, *RRA Notes*, 20, 39–46.

Grandin, B., Thampy, R. and Young, J. (1991) *Village Animal Healthcare: A community-based approach to livestock development in Kenya*, Intermediate Technology Publications, London.

Gündel, S., Hancock, J. and Anderson, S. (2001) *Scaling up strategies for research in natural resource management: A comparative review*, NRI, Chatham, UK.

Gustafson, D.J. (2002) Supporting the demand for change: recent project experience with farmer learning grants in Kenya, Paper prepared for the workshop entitled 'Extension and Rural Development: A convergence of views on international approaches', 12–15 November 2002, Washington, DC, World Bank/USAID/Neuchatel Initiative.

Hadrill, D. and Yusuf H. (1994). Seasonal disease incidence in the Sanaag region of Somaliland, *RRA Notes*, 20, 52–53.

Harrington, L.W. and Tripp, R. (1984) Recommendation domains: a framework for on-farm research, CIMMYT Economics Program Working Paper 02/84, CIMMYT, Mexico.

Heffernan, C. (1994) Livestock Healthcare for Tibetan Agro-Pastoralists: Application of Rapid Rural Appraisal Techniques, *RRA Notes*, 20: 54–57.

Heffernan, C. and Sidahmed, A. (1998) Issues in the delivery of veterinary services to the rural poor, Paper presented at the Livestock Development Studies Group Conference, The Delivery of Veterinary Services to the Poor, Reading, 12 June 1998.

Horne, P.M. and Ibrahim, T.M. (1996) 'Forage production for low and high input systems in Southeast Asia', In: Merkel, R.C., Soedjana T.D. and Subandriyo (eds), *Small Ruminant Production: Recommendations for Southeast Asia*, Proceedings of a workshop held in Parapat, North Sumatra, Indonesia, 12–15 May 1996.

Horne, P.M. and Stür, W.W. (1999) *Developing forage technologies with farmers – how to select the best variety to offer farmers in Southeast Asia*, ACIAR, Canberra, pp.80.

IDL Group and McCorkle, C. (2002) 'Community-based animal healthcare, participation, and policy: where are we now?', In: *Community-based Animal Healthcare, PLA Notes 45*, International Institute for Environment and Development, London.

Iles, K. (1994) 'The progeny history data collection technique: a case study from Samburu District, Kenya', In: IIED (1994).

International Institute for Environment and Development (IIED) (1994) *RRA Notes, 20: Special Issue on Livestock*, IIED, London.

International Institute for Environment and Development (2002) *PLA Notes 45, Special Issue on Community-based Animal Healthcare*, IIED, London.

ITDG and IIRR (1996) *Ethnoveterinary Medicine in Kenya; A field manual of traditional animal health care practices*, Intermediate Technology-Kenya and International Institute for Rural Reconstruction.

Jiggins, J. (1989) Farmer participatory research and technology development, Occasional Papers in Rural Extension No. 5, University of Guelph, Ontario, Canada.

Kaburia, H. (1998) Literature review on medicinal plants collected from Samburu District, A consultant report, ITDG (Internal Document), London.

Kaitho, R.J., Biwott, J., Tanner, J.C., Gachuiri, C.K. and Wahome, R.G. (2001) Effect of allocation of fixed amounts of concentrates on milk yields and fertility of dairy cows. *Agrippa electronic journal* http://www.fao.org/DOCREP/ARTICLE/AGRIPPA/X9500E09.HTM

Kariuki, J.N., Boer, H., Tamminga, S., Gitau, G.K., Gachuiri, C.K. and Muia, J.M. (1998a) Rumen degradation and intestinal digestion of protein in Napier grass and other Kenyan forages, *Animal Feed Science and Technology*, 31: 160–9.

Kariuki, J.N., Gitau, G.K., Gachuiri, C.K., Tamminga, S. and Muia, J.M.K. (1998b) Effect of supplementing Napier grass with Desmodium and lucerne on intake and weight gains in dairy heifers, *Livestock Production Science*, 60: 81–8.

Kariuki, J.N., Tamminga, S., Gachuiri, C.K., Gitau, G.K., and Muia, J.M.K. (1998c) Intake, DM degradation and rumen fermentation as affected by varying levels of Desmodium and sweet potato vines in Napier grass fed to cattle, *Animal Feed Science and Technology*, 31: 151–9.

Keya, N.C.O. and Karangi, D.W. (1973) The seeding and superphosphate rates for the establishment of *Desmodium uncinatum* (Jacq) DC. by oversowing in uncultivated grasslands of Western Kenya, *Tropical Grasslands*, 7, 319–325.

Keya, N.C.O., Olsen, F.J. and Holliday, R. (1971) The role of superphosphate in the establishment of oversown tropical legumes in natural grasslands of western Kenya, *Tropical Grasslands*, 5, 109–116.

Khayota, B. (1998) Literature review on ethno botanical properties of medicinal plants from Samburu District; A consultant report; ITDG-EA Internal Document.

Kiff, L., Pound, B. and Holdsworth, R. (1996) *Covercrops: A review and database for field users*, NRI, Chatham, UK, 180pp.

Leksmono, C.S. and Young, J. (2002) 'Community-based animal health workers and institutional change: the DELIVERI project in Indonesia', In: *Community-based Animal Healthcare, PLA Notes 45*, International Institute for Environment and Development, London.

Leyland, T. (1994) 'Planning a community animal health programme in Afghanistan'. In, IIED (1994).

Livestock in Development (1999) *Livestock in Poverty-focused Development*, Livestock in Development, Crewkerne, UK.

McCorkle, C., Mathias, E. and Schillhorn van veen, T.W. (1996) *Ethnoveterinary Research and Development*, Intermediate Technology Publications, London.

McCorkle, C., Rangnekar, D.V. and Mathias, M. (1999) 'Introduction: whence and whither ER&D?'. In: Mathias et al. (eds).

Mariner, J.C. (2000) Participatory epidemiology: methods for the collection of action-orientated epidemiological intelligence, *FAO Animal Health Manual 10*, FAO, Rome.

Mariner, J.C. (2001) Report on a consultancy to assist in the development of a rinderpest eradication strategy in West and East Nile Ecosystems, Community-based Animal Health and Participatory Epidemiology Unit, Pan African Programme for the Control of Epizootics, Organization of African Unity/Interafrican Bureau for Animal Resources, Nairobi.

Martin, M., Mathias, E. and McCorkle, C.M. (2001) *Ethnoveterinary Medicine: An annotated bibliography of community animal healthcare*, ITDG Publishing, London.

Mason, V., Rees, D.J., Mulira, G.L., Mbugua, J.K., Shitandi, D. and Mukasa, B. (1999) 'Training farmers groups for participatory research in animal husbandry for small holder farms in Kenya', In: *KARI/DFID NARP II Project – End of Project Conference*, Vol. 1., KARI/DFID East Africa, Nairobi, Kenya.

Mata, B.V., Travassos Dias, P., Fringe, R. and Alders, R.G. (2000) *Lessons learnt during vaccine field trials with village chickens in Mozambique*, Proceedings of the XXI World's Poultry Congress, Montreal, 20–24 August 2000, Abstract 13.08.

Mathias, M., Rangnekar, D.V. and McCorkle, C. (1999) *Ethnoveterinary Medicine: Alternatives for livestock development*, Proceedings of an international conference held in Pune, India, 4–6 November 1997, BAIF Development Research Foundation, Pune.

Matthewman, R., Ashley, S. and Morton, J. (1998) 'The delivery of information to livestock farmers in India: a case study', In: Dolberg, F. and Petersen, P.H. (eds) *Maximising the Influence of the User: Alternatives to the training and visit system – Proceedings of a workshop*, DSR Forlag, Copenhagen.

Maurya, D.M. (1989) 'The innovative approach of Indian farmers', In: Chambers, R., Pacey, A. and Thrupp, L.A. (eds) *Farmer First: Farmer Innovation and Agricultural Research*, Intermediate Technology Publications, London.

Minjauw, B, Muriuki, H.G. and Romney, D. (2002a) *Development of farm field school methodology for smallholder dairy farmers in Kenya*, Proceedings of the workshop 'International Learning Workshop on Farmer Field Schools (FFS): Emerging Issues and Challenges, 21–25 October 2002, Yogyakarta, Indonesia, International Potato Centre, Manila.

Minjauw, B., Muriuki, H.G. and Romney, D. (2002b) 'Adaptation of the farmer field school methodology to improve adoption of livestock health and production interventions', In: *Responding to the Increasing Global Demand for Animal Products: Programme and Summaries of an International Conference organised by BSAS, ASAS and MSAP*, Merida, Mexico, November 2002, BSAS, Penicuik, Scotland.

Morton, J. (2001) *Participatory Livestock Production Research in Kenya and Tanzania – Experience and Issues*, Mimeo, Natural Resources Institute, Chatham, UK.

Mugera, G.M., Bwangamoi, O. and Wandera, J.G. (1979) *Diseases of Cattle in Tropical Africa*, Kenya Literature Bureau, Nairobi.

Mulira, G.L., Mason, V., Mukasa, B., Shitandi, D. and Wekesa, D. (1999) 'Lessons learnt from participatory evaluation of worm control methods in cattle and sheep', In: *KARI/DFID NARP II Project – End of Project Conference*, Vol. 1., KARI/DFID East Africa, Nairobi, Kenya.

Mwangi, D.M. (1999) Integration of herbaceous legumes into Napier grass fodder systems in central Kenya: constraints and potential, PhD thesis, University of London, London.

Mwangi, D.M., Thorpe, W., Methu, J.N.G.M., Chui, J.N., Musembi, F.K., Lukuyu,

M., Chege, L., Mutuota, J. and Odongo, N.E. (1995) *Factors affecting the adoption of planted forages in the Nairobi milk shed: Report on participatory rural appraisals conducted in Kiambu, Kenya*, Kenya Agricultural Research Institute, National Agricultural Research Centre, Muguga, Central Province, Nairobi, Kenya.

Mwangi, D.M, Cadisch, G., Thorpe, W. and Giller, K.E. (in press) Harvesting management options for legumes intercropped in Napier grass in the Central Highlands of Kenya. *Tropical Grasslands*.

Nahdy, S. (2002) The role of extension in rural development: The Ugandan National Agricultural Advisory Services (NAADS), Paper prepared for the workshop entitled 'Extension and Rural Development: A Convergence of Views on International Approaches', 12–15 November 2002, Washington, DC, World Bank/USAID/Neuchatel Initiative.

Norman, D.W., Worman, F.D., Siebert, J.D. and Modiakgotla, E. (1995) *The Farming Systems Approach to Development and Appropriate Technology Generation*, FAO, Rome.

Norrish, P., Lloyd Morgan, K. and Myers, M. (2001) *Improved communication strategies for renewable natural resource research outputs. Socio-economic Methodologies for Natural Resources Research. Best Practice Guidelines*, NRI, Chatham, UK.

North American Research Group (1998) *Responsible Research with Communities: participatory research in primary care*, website *http://napcrg/responsibleresearch.pdf*

Okali, C, Sumberg, J. and Farrington, J. (1994) *Farmer Participatory Research: Rhetoric and reality*, Intermediate Technology Publications, London.

Okuthe, O.S., Kuloba, K., Emongor, R.A., Ngotho, R.N., Bukachi, S., Nyamwaro, S.O., Murila, G. and Wamwayi, H.M. (2002) National agricultural research systems experiences in the use of participatory approaches to animal health research in Kenya, Paper presented at the international conference Primary Animal Health Care in the 21st Century: Shaping the Policies, Rules and Institutions, 15–18 October 2002, Mombasa. African Union's Interafrican Bureau for Animal Resources, Nairobi.

Ooi, P. (1998) *Beyond the Farmer Field School: IPM and empowerment in Indonesia*, Gatekeeper Series No. 78. IIED, London.

Pasiecznik, N.M., Felker, P., Harris, P.J.C., Harsh, L.N., Cruz, G., Tewari, J.C., Cadoret, K. and Maldonado, L.J. (2001) *The* Prosopis juliflora–Prosopis pallida *complex: A Monograph*, HDRA, Coventry, UK.

Peacock, C. (1996) *Improving Goat Production in the Tropics: A manual for development workers*, Oxfam, Oxford.

Perry, B., Randolph, T.F., McDermott, J.J., Sones, K.R. and Thornton, P.K. (2002) *Investing in Animal Health Research to Alleviate Poverty*, ILRI, Nairobi, Kenya.

Peters, M., Horne, P., Schmidt, A., Holmann, F., Kerridge, P.C., Tarawali, S.A., Schultze-Kraft, R., Lascano, C.E., Argel, P., Stur, W., Fujisaka, S., Muller-Samann, K. and Wortmann, C. (2001) The role of forages in reducing poverty and degradation of natural resources in tropical production systems, AgREN Network Paper No. 117, July 2001, ODI, London.

Pretty, J. (1995) *Regenerating Agriculture: Policies and practice for sustainability and self-reliance*, Earthscan, London.

Pretty, J., Guijt, I., Thompson. J. and Scoones, I. (1995) *Participatory Learning and Action: A trainer's guide*, IIED, London.

Reategui, K., Vera, R.R., Loker, W.L. and Vasquez, M. (1995) On farm grass-legume pasture performance in the Peruvian rainforest. *Experimental Agriculture*, 31, 227–239.

Reijntjes, C., Haverjort, B. and Waters-Bayer, A. (1992) *Farming for the Future: An introduction to low-external-input and sustainable agriculture*, Macmillan, London.

Rietbergen-McCracken, J. and Narayan, D. (1998) *Participation and Social Assessment: Tools and techniques,* World Bank, Washington, DC.

Roeleveld, A. (1996a) 'The diagnostic phase in research on livestock systems', In: Roeleveld. A. and van den Broek A. (eds), *Focusing Livestock Systems Research,* Royal Tropical Institute, Amsterdam.

Roeleveld, A. (1996b) 'Issues in livestock systems diagnosis', In: Roeleveld. A. and van den Broek A. (eds), *Focusing Livestock Systems Research,* Royal Tropical Institute, Amsterdam.

Roeleveld. A. and van den Broek, A. (1996) *Focusing Livestock Systems Research,* Royal Tropical Institute, Amsterdam.

Romney, D.L., Tanner, J., Chui, J., Kenyanjui, M., Morton, J., Ndegwa, P., Kimari, A. and Thorne, P. (1998) 'Feed utilisation options for smallholder dairy farmers', In: *BSAS/KARI Proceedings of an International Conference on Foods Lands and Livelihoods, Setting Research Agendas for Animal Science,* 27–30 January 1998, Nairobi, Kenya, BSAS, Edinburgh, p43.

Roothaert, R.L. and Phengsavanh, P. (2001) Assessing the use of indigenous fodder trees in Laos, Annual Report 2001, Project PE–5 Sustainable Systems for Small-holders: Integrating Improved Germplasm and Resource Management for Enhanced Crop and Livestock Production Systems, Centro Internacional de Agricultura Tropical, Cali, pp.88–95.

Sagar, V. and Ahuja, K. (1993) *Economics of Goat Keeping in Rajasthan,* Indo-Swiss Goat Development and Fodder Production Project, Jaipur.

Saka, A.R., Haque, I., Said, A.N., Lupwayi, N.Z. and El-Wakeel, A. (1994) Forage legumes in crop-livestock systems of Sub-Saharan Africa., Soil science and plant nutrition section, Working document No. 24, International Livestock Centre for Africa (ILCA).

Scoones, I. (1994) 'Browse ranking in Zimbabwe', In: IIED (1994).

Shehu, Y. and Akinola, J.O. (1995) The productivity of pure and mixed grass-legume pastures in the Northern Guinea Savanna zone of Nigeria, *Tropical Grasslands,* 29, 115–121.

Sidahmed, A. (1995) 'Livestock and feed development and improvement, research needs in West Asia and North Africa', In: Gardiner, P. and Devendra, C. (eds), *Global Agenda for Livestock Research: Proceedings of a consultation,* International Livestock Research Institute, Nairobi.

Staal, S.J., Chege, L., Kenyanjui, M., Kimari, A., Lukuyu, B., Njubi, D., Owango, M., Tanner, J., Thorpe, W. and Wambugu, M. (1998a) Characterisation of dairy systems supplying the Nairobi milk market A pilot survey in Kiambu district for the identification of target producers, KARI/MoA/ILRI Collaborative Research Project Report.

Staal, S., Chege, L., Kenyanjui, M., Kimari, A., Lukuyu, B., Njubi, D., Owango, M., Tanner, J., Thorpe, W. and Wambugu, M. (1998b) A cross-sectional survey of Kiambu district for the identification of target groups of smallholder dairy producers, KARI/ILRI collaborative project research project report, Nairobi, Kenya.

Statistical Services Centre (2000) *One Animal per Farm – A guide to resolving the statistical difficulties encountered by on-farm researchers working with small livestock numbers in the developing world,* University of Reading, Reading, UK.

Steinfeld, H. (2002) 'Increasing global demand for animal products', In: *Responding to the Increasing Global Demand for Animal Products,* Programme and Summaries of an International Conference organised by BSAS, ASAS and MSAP, Merida, Mexico, November 2002.

Stewart, S. (2002) 'Community-based animal health training and creative change in Bolivia', In: *Community-based Animal Healthcare, PLA Notes 45*, International Institute for Environment and Development, London.

Sutherland, A. and Kang'ara, J.N. (2000) 'Experiences in applying FSR in semi-arid Kenya', In: Collinson, M. (ed.), *A History of Farming Systems Research*, Food and Agriculture Organization of the United Nations, Rome and CABI Publishing, Wallingford, UK.

Sutherland, A. and Martin, A. (1999) Institutionalizing farmer participatory research – key decisions based on lessons from projects in Africa. In: Grant, I. and Sears, C. (eds), *Decision Tools for Sustainable Development*, NRI, Chatham, UK.

Sutherland, A., Martin, A and Rider-Smith, D. (2001) *Dimensions of Participation: Experiences, Lessons and Tips from Agricultural Research Practitioners in Sub-Saharan Africa*, NRI, Chatham, UK.

Tewari, J.C., Harris, P.J.C., Harsh, L.N., Cadoret, K. and Pasiecznik, N.M. (2000) *Managing* Prosopis juliflora *(Vilayati babul): A Technical Manual*, CAZRI, Jodhpur, India and HDRA, Coventry, UK.

Thakur, Y.A., Joshi, A.L., Conroy, C., Desai, P.R. and Halli, M.D. (2002) Improving productivity of goats during the rainy season in rural Karnataka, Paper presented at International Workshop on *Browse Plants and Small Ruminant Productivity in the Tropics*, Sokoine University of Agriculture, Morogoro, Tanzania, 7–10 January 2002.

Thomas, D. and Sumberg, J.E. (1995) A review of the evaluation and use of tropical forage legumes in sub-Saharan Africa, *Agriculture, Ecosystems and Environment*, 54, 151–163.

Thornton, P.K., Kruska, R.L., Henninger, N., Kristjanson, P.M., Reid, R.S., Atieno, F., Odero, A.N. and Ndegwa, T. (2002) *Mapping Poverty and Livestock in the Developing World*, ILRI, Nairobi, Kenya.

Tripp, R. (1991) 'The farming systems research movement and on-farm research', In: Tripp, R. (ed.), *Planned Change in Farming Systems: Progress in on-farm research*, John Wiley, Chichester.

Turton, C. with Birardar, N., Ramamurthy, V., Singh, J.P. and Mishra, A.K. (1996) *Opportunities and Constraints for Fodder Development in Rain-Fed Areas of India: Developing linkages with smallholder farmers*, An Overseas Development Institute/and Indian Grassland and Fodder Research Institute Collaborative Study, ODI, London and Indian Grassland and Fodder Research Institute, Jhansi, India.

Veldhuizen van, L., Waters-Bayer, A. and de Zeeuw, H. (1997) *Developing Technology with Farmers: A trainer's guide for participatory learning*, Zed Books/ETC Netherlands.

Wambugu, M. (2000) Extension and its effect on dairy cattle nutrition and productivity in smallholder dairy enterprises in Kiambu district, MSc thesis, Nairobi University.

Wandera, J.L. (1995) Pasture/Fodder Research Program, Kenya Agricultural Research Institute (KARI), National Agricultural Research Centre – Kitale, Kenya.

Wanyama, J.B. (1997) *Confidently Used Ethnoveterinary Knowledge Among Pastoralists of Samburu, Kenya, Book One: Methodology and Results*, Intermediate Technology Kenya, Nairobi.

Waters-Bayer, A. (1989) 'Trials by scientists and farmers: opportunities for co-operation in ecofarming research', In: Kotschi, J. (ed.), *Ecofarming Practices for Tropical Smallholdings*, Margraf Verlag, Leiden.

Waters-Bayer, A. and Bayer, W. (1994) *Planning with Pastoralists: PRA and more – a review of methods focused on Africa*, GTZ, Eschborn.

Waters-Bayer, A. and Bayer, W. (2002) 'Animal science research for poverty allevia-
tion in the face of industrialisation of livestock production', In: *Responding to the
Increasing Global Demand for Animal Products*, Programme and Summaries of an
International Conference organized by BSAS, ASAS and MSAP, Merida, Mexico,
November 2002.

Wood, P.D.P. (1979) A simple model of lactation curves for milk yield, food requirement
and body weight, *Animal Production*, 28, 55–63.

Young, J., Dijkema, H-P., Stoufer, K., Ojha, N., Shrestha, G. and Thapa, L. (1994)
Evaluation of an animal health improvement programme in Nepal, *RRA Notes*, 20,
58–66.

Index